Safavid Iran and Her Neighbors

Safavid Iran and Her Neighbors

Edited by

MICHEL MAZZAOUI

THE UNIVERSITY OF UTAH PRESS

SALT LAKE CITY

First paperback edition 2014

The Defiance House Man colophon is a registered trademark of the University of Utah Press. It is based upon a four-foot-tall, Ancient Puebloan pictograph (late PIII) near Glen Canyon, Utah.

18 17 16 15 14
5 4 3 2 1

LIBRARY OF CONGRESS CATALOGING-IN-PUBLICATION DATA

Safavid Iran and her neighbors / edited by Michel Mazzaoui.
p. cm.
Includes bibliographical references and index.
ISBN 978-1-60781-251-7 (pbk. : alk. paper)
1.Iran—History—Safavid dynasty, 1501–1736. I. Mazzaoui, Michel M., 1926–
DS292.S236 2003
955'.03—dc21 2003006423

Contents

Preface

The Safavid period occupies a central place in Persian history. It covers the two and a quarter centuries between A.D. 1501, when the first Safavid ruler, Shah Ismā'īl, came to power, and 1722, with the last effective ruler, Shah Sulṭān Ḥusayn. This period constitutes a glorious chapter in the long history of Iran, with such figures as Shah 'Abbās the Great and the city of Isfahan associated with his reign. For the first time since the Muslim conquest of Iran in the seventh century, Iran became an identifiable entity in the heart of the Middle East region, where the Safavid rulers established Shi'ism as the dominant branch of Islam. Iran still occupies the land where the Safavid shahs ruled, and Shi'ism is still the Muslim faith observed by the majority of Iranians.

To the east and to the west of Safavid Iran were four more or less contemporary states: the Ottomans in Anatolia and the Balkans, the Mamluk state in Egypt and Syria (both to the west), the Mughal state of India, and the Uzbek state in Central Asia (both to the east). These powers plus the Safavids constituted the five entities into which the central part of the Middle East was divided in the post-Caliphal, post-Mongol period during the 250 years prior to A.D. 1500.

During the Safavid period, military engagements often took place, particularly between the Safavids and the Ottomans in the west and the Safavids and the Uzbeks in the east. Iran had adopted Shi'ism, while the other four entities herein mentioned were considered Sunni, which was often viewed as a factor in the struggle between Iran and her neighbors. Perhaps more important were claims and counterclaims along border areas, frequently expressed in the term *mulk-i mawrūth* (inherited possessions). This is clearly seen in the Ottomans' continuous attempts to incorporate Tabriz in the Turkish-speaking region of Azerbayjan and the Iranian attempts to annex Herat, a major center in Khurasan. (Iran ultimately kept Tabriz but lost Herat!)

The situation in the Middle East circa A.D. 1500 centering on Safavid Iran was the theme of the symposium held in Salt Lake City at the University of Utah on May 8 and 9, 1998. It was administered by the university's Middle East

Center with support from the College of Humanities, the Obert C. and Grace A. Tanner Humanities Center, the Department of History, and the University of Utah Press.

Four persons from the University of Utah assisted in chairing the four sessions of the symposium: Bernard Weiss, Department of Languages; Jeff Grathwohl, director of the University of Utah Press; Anand Yang, Department of History; and Peter von Sivers, Department of History. In bringing these scholars together, and in providing a forum for the exchange of ideas, the symposium may be considered a success.

From the very beginning of the project, and through the various stages of its development, it was understood that an effort would be made to publish the papers of the symposium in book form. The director of the University of Utah Press, who participated in the proceedings, thought the symposium was "very successful" and demonstrated an interest in publishing the papers. The slow process of communicating with the participants and collecting the finished drafts of their contributions began. Some of the participants decided not to be included in this publication: they either thought their papers required more research and thus were not ready to be committed to print or had plans to publish their papers elsewhere. Finally, eight out of the original fourteen contributions were received in near-final form, and the collection was subsequently peer reviewed and further revised.

The eight articles included in the present volume deal with a variety of topics related to the main theme of the symposium: religious, artistic, literary, and social. The remaining six contributions not included in this volume are by Rosemary Stanfield-Johnson, Cornell H. Fleisher, Sholeh Quinn, John E. Woods, Kathryn Babayan, and the late Touraj Noroozi.

Hamid Algar's article deals with the relations between the new Safavid "system" with its Shiʿite tendencies and the Naqshbandī Sufi order with its "quintessentially Sunni nature." Juan Cole's contribution deals with miniature paintings of the Mughal Sultan Jahangir and the Safavid Shah ʿAbbās. Copies of the miniatures are included in the present volume. The analytical discussion of the significance of these miniatures touches upon concepts of power and submission and is an original interpretation of Persian miniature painting both as an art form and as an expression of the painter's inner world.

A literary phenomenon that prevailed during the Safavid period was the emigration of many Iranian poets to the Indian subcontinent. Numerous reasons have been submitted to explain this phenomenon: Stephen Dale in his article on the Indian poems of Ashraf Mazandarani (d. 1704) gives persuasive comments on this subject.

Shireen Mahdavi's discussion of family values and the Safavids summarizes early references to women in European travel literature. She focuses on the high Safavid period and the chief religious interpreter, Mulla Muhammad Baqir Majlisi, including a detailed analysis of Majlisi's views on the subject in his original work *Ḥilyat al-Muttaqīn.* After the completion and publication of her work on Amin al-Zarb, Dr. Mahdavi has dealt with various aspects of the history of changes in the role of Iranian women and the social and family values associated with their role in Persian society.

Professor Rudi Matthee's contribution on diplomatic relations between Iran and Russia during the high Safavid period (1587–1639) adds a new dimension to the geographic region treated in this symposium. He analyzes "the geopolitical status of the Caucasus as a frontier region where the territorial claims of adjoining powers—Safavids, Ottomans, and eventually the Russians as well—collided." Dr. Matthee also discusses commercial relations between Iran and Russia in some detail. In 1999 he published a major work entitled *The Politics of Trade in Safavid Iran,* dealing with important questions of commercial activity during the Safavid period.

Professor R. D. McChesney's contribution on pilgrimage/ḥajj routes from Central Asia—mainly Uzbek territory—is a significant contribution on a little-researched topic. He describes various routes (around the Caspian via Astrakhan, through India, and via Iran), discusses the various obstacles involved, and tracks down actual travelers from Central Asia who came on these pilgrimages. Among several critical observations, he refutes the notion that the Safavids "made it impossible for Sunni pilgrims from Central Asia and India to cross their territory."

Vera B. Moreen has published quite extensively on the subject of Judaism in Safavid Iran, including the recently published anthology *In Queen Esther's Garden: An Anthology of Judeo-Persian Literature.* In the present volume she considers the polemical remarks by Rabbi Yehudah b. El'azar, a Jewish scholar (born in Kashan), regarding Jews, Christians, and Muslims.

Finally, Devin Stewart's paper on al-Shahīd al-Thānī (the second martyr in Shi'ite Ithnā'asharī views) Zayn al-Dīn al-'Āmilī (d. 1558) considers his work within the controversy in the Shi'ite tradition between the Akhbārī and the Uṣūlī approach to Islamic jurisprudence. Zayn al-Dīn is best known in Shi'ite scholarly circles as the greatest commentator on a work written two centuries earlier by the first martyr, Ibn Makkī al-'Āmilī (d. 1384).

These short descriptions of the contents of the present volume do not do justice to the discussions in the essays themselves. They are intended to help readers decide which of these essays interest them most. The value of this research on the subject of the symposium remains in the readers' hands.

TRANSLITERATION

The transliteration system followed in the essays is based on *The Encyclopaedia of Islam, International Journal of Middle East Studies* (*IJMES*), or *Encyclopaedia Iranica.* Some of the writers, however, have chosen a modified form of the standard systems.

ACKNOWLEDGMENTS

In the early stages of the project, Professor Peter Sluglett (then director of the Center of Middle East Studies) assisted in the planning of the symposium and in ensuring its ultimate success. Kathy Wyer, graduate student in Middle East Studies, at one time considerably and almost single-handedly moved the action on. After the symposium, Kathy was helpful in procuring final copies of the papers from the participants. Matt Malczycki, graduate student in Middle East Studies, assisted in the final editorial process. Finally, Jeffrey L. Grathwohl, director, University of Utah Press, was more responsible than anybody else for seeing this project come to fruition and for its ultimate appearance in book form. Thanks, Jeff, for everything!

Michel Mazzaoui
Department of History
University of Utah, Salt Lake City

The Safavid Phenomenon

An Introductory Essay

Michel Mazzaoui

The leading Safavid historian Roger Savory has remarked that "the establishment of the Safawid state in 907/1501 by Shah Isma'il I ... marks an important turning point in Persian history."[1] Along these lines, a large number of historians have devoted much effort toward explaining the meaning and significance of this "turning point." Several important ideas have been presented, which cover a wide spectrum of analysis and interpretation of what is undeniably a major event in the long history of Iran.

Yet some of these ideas and interpretations seem to conflict with each other, especially as several modern historians see in the rise of the Safavid state a manifestation of Persian national consciousness. This *vaḥdat-e millī* or nationalism did not exist in Iran or, for that matter, anywhere else in the world circa A.D. 1500. The concept took shape in Europe after 1500, grew dramatically during the Age of Enlightenment, and ultimately matured toward the end of the eighteenth century with the French Revolution in 1789. Only after 1800, when Europe overwhelmed the Islamic countries of the Middle East (usually dated from the French naval expedition against Egypt under Napoleon Bonaparte in 1792), did ideas of nationalism start to influence the course of events in Iran and elsewhere in the region.

Explanations for the rise of the Safavid state and investigations concerning several aspects of Persian history during the Safavid period continue to engage the attention of a contingent of younger scholars who, in many ways, have challenged the classical views of their predecessors. In fact, one of these predecessors, Jean Aubin (who may be considered the doyen of Safavid studies since the death of Vladimir Minorsky), recently wrote a long article expressing new thoughts and reconsiderations of the Safavid period.[2] (I personally would welcome the chance to review my own thoughts on the rise of the Safavid dynasty published more than a quarter of a century ago!)[3]

Thus, the field of Safavid research is quite active, and there is possibly some justification for revisiting the conditions that brought about this "turning point" in the history of Iran.

Rather than going over material already carefully and skillfully argued by Safavid scholars, it is perhaps more rewarding to go back to the Persian contemporary sources, who—after all is said and done—were the prime movers in the undertaking. As we know, the period is very rich in Safavid primary material. The present discussion, however, is limited (not quite arbitrarily as may readily be seen) to three Persian historians who appear to have differing views on the political, social, and cultural forces that led to the rise of the Safavid state. Obviously, these historians could not look back, as we can, to give an overall interpretation. They were part of the history as it unfolded. But in each case they seem to have been aware of a great change that was taking place, which they tried to express and explain rather clearly. Their historical accounts invariably appeared in the form of a chronicle.

The three historians are Faḍl Allāh ibn Rūzbihān Khunjī, the author of *Tārīkh-i ʿĀlam-ārā-yi Amīnī,* which was written before the accession of Shah Ismāʿīl and describes the last years of the Aqqoyunlu Turkman dynasty (especially the reign of Sultan Yaʿqūb); Ḥasan-i Rūmlū, author of *Aḥsan al-Tavārīkh,* the standard work on the periods of Shah Ismāʿīl and Shah Ṭahmāsb; and Iskandar Beg Turkmān Munshī, who as the court historian wrote his great *Tārīkh-i ʿĀlam-ārā-yi ʿAbbāsī* during the reign of Shah ʿAbbās.[4] The discussion presented here with reference to these three historians covers the *ghāzī-jihād* concept as seen in Khunjī's work; the Shīʿī-religious basis of the state as expressed in Rūmlū's work; and the heroic-nationalist pride that can be read between the lines of Iskandar Munshī's robust prose.

One cannot find an exact term of reference let alone a thesis or theme for each of these three historians. They wrote in the traditional style of annalistic chronicles, extolling the rulers under whose aegis they lived and worked. But as they wrestled with what they must have sensed was a major event in their country's history, they arrived at three different interpretations that—although not fully elaborated—still give an impression of what these perceptive individuals felt had taken place.[5]

I

Khunjī's usefulness in our understanding of Safavid history—which hinges on the detailed information he provides for the activities of Junayd and Ḥaydar (the grandfather and father respectively of Shah Ismāʿīl) leading to the establishment of the Safavid state—simply cannot be properly appreciated.

There is no need here to go over the argument of how a contemplative Ṣūfī order, founded by the venerable Shaykh Ṣafī al-Dīn Isḥāq Ardabīlī in post-Mongol Azerbayjan,[6] was transformed into a fighting force under Junayd and Ḥaydar, thus preparing the way for the young Ismāʿīl. Khunjī reflects on this and says (in the words of his translator, V. Minorsky): "...what a pity that, while Safi al-Din preserved his being from a doubtful repast, he did not restrain his children from the vanities of this world. As a result, his progeny forsook poverty and humility for the throne of a kingdom."[7] He adds a little later: "When the boon of succession reached Junayd, he altered the way of life of his ancestors: the bird of anxiety laid an egg of longing for power in the nest of his imagination. Every moment he strove to conquer a land or a region."[8]

To achieve their quest for power Junayd and Ḥaydar began to engage in what is one of the surest ways to power and authority within an Islamic context: conducting *ghāzī* activity against neighboring Christian infidels. The Arabs did it in their wars of expansion in early Islam (hence the *maghāzī* literature); the Turks did it in their push against Byzantium, first in Anatolia and subsequently across the Straits in the Balkan region;[9] and now the Iranians (actually Qizilbāsh Turks under Junayd and Ḥaydar) were conducting this same type of *ghazā* against the Byzantine Christian enclave of Trebizond on the Black Sea and, more extensively, against Cherkes territory in Georgia and the Caucasus in general. Suddenly, the *murīd*s of the Ṣūfī order of Ardabil became the *ghuzāt-i Ṣūfiyah* under Junayd and Ḥaydar. "Thence," says Khunjī, "with a small number of heterogenous elements, and hiding his intentions under the pretext of a holy war against the Cherkes, he [Junayd] crossed the Kur river and hurried to the province of Tabarsaran."[10]

About the *ghāzī* activity of Ḥaydar, Khunjī gives more details: "With some 10,000 men the Shaykh passed through Darband to the country of the infidel Cherkes. Having wrought havoc and taken captives (in one such campaign he brought back with him some 6,000 captives), he triumphantly returned to Ardabil."[11] At some point, Ḥaydar wrote to the Aqqoyunlu sultan (Yaʿqūb, who began to suspect this *ghāzī* activity), telling him that his men, "having exerted themselves [*ijtihād*] in various religious exercises and duly completed the great *jihād*, which is the assault on one's own soul, ... claimed the right to distinguish themselves in the lesser *jihād*," which is to fight the infidels. "Should the sovereign permit, they would begin the holy war against the Cherkes."[12]

2

Stressing the *jihād-ghāzī* activity in explaining the establishment of the Safavid state is quite convincing if one accepts the details in Khunjī (while making some allowance, however, for the fact that our historian was avowedly anti-Safavid). In contrast, the religious-Shīʿī (Ithnāʿasharī) factor in the creation of the state, as expressed by Ḥasan-i Rūmlū in his *Aḥsan al-Tavārīkh* (and by other contemporary historians) and accepted almost wholeheartedly by most modern scholars, is a more problematic matter. Who said that Iran or rather the Iranian people were ready to become Shīʿī? After all, the country was still predominantly Sunni when Ismāʿīl came to power. And how does one explain the transformation in the leadership of the Ṣūfī order of Ardabil from a Sunni-Shāfiʿī founder, Shaykh Ṣafī al-Dīn, to the extreme *ghulāt* views of *ilāh* and *ibn-Allāh* with reference to Junayd and Ḥaydar and to the poetic utterances of Shah Ismāʿīl, who "used to abide with God, but now he has appeared in the world?"[13] Nevertheless, Rūmlū tells us in no uncertain terms: "Shah Ismāʿīl, at the start of his accession, ordered that the muezzins of all the provinces should recite the *adhān* in accordance with the system established by the Ithnāʿasharī Imams. . . . [By adding] I testify that ʿAlī is the walī of Allāh, and hasten to the best of deeds."[14] And after doing some calculations, Rūmlū adds: "These words have not been heard in the world of Islam ever since the arrival [in Baghdad] of Toghrul Beg ibn Mikāʾīl ibn Saljūq and the escape of Basāsīrī, which from that date till the said year [i.e., 907/1501] totals five hundred and twenty-eight years."[15]

There is no doubt that the proclamation of Shiʿism as the "established church" was the most distinctive character of the new order. Evidently, it required some time for it to take root; and some writers (like Alessandro Bausani) maintained that Iran became fully Shīʿī only much later. "It is a fact," he says, "that when the Safavids arrived the majority of the Persian population was Sunnite, and the change to Shiʿism was a conscious and deliberate policy carried out by the Safavids themselves." "The effective conversion of the mass of the Persian people to Shiʿism," he adds, "probably occurred in the eighteenth century."[16]

3

Finally, when one reads Munshī's magisterial *Tārīkh-i ʿĀlam-ārā-yi ʿAbbāsī*, one gets the impression that here was a writer or historian consciously reflecting on the heroic origins of a state that has (in the reign of Shah ʿAbbās and proudly chronicled by Munshī the court historian) reached a golden age of grandeur and stability whose physical manifestation was the structurally and symmetrically beautiful and awe-inspiring Maydān-i Shāh in Isfahan.

In the first *jild* of Munshī's *Tārīkh,* the author traces the origins and rise to power of the Safavid dynasty in a grandiose style. He sums up the history of the reigns of the ancestors of Shah ʿAbbās from their Ṣūfī origins, to the founding of the state by Shah Ismāʿīl, through Ṭahmāsb, Ismāʿīl II, and Khudābanda. This is perhaps the best summary account we have of the pre-ʿAbbās period. There is a sense of inevitability in the telling of the story. To Munshī, the rise of the Safavids on the Iranian plateau between the Ottoman Turks in the West and the Uzbek Turks in the East (with the Mamluks in Egypt in the southwest and the Mughals of India in the southeast) was a natural and preordained event. The land mass where this took place was after all "Īrān-zamīn," the ancestral home of the Iranian people. (Never mind the fact that the military power that made it possible was Qizilbāsh Turkic, the court language Azeri Turkish, and he himself was Iskandar Beg Turkmān—i.e., of Turkish descent!)

Specifically, Munshī begins to conjure up images of ancient Iran of the era of the Khahāmenashī (Achaemenians). On the accession of Shah Ṭahmāsb, for example, he expresses himself as follows: "Of the sons of Shah Isma'il, Tahmasp, the eldest son, was most fit to succeed him on the throne of Khosrow and Kay-Qubad."[17]

On another occasion, the shah (Ṭahmāsb, in 939/1532–33) was coming to relieve Herat from Uzbek pressure. A poet sang in celebration: "O Pretender! Have you not heard that our Shah, who is like the stars in majesty and is revered like Jamshid, is approaching?"[18]

It is perhaps with Munshī that one begins to sense a pride in Iran's heroic past (some would even call it a revival). It is not "national" pride as much as reverberations of a nostalgia for earlier times. (After all, the most famous *Shāhnāmah* ever done was made at the royal workshops of Shah Ṭahmāsb by some of the greatest Safavid miniature painters.)[19]

With Ismā'īl it was *ghazā* and conquest; now we begin to look for recovery of *mulk-i mawrūth* (inherited possessions) as justification for conducting military campaigns. The country remained united in spite of pressures from the West and East. Although it may have lost Baghdad to the dreaded Turks, it kept Tabriz as part of Īrān-zamīn and Khurasan and Herat in the East, plus its possessions in the Caucasus and the Persian Gulf.

To Munshī, therefore, the *ghāzī* origins of the state were a thing of the past; and the Shī'ī-Ithnā'asharī foundations became the "established church" defended by the royal dynasty. But most of all, the Safavid state to him occupied its rightful place in the central part of the Middle East, where the Iranians, no matter how difficult it is to define them at this or any other time, will ultimately occupy their position among the nations of the world.

4

A concluding remark: the three interpretations of the rise of the Safavids briefly discussed here—namely, the *ghāzī* backgrounds, the Shī'ī-Ithnā'asharī faith, and the heroic nostalgia for a golden age—are in some way interrelated. The three forces worked together on the Iranian plateau to create, during the post-Caliphal, post-Mongol period, the beginning of a "nation state" that for some time served as a link between the later Middle Ages and the early modern times.

NOTES

1. Roger Savory, "Ṣafawids," in *Encyclopaedia of Islam,* 2nd ed. (*EI*²), 8:765.

2. Jean Aubin, "L'Avènement des Safavides reconsidéré," *Moyen Orient et Océan Indien* 5 (1988): 1–130.

3. Michel M. Mazzaoui, *The Origins of the Ṣafawids: Šī'ism, Ṣūfism, and the Ġulāt* (Wiesbaden: Franz Steiner, 1972).

4. The three historians: Faḍl Allāh ibn Rūzbihān Khunjī, *Tārīkh-i 'Ālam-ārā-yi Amīnī;* trans. V. Minorsky: *Persia in A.D. 1478–1490,* Royal Asiatic Society (London: Luzac, 1957); Ḥasan-i Rūmlū, *Aḥsan al-Tavārīkh,* ed. 'Abd al-Ḥusayn Nāva'ī (Tehran: Intishārāt-i Bābak, 1357/1979); trans. C. N. Seddon as *A Chronicle of the Early Safawis* (Baroda: Oriental Institute, 1931); Iskandar Beg Munshī, *Tārīkh-i 'Ālam-ārā-yi 'Abbāsī,* ed. Īraj Afshār (Tehran: Amīr Kabīr, 1334–35 Sh./1995–96); trans. R. Savory, *History of Shah 'Abbas* (Boulder: Westview Press, 1978).

5. Modern historians, especially the celebrated E. G. Browne, have discussed the rise of a spirit of Iranian nationalism during the Safavid period. This concept of *vaḥdat-e millī* is difficult to prove at this time. See the section "Nationality" in Browne's *A Literary History of Persia,* 4 vols. (Cambridge: Cambridge University Press, 1953), 4:12ff.

6. Shaykh Ṣafī al-Dīn became very famous as a Ṣūfī master during the post-Mongol period (d. A.D. 1334). *Ṣafvat al-Ṣafā,* on the life and times of Shaykh Ṣafī al-Dīn, has recently been edited by Ghulam-reza Tabataba'i Majd (Tabriz: published by the editor, 1373 Sh./ 1995).

7. From Minorsky's translation of Khunji's work, *Persia in A.D. 1478–1490,* p. 63.

8. Ibid.

9. Mustafa Kemal did it against the Greeks in Anatolia after the First World War and gained the honorific "ghāzī."

10. Khunjī/Minorsky, *Persia in A.D. 1478–1490,* p. 64.

11. Ibid., p. 69.

12. Ibid., p. 68.

13. V. Minorsky, "The Poetry of Shah Isma'il," *Bulletin of the School of Oriental and African Studies* 10 (1940–43): 10006a–1053a; quoted in Mazzaoui, *The Origins of the Ṣafawids,* p. 85.

14. Rūmlū, *Aḥsan* in Mazzaoui, *The Origins of the Ṣafawids,* pp. 1–2.

15. Rūmlū, *Aḥsan* in Mazzaoui, *The Origins of the Ṣafawids,* p. 2.

16. Alessandro Bausani, *The Persians* (New York: St. Martin's Press, 1971), p. 139.

17. Munshī/Savory, *History of Shah 'Abbas,* 1:145/1:75.

18. Ibid., 1:60/1:99.

19. The famous Houghton *Shahnamah,* done in a royal edition by Martin B. Dickson and Stuart Cary Welch, 2 vols. (Cambridge, Mass.: Harvard University Press, 1981.)

I

Naqshbandīs and Safavids

A Contribution to the Religious History of Iran and Her Neighbors

Hamid Algar

The circumstances surrounding the genesis of a Sufi order rarely give any hint of the ultimate scope of its diffusion—whether it is to remain local, expand regionally, or become quasi-universal. Thus the Naqshbandiyya first emerged as a crystallization of Sufi lineages, collectively known as the Khwājagān, that for six generations had been restricted to Transoxiana and Khwarazm. Most followers of the eponym, Bahā' al-Dīn Naqshband (718–91/1318–89), lived in the city of Bukhara or its surrounding villages; and there was little if any indication in his lifetime of the order's potential for diffusion throughout Central Asia and beyond.[1] The broader propagation of the order began with several of Bahā' al-Dīn's immediate successors: Khwāja 'Alā' al-Dīn 'Aṭṭār (d. 802/1400), for example, had among his disciples a certain 'Abdullāh Imāmī Iṣfahānī, and his son and successor, Ḥasan 'Aṭṭār (d. 826/1423), extended the influence of the order south to Herat.[2]

It was not until late in the ninth/fifteenth century, however, that the true expansion of the order began, principally although not exclusively at the hands of Khwāja 'Ubaydullāh Aḥrār (806–95/1404–90). His disciples propagated the Naqshbandiyya throughout much of Central Asia and took it west to Ottoman Turkey, Syria, and the Hijaz. Among the places where the order now made its appearance were also certain areas of Iran, a land soon to be submerged by the violent tides of Safavid Shi'ism; the lifespan of the Naqshbandiyya in places such as Tabriz and Qazvin was therefore destined to be relatively brief. The Naqshbandī presence in pre-Safavid and early Safavid Iran nonetheless deserves to be studied in some detail, as a topic of importance both for the overall history of the Naqshbandiyya and for the religious transformation of Iran that accompanied the foundation of the Safavid state.

THREE PUPILS OF AḤRĀR IN TABRIZ

Three followers of Aḥrār are known to have lived in Tabriz, the city that was to be the first capital of the Safavid state, in the late Aqqoyunlu period. They are virtually unmentioned in the principal sources on Aḥrār, notably Fakhr al-Dīn 'Alī Ṣafī's *Rashaḥāt-i 'Ayn al-Ḥayāt,* and it is therefore unlikely that they were particularly close to him.[3] Moreover, none of them were native to the city, and it is unclear when and why two of the three chose to settle there. It is tempting to hypothesize that they did so in obedience to directives of Aḥrār aimed at establishing a Naqshbandī presence in the Aqqoyunlu capital, given his own attempts to establish ascendancy over the Timurids. There is nothing in their biographies to support such a hypothesis, however; nor is there any evidence of coordination of activity or even mutual acquaintance among the three pupils of Aḥrār in pre-Safavid Tabriz.

The first of the trio, Khwāja Muḥammad Amīn Bulghārī, was a native of Kazan and as such probably the first person from the Volga-Ural region to acquire a Naqshbandī affiliation. Why he settled in Tabriz instead of returning to his homeland after completing his training with Aḥrār is unknown. He does not appear to have devoted any energy to propagating the Naqshbandiyya in Tabriz. He is related to have spent much of his time reading and copying out works of Sufi literature and keeping the company of a Kubravī shaykh, Badr al-Dīn Aḥmad Lālā'ī (d. 912/1506), whose esteem for him was such that he permitted him the use of his personal retreat at a *khānaqāh* in the significantly named village of Darvīshābād.[4] This intimacy was due in part, no doubt, to Bulghārī's prior acquaintance with Lālā'ī's own master, Mīr Sayyid 'Abdullāh Barzishābādī (d. ca. 856/1452).[5] Credited with numerous miraculous feats (*khavāriq-i 'ādāt*) as well as a firm command of both the exoteric and esoteric sciences, Bulghārī left no initiatic descendants when he died sometime in the reign of Rustam Shah Aqqoyunlu.[6]

Another former associate of Aḥrār resident in Tabriz in the immediate pre-Safavid period was Bābā Ni'matullāh b. Shaykh Maḥmūd Nakhchivānī, also known as Shaykh 'Alvān.[7] Little is known of his activity there except that he, too, had collegial relations with Sufis of other affiliations, especially the Khalvatī Dede 'Umar Raushanī (d. 892/1487), whom he visited on his deathbed.[8] It was also in Tabriz, in 902/1496, that Nakhchivānī completed a well-regarded Arabic commentary on the Qur'ān, *al-Fawātiḥ al-Ilāhiyya wa 'l-Mafātīḥ al-Ghaybiyya,* a work of considerable stylistic beauty marred only by occasional Persianisms.[9] Written without consulting any existing commentary, this *tafsīr* appears at first sight to have few specifically Sufi features, given its general avoidance of technical vocabulary; it is nonetheless pervaded by the themes of moral purification and spiritual advancement. Further, it displays an attention to thematic continuity from one *sūra* to the next rarely encountered in premodern commentaries and is additionally distinguished by treating the *bismillah* at the beginning of each *sūra* as syntactically connected to its opening verse and thus bearing a slightly different meaning on each occasion.[10]

Nakhchivānī left Tabriz for Anatolia in 904/1498 and settled the following year in Akşehir, which had come definitively under Ottoman rule in 867/1463; he died there in 920/1514. This final migration may have been prompted by dismay at the progressive disintegration of the Aqqoyunlu state. Neither in Tabriz nor in Akşehir does Nakhchivānī appear to have done anything to propagate the Naqshbandī path. In apparent violation of the Naqshbandī principle of "seclusion within society" (*khalvat dar anjuman*), he was much given to withdrawal and isolation, to the degree that Taşköprüzade remarks of him that "he was wont to conceal himself" (*kāna yukhfi nafsahu*).[11] An aversion to the tasks of spiritual guidance can be deduced, too, from Nakhchivānī's expression of regret that Dede ʿUmar Raushanī had seen fit to burden himself with the administration of the *khānaqāh* established for him by Saljūq Khātūn, mother of Sultan Yaʿqub Aqqoyunlu.[12]

The life of a third disciple of Aḥrār active in Tabriz, Mīr Sirāj al-Dīn ʿAbd al-Vahhāb Hamadānī, is known in far greater detail; but it conveys a similar impression of disinclination to spread the *ṭarīqa* or even of alienation from it. The Naqshbandī element in his life is, in fact, restricted to a period of study with Aḥrār of unknown length and intensity.[13] His father, Najm al-Dīn ʿAbd al-Ghaffār Ṭabāṭabāʾī, a well-regarded *sayyid,* was closely connected to the Aqqoyunlu dynasty. Meeting Uzun Ḥasan in Diyarbekir before his rise to power, he had foretold his conquest of Azerbayjan, Fars, and Baghdad; and he was rewarded with appointment as Shaykh al-Islām of Tabriz when the prediction came true. He is said at the same time to have been fully engaged in the practice of Sufism, albeit under the Ḥurūfī-tainted auspices of Qāsim-i Anvār (d. 837/1433–34).[14] ʿAbd al-Ghaffār must have spent considerable time in Samarqand before settling in Tabriz, for it was there that his son ʿAbd al-Vahhāb was born, grew to maturity, and became a follower of Aḥrār. Summoned to Tabriz to join his father, ʿAbd al-Vahhāb Hamadānī had the misfortune to arrive there just after his death but the good fortune, as a scholar of superior accomplishments, to inherit his position as Shaykh al-Islām and to hold it continuously until the end of Aqqoyunlu rule.

There is no evidence whatsoever to suggest that ʿAbd al-Vahhāb manifested any sign of Naqshbandī identity after coming to Tabriz, let alone that he used his office to propagate the *ṭarīqa.* It is possible, although by no means proven, that he nurtured a hidden inclination to Shiʿism; this would not only explain his lack of enthusiasm for the Naqshbandiyya but also help to account for his later rallying to the cause of Shah Ismāʿīl. This possibility is raised most insistently in Muhyi Gülşenî's *Menâkıb-ı Ibrahim Gülşenî*—a hagiographical account of Shaykh Ibrahim Gülşenî (d. 940/1533), founder of a branch of the Khalvatiyya named after him—that was written about sixty-seven years after the shaykh's death. The author portrays ʿAbd al-Vahhāb Hamadānī as a malicious, obstinate, but ultimately powerless antagonist of Gülşenî, motivated primarily by base *"rāfiḍī"* (i.e., Shiʿite) tendencies.

The first contest between the two men described in the *Menâkıb* took place in the presence of Sultan Yaʿqūb (r. 883–896/1478–90), when Gülşenî was discoursing on the meaning of Qurʾān 2:152: "Remember Me and I will remember you" (*faʾdhkurūnī adhkurkum*). The qadi of Yazd, a protégé of ʿAbd al-Vahhāb who had come to court in order to present a petition, sought to undermine the shaykh's homily by citing the *ḥadīth* "whosoever says *lā ilāha illāh ʾllāh* shall enter Paradise" as evidence that mere verbal utterance of the creed is enough to gain divine favor. ʿAbd al-Vahhāb concurred with the qadi's argument and, unwisely spurning Gülşenî's charitable attempt to gloss over the crude error it contained, found himself embarrassed before the sultan.[15]

A series of more dangerous confrontations ensued when Gülşenî decided to go on the hajj in 900/1494 (because "the signs of turbulence were appearing"), and ʿAbd al-Vahhāb insisted on accompanying him. His primary aim was to have Amīr Zakariyā Baghdādī (the *amīr al-ḥajj* appointed by Sultan Rustam) replaced by a Shiʿite of his own acquaintance, Sayyid Muḥammad Mukavvanī, so that the pilgrims from Tabriz would be compelled to make the hajj under Shiʿite leadership; for ʿAbd al-Vahhāb was "outwardly a Sunni, but inwardly a *rāfiḍī*."[16] When he failed to accomplish this, he sought—after arriving in Baghdad—to persuade the pilgrims that the route before them was swarming with locusts, that the wells had dried up, and that bandits belonging to the Mushaʿshaʿ sect of Khuzistan would seek to enslave them. The majority of the pilgrims nonetheless continued to put their trust in Gülşenî, and ʿAbd al-Vahhāb therefore plotted to have him assassinated by a Shiʿite fanatic once the pilgrims reached Karbala. The would-be assassin was caught by servants of the shaykh, who forgave and released him. The attempts that ʿAbd al-Vahhāb made at Najaf and Rahba to sabotage the progress of the hajj caravan under Gülşenî's leadership were similarly unsuccessful; ultimately, as a result of the shaykh's earnest prayers, ʿAbd al-Vahhāb even repented of his evil ways and entered Medina as a *murīd* of Gülşenî. This repentance plainly entailed a renunciation of his crypto-Shiʿism, for in the dream that led to his change of heart he saw four figures whom Gülşenî helpfully identified for him as the Four Righteous Caliphs of Sunni belief.[17]

The purely hagiographical aspects of this narrative are clearly questionable as a source of historical fact; in particular, no other contemporary or near-contemporary account identifies ʿAbd al-Vahhāb as ever having become a follower of Gülşenî. Significant, nonetheless, are the absence in the *Menâkıb* of any reference to ʿAbd al-Vahhāb as a Naqshbandī and the depiction of him as an enemy of Gülşenî, which must at least reflect some tension between the two men; this contrasts strongly with the respect Nakhchivānī had shown Dede ʿUmar Raushanī, Gülşenî's master, as a fellow Sufi. The attribution in the *Menâkıb* of Shiʿite tendencies to ʿAbd al-Vahhāb is not entirely implausible, given his later entry into the service of Shah Ismāʿīl. Ibn al-Karbalāʾī's *Rauḍāt al-Jinān,* the most detailed and reliable source available on the Sufis of pre-Safavid Tabriz, however, does not attribute any such tendencies to ʿAbd al-Vahhāb. Moreover, if he had been a secret Shiʿite, simply biding his time until the establishment of Shiʿite supremacy in Tabriz, he would presumably have offered his services to Shah Ismāʿīl as soon as he captured the city. Yet, according to precisely the *Menâkıb,* ʿAbd al-Vahhāb was one of those in Tabriz who as a measure of caution donned the Qizilbash headgear in anticipation of Shah Ismāʿīl's arrival, only to remove it gleefully when Alvand Khān, ʿAbd al-Vahhāb's brother-in-law, slowed Ismāʿīl's advance on the city by defeating him at Marand. When Shah Ismāʿīl recovered from this setback and resumed his march on Tabriz, ʿAbd al-Vahhāb fled in fear of his wrath.[18]

ʿAbd al-Vahhāb made his way from Tabriz to Herat, where he was hospitably received at the Timurid court as a *sayyid* of high rank, possibly as a result of links he had established while in Samarqand. But when Ḥusayn Mīrzā Bāyqarā died in 912/1506, ʿAbd al-Vahhāb wrote to Shah Ismāʿīl to inquire about the possibility of a safe return to Tabriz. He received an encouraging response; bidding farewell to Badīʿ al-Zamān Mīrzā, the last of the Timurids to rule over Herat, he left the city shortly before it fell to Muḥammad Shībānī the Uzbek. Back in Tabriz, he not only resumed his functions as Shaykh al-Islām, now under the auspices of the Safavid regime, but also enjoyed the personal favor of Shah Ismāʿīl, despite the general distaste for keeping the company of *sayyid*s revealingly attributed to him by Ibn al-Karbalāʾī.[19] ʿAbd al-Vahhāb reciprocated by remaining loyal to Shah Ismāʿīl when he fled his capital after the Battle of Çaldıran and during the eight-day Ottoman occupation of Tabriz that followed.

It is nonetheless plain that ʿAbd al-Vahhāb was also respected by the Ottomans, for Sultan Selim mentioned him alone by name (and by epithet, as "the pride of the *sayyid*s [*fakhr al-sādāt*]") in the letter he sent to the notables of Tabriz on 2 Rajab 920/August 23, 1514, announcing the impending arrival in their city of an Ottoman army under the command of Dukakinzade Ahmed Paşa.[20] It may have been because of ʿAbd al-Vahhāb's apparent acceptability to the Ottomans that Shah Ismāʿīl entrusted him with a diplomatic mission to Istanbul that was designed primarily to win the return of Tājlū Khānum, one of his wives who had been abducted by the Ottomans after the Battle of Çaldıran.[21] The party reached Amasya safely on 11 Shavvāl 920/November 29, 1514, but one week later ʿAbd al-Vahhāb Hamadānī and other members of his group were arrested and taken to Istanbul in chains.[22] ʿAbd al-Vahhāb was imprisoned at Rumeli Hisar until Kânûnî Süleyman succeeded Selim in 926/1520; but he remained in Istanbul, perhaps voluntarily, until death supervened either as early as the next year or sometime after 930/1524; in either case, his final resting place was the cemetery at Eyüp.[23]

ʿAbd al-Vahhāb's ability to serve successively Aqqoyunlu, Timurid, and Safavid rulers—as well as to gain the favor of Sultan Selim, at least until the ill-fated diplomatic mission of 920/1514—might be taken at first sight as a consummate form of opportunism, a Talleyrandesque ability to survive and even benefit from changes of regime. With the exception of the *Menâkıb-ı Gülşenî,* however, all contemporary or near-contemporary sources speak of him with respect as a religious scholar of real merit and learning, and the testament he wrote to his sons from his place of confinement reveals delicacy of spirit and genuine erudition. The reason for his broad acceptability may have lain rather in his status as a *sayyid* of high rank in an age when veneration for descendants of the Prophet was still an important part of Sunni—not to mention Shiʿite—spirituality.[24] Thus Ḥusayn Mīrzā Bāyqarā appointed him overseer of the *sayyid*s of Herat;[25] Sultan Selim addressed him as "pride of the *sayyids*";[26] Shah Ismāʿīl described him as "refuge of the rank of *sayyid* and stewardship [*niqābat*] ... and light of the quality of *sayyid* [*nūr al-siyāda*]";[27] and Ibrahim Paşa, Selim's grand vizier, objected to his master's inhospitable treatment of ʿAbd al-Vahhāb partly on the grounds that he was a "*sayyid* of authentic lineage [*seyyid-i sahihü 'n-neseb*]."[28]

As for ʿAbd al-Vahhāb's confessional loyalties, there is no firm evidence that he ever abandoned Sunnism. His entry into the service of Shah Ismāʿīl is not automatic proof of the contrary; it may well be that the first Safavid ruler, for all his virulent hatred of Sunni Islam, thought it politic to install in a position of influence a well-regarded Sunni notable who might reconcile the citizens of Tabriz to the new order being imposed on them. Motivated by a hostility to ʿAbd al-Vahhāb, the reasons for which are difficult to discern, the author of the *Menâkıb-ı Gülşenî* may have deduced from ʿAbd al-Vahhāb's agreement to serve as Shah Ismāʿīl's Shaykh al-Islām an embrace of Shiʿism, which he then projected back into the Aqqoyunlu past. It is probable that Sultan Selim's initial regard for ʿAbd al-Vahhāb rested on the assumption that he was Sunni and that his imprisonment of him in Istanbul, in violation of the prevalent diplomatic norms, was motivated at least in part by disapproval of a Sunni representing the heretical Safavid state.[29] The only textual evidence to survive from ʿAbd al-Vahhāb, the testament that he addressed from Istanbul to his sons in Tabriz, is ambiguous. On the one hand, it cites several traditions of Imam Jaʿfar al-Ṣādiq, following the mention of his name with the invocation *ʿalayhi ʾl-salām* ("upon whom be peace"), which is normally used only by Shiʿites in such a context. On the other hand, it also cites a *ḥadīth* transmitted by Abū Hurayra, a narrator universally condemned as unreliable, even fraudulent, by Shiʿite scholars of tradition.[30]

It may be that ʿAbd al-Vahhāb Hamadānī was in an intermediate or transitional state between Sunnism and Shiʿism or that he had elaborated a personal amalgam of the two positions; there may well have been others among his contemporaries who sought to solve in similar fashion the acute religious and political dilemma with which they were faced.[31] But as for the descendants of ʿAbd al-Vahhāb, they were indubitably Shiʿite and had no connection to the Naqshbandiyya.[32]

ṢUNʿULLĀH KŪZAKUNĀNĪ AND HIS DESCENDANTS

Despite their affiliations with Khwāja Aḥrār, the depth and duration of which cannot be reliably measured, none of the three individuals reviewed manifested any concern for the implantation of the Naqshbandiyya as a functioning *ṭarīqa* in pre-Safavid Tabriz. In any event, Bulghārī had died, and Nakhchivānī had migrated to Akşehir, several years before Shah Ismāʿīl's entry into Tabriz; and despite initial misgivings, ʿAbd al-Vahhāb entered his service. It was a Naqshbandī from a different lineage, Ṣunʿullāh Kūzakunānī (d. 929/1522–23), who was active in spreading the *ṭarīqa* in the Tabriz region both before and after the change of regime. His career therefore illustrates far more clearly the challenges faced by the Naqshbandiyya under the nascent Safavid dispensation.

Born in the village of Kūzakunān in the Urūnāq district, some twelve *farsakh*s from the city of Tabriz, Ṣunʿullāh acquired proficiency in the rational and transmitted sciences from unnamed teachers before setting out for Khurasan, "the source of the saints and the mine of the pious," in search of a spiritual master.[33] Arriving in Herat, he attached himself to the circle of ʿAbd al-Raḥmān Jāmī (d. 898/1492), took up residence in a *madrasa* he administered, and acted as his personal *imām*. In accordance with his customary reluctance to act as preceptor, however, Jāmī referred Ṣunʿullāh for purposes of spiritual training to Maulānā ʿAlāʾ al-Dīn Ābīzī Maktabdār, who like himself had been initiated into the Naqshbandiyya by Saʿd al-Dīn Kāshgharī (d. 860/1456).[34] Kāshgharī's descent from the eponym of the order was by way of Khwāja ʿAlāʾ al-Dīn ʿAṭṭār and Maulānā Niẓām al-Dīn Khāmūsh (d. ca. 853/

1449) and differed, therefore, from that of his better-known contemporary Aḥrār, with whom he was nonetheless in friendly contact.

Early in the reign of Ya'qūb Mīrzā (883–96/1478–90), Ṣun'ullāh returned to Tabriz, where he immediately gained the approbation of Badr al-Dīn Lālā'ī, the same Kubravī shaykh with whom Muḥammad Amīn Bulghārī had associated. After performing the hajj, Ṣun'ullāh took up residence in the Naubar district of Tabriz, built a mosque near the Chahār-sū-yi 'Arabān, and set about propagating the path of the Naqshbandī masters. In this he was evidently successful, and he gained a reputation for piety that was much enhanced when he refused to leave Tabriz during an outbreak of the plague, remaining in the city to care for the sick and the dying and to help bury the dead. Indeed, his prestige was such that he was always able to intervene with the rulers "in speech, deed, and writing," on behalf of the victims of injustice, and he came to expect their deference to him as a matter of course. When Aḥmad Gövde (r. 902–3/1497) neglected to pay him his respects on the eve of a campaign in Iraq, Ṣun'ullāh was offended; despite entreaties by other members of the Aqqoyunlu family, he refused to pray for Gövde's victory and remarked: "Neglect of the dervishes, particularly the followers and servants of 'Abd al-Khāliq Ghijduvānī, does not lead to good results." The inevitable consequence was that Aḥmad Gövde suffered a prompt defeat near Khwānsār.[35]

When Shah Ismā'īl took Tabriz in 907/1501, Ṣun'ullāh clearly thought it best not to rely on his own occult powers for protection. He fled to Bitlis, where he remained for a number of years until nostalgia brought him back to Tabriz. Unlike 'Abd al-Vahhāb, he did not take the precaution of obtaining a guarantee of safety from Shah Ismā'īl before returning and when brought into his presence even refused the full prostration required by court protocol. This display of courage is said to have impressed the shah favorably, and he consented to the suggestion of the *ṣadr* Mīr Jamāl al-Dīn Iṣfahānī that Ṣun'ullāh be released. Ṣun'ullāh lived out the rest of his life unmolested in Tabriz, and it can even be deduced from Khwāndmīr's *Ḥabīb al-Siyar*, written between 927/1521 and 930/1524, that little if any attempt was made to curtail his influence: "From the early days of the reign of Ya'qūb Mīrzā down to the present day, he [Ṣun'ullāh Kūzakunānī] has been seated on the carpet of piety and abstemiousness in the noble city of Tabriz and is celebrated among the people of that region for the purity of his soul and the clarity of his spirit."[36] He died peacefully in 929/1523 and was buried in the cemetery at Surkhāb.[37]

Ṣun'ullāh Kūzakunānī's ability to function with some degree of freedom is confirmed by the fact that he was survived by two *khalīfa*s. The more important of them was Darvīsh Jalāl al-Dīn Akhī Khusraushāhī, who several years earlier, after turning his back on a life of youthful profligacy that had brought him within an inch of the gallows, had joined the following of Bāyazīd Khalkhālī, a follower of the Kubravī Sayyid Muḥammad Nūrbakhsh (d. 869/1465). When Nūrbakhsh proclaimed himself the Mahdī, Khalkhālī broke with him and dissolved his own following. Thereupon Khusraushāhī transferred his loyalties to Ṣun'ullāh Kūzakunānī, continuing to practice the vocal *dhikr* he had acquired from his first affiliation instead of the silent *dhikr* that was normative for the Naqshbandīs; it is probable that this, too, was the method of invocation he transmitted to his spiritual descendants. He spent the rest of his life in his native village of Khusraushāh; the date of his death is unknown.[38]

Khusraushāhī was succeeded in turn by Maulānā Ilyās Bādāmyārī, a *khalīfa* who had acquired two *ṭarīqa* affiliations before coming to the Naqshbandiyya. In his birthplace of Gāvrūd, Maulānā Ilyās was first initiated into a Nūrbakhshī lineage by his father, Shaykh 'Īsā, after whose death he joined the following of 'Abd al-Ḥayy Gīlānī, a Kubravī shaykh.[39] It seems that he passed on this multiple ancestry to his own initiatic descendants, for one of them, Açıkbaş Mahmud Efendi, wrote a treatise entitled *Risāla-yi Nūrbakhshiyya* in which he detailed the litanies recited by Kubravīs and Nūrbakhshīs as well as Naqshbandīs.[40] This joint cultivation of Kubravī and Naqshbandī tradition by the line descending from Maulānā Ilyās is not particularly remarkable, similar instances being encountered, for example, in Central Asia.[41] The Nūrbakhshiyya, however, an offshoot of the Kubraviyya, espoused a variety of Shi'ism (albeit initially an extremely eccentric one) that seems difficult to reconcile with the assertively Sunni identity of almost all Naqshbandīs. Whatever may be the explanation of the compound he bequeathed to his descendants, Maulānā Ilyās died and was buried in Bādāmyār in Shavvāl 965/May–June 1558, aged well over a hundred.

The other known *khalīfa* of Ṣun'ullāh Kūzakunānī was Maulānā 'Alī-jān Bādāmyārī, concerning whom nothing is reported other than his death in 967/1560 at Akhtarīn, a village two *farsakh*s from Aleppo.[42] This detail may suggest, however, that by the middle of the tenth/sixteenth century the relative tolerance from which the Naqshbandīs of the Tabriz region had benefited was coming to an end, for there are two other instances of Naqshbandī migration to Ottoman territory at about the same time.

Concerning the first of these migrants, Ahmed Mumcu Paşa Efendi, another *murīd* of Khusraushāhī, nothing is recorded other than that he died at Çiçekli near Giresun on the coast of the Black Sea.[43] Considerably more is known of the other, Abū Sa'īd Kūzakunānī, the son of Ṣun'ullāh, thanks to the detailed and vivid biography provided by Nevîzade Ataî in the *Hadâikü 'l-Hakâik;* his account shows clearly how the fate of some Naqshbandīs became enmeshed in the struggle between the Safavids and the Ottomans. Born in Tabriz on 8 Dhū 'l-Qa'da, 920/December 25, 1514, soon after his father's return from exile in Bitlis, the child was optimistically named after the celebrated early Khurasanian Sufi Abū Sa'īd b. Abī 'l-Khayr (d. 440/1049); a chronogram composed to honor his birth called him indeed "the second Bū Sa'īd-i Abū 'l-Khayr." He studied with his father and a number of scholars, the most prominent of whom was Ghiyāṣ al-Dīn Manṣūr, but there is no indication that he sought himself to continue his father's initiatic line. He nonetheless found it advisable to flee to Anatolia on the pretext of making the hajj, in the company of an uncle, Shaykh 'Azīz. Shah Ṭahmāsp discovered his plans and had him imprisoned, imposing on him a fine of 10,000 gold dinars (*dīnār-i surkh*) in order to discourage similar attempts to flee by others. In order to pay the fine Abū Sa'īd sold off all his property, for whatever he could get; and when the proceeds proved insufficient, he engaged in hard labor to pay off the balance, remaining all the while under close surveillance. Finally, with the help of persons "close to Islam" (by which Nevîzade presumably means crypto-Sunnis), Abū Sa'īd was able to escape Tabriz and to take refuge at the tomb of Shaykh Ṣafī al-Dīn, ancestor of the Safavid family, at Ardabil. (That this Safavid shrine, which for long counted as an *imāmzāda* thanks to the Mūsawī genealogy attributed to the family, should provide inviolable sanctuary for a Sunni fleeing the wrath of Ṭahmāsp is not without its irony; it is almost as if Shaykh Ṣafī al-Dīn were posthumously extending his protection to a person with whom he had more in common than with his own descendants.)

Abū Sa'īd remained in Ardabil for two years, in the service of (or possibly studying with) a certain Mullā Ḥusayn Ardabīlī. He emerged from the shrine in 955/1548—when Kânûnî Süleyman, encouraged by the Safavid renegade Alqāṣ Mīrzā, launched another Ottoman invasion of Azerbayjan—and made his way to the Ottoman camp. He was granted immediate protection and accompanied the Ottoman army as it withdrew from Azerbayjan by way of Diyarbekir. Thence he proceeded to Aleppo, where he was provided with a modest allowance. Unhappy with the amount, he let it be known that he was contemplating a move to India to attach himself to the Mughal emperor Humāyūn.[44] Thereupon Rüstem Paşa arranged for him to live in Istanbul with a provisional allowance of fifteen *akçe* on the understanding that it was to be gradually increased to thirty-five *akçe;* in fact it ultimately reached 100 *akçe* during the vizierate of Ali Paşa. Apart from performing the hajj in 971/1564, Abū Sa'īd remained in Istanbul until his death in Jumādā 'l-Ūlā 980/September 1572, and he was buried next to the mosque of Şeyh Vefa.

A somewhat eccentric recluse, the son of Ṣun'ullāh Kūzakunānī seems to have done little to justify his sobriquet of "the second Abū Sa'īd." He was learned in the rational and transmitted sciences; and *tafsīr* appears to have been his principal interest, for he compiled a biographical dictionary of *mufassirīn* and made a translation (presumably into Turkish) of the *tafsīr* of Bayḍāwī.[45] He did not show much interest in Sufism, despite the Naqshbandī training he had received from his father. Obsessively fastidious in matters of ritual purity, he constantly washed his clothes and eating vessels and brushed his boots to remove all trace of imagined pollution. He would also wash immediately after he had shaken hands with anyone. It is not therefore surprising that he never showed the taste for mingling with his fellows that the function of Sufi shaykh would have required, nor even married.[46]

Another indication of the conditions that had impelled Abū Saʿīd Kūzakunānī to flee Safavid territory was that Sayyid Muḥammad Bādāmyārī, a relative and *khalīfa* of Maulānā Ilyās Bādāmyārī, found himself obliged to quit the region of Tabriz and to seek refuge, with all his relatives and followers, in Urūmiya. It is worth noting that there, too, he was not free of polemical attention from Shiʿites; but in that largely Kurdish city they were obliged for the time being to restrict themselves to inconclusive debate.[47] Indeed, the Bādāmyārī line persisted there for some three generations.[48]

Muḥammad Bādāmyārī was first succeeded in Urūmiya by his son Sayyid Aḥmad (or, according to some sources, Muḥammad), commonly known as Koç Baba or Koçağa Sultan (d. 1016/1607), whose posthumous fate is described by Evliyâ Çelebi in his account of a visit to Urūmiya in 1056/1646.[49] He reports that Koçağa Sultan's tomb was "an exalted threshold" (*bir ulu asitane*), surrounded with gardens and so richly endowed that the more than 300 resident dervishes were able to entertain lavishly all who came to visit the shrine. It so happened that the governor of Urūmiya, a certain Tuqmāq Khān —for by now the Safavids were in control of the city—coveted the wealth of one of Koçağa Sultan's followers, which he thought he could more easily possess if he put the man to death. The man pleaded for his life by invoking the spirit of Koçağa Sultan, which enraged Tuqmāq Khān to the point that he not only had him killed forthwith but also ordered the disinterment of Koçağa Sultan's remains. The body proved to be miraculously intact, so the command was given for it to be burnt, the only result being that it was heard to proclaim: "I am the second Abraham, O Eternally Living One!"[50] The body was therefore reburied, with the funeral prayers performed over it anew, and flowers exuding a uniquely exquisite perfume sprang up on the site of the abortive immolation. Still intent on his evil design, Tuqmāq Khān proposed to the Safavid monarch, Muḥammad Khudābanda, that attempts be resumed to destroy "the *tekke* of the Sunnis," but the shah told him to desist.[51]

Quite apart from its hagiographical aspects, Evliyâ Çelebi's account is plainly inaccurate in at least one respect: the reign of Muḥammad Khudābanda came to an end in 996/1588, some thirty years before the death of Koçağa Sultan. It may nonetheless be permissible to deduce from it a story of Safavid determination to destroy a much frequented Naqshbandī shrine in the face of popular resistance. The story ends with the posthumous triumph of Koçağa

Sultan, and his line is known to have continued in Urūmiya for three more generations: he was succeeded first by his son Sayyid ʿAlī and then by his grandson Sayyid Ṣiddīq, who was followed by his son Sayyid Abvābī ʿĀjizī.[52] Nevertheless, another of Koçağa Sultan's sons, Shaykh Maḥmūd, evidently regarded Safavid hostility as reason enough to abandon Urūmiya and migrate to Diyarbekir, a destination that in the long run also proved no haven.

THE SHAYKH FROM URŪMIYA AND HIS DESCENDANTS IN DIYARBEKIR, BURSA, AND ERZURUM

It was probably the reconquest of Urūmiya by Shah ʿAbbās in 1012/1603, resulting in the definitive incorporation of the area into the Safavid realm after a quarter-century of Ottoman rule, that prompted the departure of Shaykh Maḥmūd. Once arrived in Diyarbekir, where he was sometimes known as *Rumiye şeyhi* or *şeyh-i Rumi* (the shaykh from Urūmiya) but more commonly as Şeyh Aziz, he quickly won a fame that radiated far beyond the city. "Military commanders and pashas visited his *tekke*," writes the historian Naîmâ. "From the lands of Tabriz and Erivan, from all the districts of Kurdistan, from Erzurum and Mosul, from Urfa and Van, people flocked to his feet."[53] It was precisely this imposing following, with its threatening insurrectionary potential, that led to the downfall of Şeyh Aziz.

The first hint of trouble came in 1045/1635 when Sultan Murad IV was preparing to besiege the citadel of Erivan. Şeyh Aziz accompanied the army, whether on his own initiative or by invitation; and such was his fame that many people came to the camp expressly in order to see him, arousing the anger of the sultan.[54] Matters were made worse by the suggestions of intriguers in the royal camp that the shaykh, "with his 40,000 powerful followers, vociferously proclaiming their divine love," might be tempted to rebel like the Mahdī (*mehdi gibi sahib-i huruc ola*). Murad initially paid no heed to these warnings but had occasion to remember them three years later when he passed through Diyarbekir on his way to Baghdad. The shaykh, accompanied by 3,000 immaculately dressed dervishes, was among the notables of the city who came out to meet him, addressing him as *hünkâr* ("sovereign" but also, according to a popular etymology, "shedder of blood"), with particular emphasis on the first syllable (*hün* = Persian *khūn*).[55] Asked to explain this intonation, the shaykh replied that Murad would conquer Baghdad after a forty-day siege and justly shed the blood of many Qizilbash but that on his return he would pay heed to the calumny of intriguers and shed blood unjustly in Diyarbekir. Disregarding this prediction, Murad replied that on his return from Baghdad he would set about the conquest of Malta.[56]

Şeyh Aziz's prediction of the conquest of Baghdad, complete with the slaughter of 42,000 Qizilbash in the space of seven hours, predictably came true; and Murad decided to reward him richly on his return to Diyarbekir. The intriguers therefore redoubled their efforts, reporting to Murad that the shaykh could now produce unlimited amounts of gold, having mastered the art of alchemy, and was therefore even more likely than before to revolt.[57] Intrigued, Murad asked the shaykh for a demonstration of his alchemical skill; with the assistance of the daughter of a Druze chieftain resident in the women's quarters of his house, he obliged, much to his own detriment. For after brief reflection, Murad decided to have the shaykh strangled, together with his Druze assistant.[58]

A quite different explanation for Şeyh Aziz's execution is put forward by the historian Peçevî (who, it may be noted, had attended his gatherings while serving in Diyarbekir as *defterdar* and shared in the general reverence he inspired). The shaykh had invited Hâseki Sultan, a lady in the royal household, to visit him; but disturbed by some aspect of her demeanor (*bir vaz'ına gayet bî-huzur olmuş*), he was imprudent enough to strike her with a mace. The enraged sultan cursed him roundly and had him put to death forthwith.[59]

Whatever the motives that led to Şeyh Aziz's execution (primarily, no doubt, a paranoid fear inspired by the activities of a shaykh with a large and variegated following in the unstable lands of Eastern Anatolia), Murad is said to have regretted his deed profoundly, to the extent that, according to Evliyâ Çelebi, he died with the words *Ah, Şeyh-i Rumi!* on his lips.[60] According to rumors that Peçevî heard after the event in distant Temesvar, Murad's own person was miraculously punished for his misdeed: the gout that had begun to afflict him during the Erivan campaign paralyzed him on the very day of the shaykh's execution; as a result he was never able to mount a horse again, and he died the following year.[61] Nature itself bore witness to the injustice that had occurred: a spring in Diyarbekir turned blood-red as soon as the deed was done.[62]

Şeyh Aziz left behind a book of some length as testimony to his teachings.[63] More important for the perpetuation of his memory, however, were his various *khalīfa*s, beginning with his musically gifted son Ismail. Born in 1020/1611, he fell heir both to his father's rank as shaykh and to the high regard he had enjoyed. At the time of Evliyâ Çelebi's visit in 1065/1655, the ceremonies of *dhikr* performed at the *tekke* that Şeyh Aziz had founded aroused the great traveler's admiration as unparalleled in any other land.[64] In addition, the *tekke*'s resources were still considerable enough to provide lavishly both for resident *murīd*s and for travelers.[65] On Ismail's death in 1080/1670, he was similarly succeeded by his son Ahmed, of whom it is recorded that he also inherited the musical talents of his father.[66] He was evidently the last of his family to exercise the function of shaykh in Diyarbekir, for no successor has been ascribed to him.

Meanwhile, another of the successors of Şeyh Aziz, his nephew Açıkbaş Şeyh Mahmud Efendi, had carried this branch of the Naqshbandiyya to Bursa. Born in Diyarbekir, he served for a while as the *voyvoda* of Mardin before leaving government service and embarking on a series of travels that took him as far as Cairo and Baghdad. Settling in Bursa, he dispensed the teachings of this branch of the *ṭarīqa* from what came to be known as the Nakşibendî-i Atîk Dergahe, while attaining great popularity as a preacher in the Dâye Hatun mosque and the Ulu Cami.[67] Açıkbaş Mahmud Efendi also attained some renown as a poet, using either Resmî or Âcizî as a *mahlas*. More interesting than his poetry are, however, his *Risâle-i Nurbahşiyye,* in which he provides the litanies recited by Kubravīs and Naqshbandīs as well as Nūrbakhshīs, and his translation with commentary of the *Aurād-i Fatḥiyya,* a litany ascribed to a Kubravī master, Sayyid ʿAlī Hamadānī (d. 786/1384).[68] He also wrote a work on twelve sciences that he dedicated to Köprülüzade Ahmed Paşa.[69] Açıkbaş Mahmud Efendi is said to have been highly regarded by Sultan Mehmed IV, evidently on account of the loyalty he displayed during the occupation of Bursa by Hasan Paşa, a Celalî rebel. This royal favor may have encouraged him to commit the near-fatal mistake of speaking unguardedly during an audience with Köprülü Mehmed Paşa that was originally designed to settle a dispute he had with a certain Narcıoğlu. He was imprisoned and ordered to quaff a cup of poison; he complied without hesitation and then proceeded to expel the poison from his system by means of copious perspiration. Duly impressed, his captors released him and returned him respectfully to Bursa.[70]

On his death in 1077/1666, Açıkbaş Mahmud Efendi was succeeded at the *tekke* he had founded first by his nephew Ahî Mahmud Efendi b. Seyyid Kasım (d. 1090/1679), originally of Van, and then by his nephew's son Mustafa Efendi (d. 1110/1698).[71] The next *postnişin* at the *tekke,* Abdülkerim Efendi (d. 1138/1725), was not a part of the family lineage and received his initiation from Shaykh Muḥammad Murād (d. 1141/1729), the main propagator in the Ottoman lands of the Mujaddidī branch of the Naqshbandiyya.[72] It may therefore be presumed that subsequent *postnişin*s at the *tekke,* which continued to function until the closure of all Sufi institutions decreed by the law of 1925, were also Mujaddidī.[73]

Less well known and significant than the offshoot in Bursa was a branch of Şeyh Aziz's lineage in Erzurum. There he is said to have appointed two *khalīfas*, Şeyh Hacı Mehmed Efendi and Şeyh Karaman. The former initiated in turn three of his nephews, Mehmed Emin Efendi, Seyfî Çelebi, and Seyyid Ömer; and the latter initiated his son Ebubekir Efendi.[74] Nothing is known of these individuals except their names, and the sole source in which they are mentioned is demonstrably erroneous in a number of respects. There is nonetheless no reason to question the likelihood of an extension of Şeyh Aziz's initiatic lineage to Erzurum, however short-lived it may have been. Similar remarks apply to Van, where Vanlı Kara Abdullah, another *khalīfa* of Şeyh Aziz, was active for a while.[75]

Nowhere, then, did the distinctive Naqshbandī lineage transplanted from Urūmiya to Anatolia survive for more than three generations. For whatever reason, the descendants of Şeyh Aziz proved unwilling or unable fully to institutionalize the widespread appeal that he himself had enjoyed—an appeal that was enhanced, moreover, by what was widely perceived as his martyrdom at the hands of Sultan Murad IV. It was other Naqshbandī lineages, not of Iranian derivation, that were destined to take firm root in Ottoman soil.

SHAYKH ʿALĪ KURDĪ AND THE NAQSHBANDĪS OF QAZVIN

Such was the ultimate fate of the Naqshbandī line first established in Tabriz by Ṣunʿullāh Kūzakunānī. Its disappearance from Iran had not followed immediately on the first Safavid conquest; a full half-century elapsed before the situation in the Tabriz region became untenable for Naqshbandīs, and the offshoot in Urūmiya survived for at least another fifty years. Perhaps more surprising than this relative longevity is that the implantation of the *ṭarīqa* in another city of northwest Iran, Qazvin, actually started after the Safavids had taken control. This can be deduced from the fact that Maulānā Qāḍī Mīrak Khālidī, who had temporarily fled the city in 911/1505–6, became after his return the follower of Sayyid ʿAlī Kurdī, a Naqshbandī shaykh who arrived there at about the same time.[76] Sayyid ʿAlī Kurdī's choice of Qazvin as a center for Naqshbandī activity is particularly remarkable in that the Safavids had already provided a sample of their intolerance by massacring all the descendants of Khālid b. al-Walīd (a companion of the Prophet traditionally execrated by Shiʿites) on whom they could lay their hands in the city; this, indeed, was the atrocity that had prompted the flight of Maulānā Qāḍī Mīrak, for he belonged precisely to that lineage.[77] It may be that Sayyid ʿAlī Kurdī nonetheless regarded the advent of the Safavids as a passing and aberrant storm that could be stoically endured until conditions returned to Sunni normalcy. Alternatively, he may have considered Qazvin, a city that for a long time remained known for its obstinate attachment to Sunnism, as a suitable base for actively opposing the religious policies of the Safavids by propagating the Naqshbandī path.[78] In any case, it is plain that he miscalculated.

A native of ʿAmādiyya in Kurdistan, Sayyid ʿAlī Kurdī had been employed by Aḥrār as tutor to one of his sons; whether he stayed on in Samarqand after the death of Aḥrār in 895/1490 is unknown. His early years in Qazvin were marked by great success in acquiring followers, "from elite and commonalty alike," and it may well have been this that prompted an ominous summons to Tabriz in 925/1519. He is said to have foreseen that he would be executed on arrival, but he went nonetheless, "in accordance with submission to fate, which is the norm of the prophets and the custom of the saints."[79] Muḥammad b. Ḥusayn Qazvīnī's *Silsila-nāma-yi Khwājagān-i Naqshband,* the sole source concerning Sayyid 'Alī Kurdī, blames his death on "the opponents of the path of certainty" (*mukhālifān-i ṭarīq-i yaqīn*). This expression probably denotes the Safavids and their followers, although Qazvīnī generally calls them Qizilbash, a pejorative term for him and many of his contemporaries. It can hardly be a coincidence that in precisely the same year one of Sayyid 'Alī Kurdī's disciples, Shaykh 'Abdullāh Qazvīnī, who had abandoned an ancestral loyalty to the line of Shaykh Zāhid Gīlānī in order to follow him, thought it politic to depart on the hajj; this was a pretext that, as we have seen, was sometimes used to facilitate flight from Safavid persecution. Shaykh 'Abdullāh Qazvīnī died in the desert without reaching his destination, in Rabī' al-Thānī 925/April 1519.[80]

Safavid persecution of the Naqshbandīs of Qazvin cannot yet have been thorough or consistent, however, for five other *khalīfa*s of Sayyid 'Alī Kurdī appear to have died natural deaths in Qazvin without suffering notable harassment in their lifetimes. Thus Abū Sa'īd (son of Bāyazīd Khalkhālī, the erstwhile preceptor of Darvīsh Akhī Khusraushāhī) died in 931/1524 and was buried near the tomb of Aḥmad Ghazālī, as was another *khalīfa,* Shaykh 'Alī Qāḍī Qazvīnī (a Ḥasanī *sayyid* and one of the leading *'ulamā'* of the city).[81] A third *khalīfa,* Shah 'Alī Qazvīnī (described as "following the path of the Malāmatiyya"), died in 949/1542 and was buried in the old cemetery of Qazvin.[82] Maulānā Nafīs Ḥakīm Qazvīnī, a Sufi said to have been permanently lost in a state of contemplative absorption (*istighrāq*), was the fourth of Sayyid 'Alī Kurdī's followers to survive him. He died and was buried at a date unknown near the *imāmzāda* popularly known as Shāhzāda Ḥusayn, which was long established as one of the principal sites of visitation and burial in Qazvin for Sunnis and Shi'ites alike; his burial there suggests that the Shi'ites of the city had not yet attempted to monopolize use of the shrine.[83] As for Maulānā Qāḍī Mīrak Qazvīnī Khālidī, who had fled the city to escape the massacre of his kinsfolk, he lived on peacefully until 969/1561–62, despite his general renown as the most favored disciple of Sayyid 'Alī Kurdī; he too was buried close to the shrine of Shāhzāda Ḥusayn.[84]

In Qazvin, as in the region of Tabriz, the climate appears to have changed for the worse soon after the middle of the tenth/sixteenth century, in part perhaps because of the transfer of the capital there by Shah Ṭahmāsp in 955/1548. In 973/1565–66 a Naqshbandī of a different line, Maulānā Ḥusayn Qazvīnī, saw himself obliged to quit the city in order to escape "the commanding of evil and the forbidding of good practiced by the Qizilbash."[85] His initiatic descent was from Sa'd al-Dīn Kāshgharī by way of 'Alā' al-Dīn Kirmānī and 'Abd al-Ghafūr Sāvajī (d. 977/1569–70). The latter had escaped the hostile attentions of the Safavids by quitting his native city of Sāva in central Iran and traveling continuously, mostly to the east, and it was in Marv-i Shāhjahān that he initiated Maulānā Ḥusayn Qazvīnī into the Naqshbandiyya. Maulānā Ḥusayn also had a second Naqshbandī affiliation, acquired presumably in Bukhara, from Khwāja Muḥammad Islām Jūybārī (d. 971/1563), an initiatic descendant of Aḥrār by a purely Central Asian line. After leaving Qazvin, Maulānā Ḥusayn made for Damascus, which tradition recommended as a place of refuge in times of extreme evil.[86] When he died is not known, nor whether he initiated anyone into the Naqshbandiyya; but to his son Muḥammad is due the *Silsila-nāma-yi Khwājagān-i Naqshband,* which is the primary, and in some cases only, source for these forgotten Naqshbandīs of early Safavid Iran.

IBRĀHĪM SHABISTARĪ AND TWO MORE 'ABD AL-VAHHĀB HAMADĀNĪS

The roster of known Naqshbandīs from western Iran in the pre-Safavid and early Safavid periods may be completed with a mention of three apparently isolated individuals, one from Shabistar and two from Hamadan.

The first of these was Burhān al-Dīn Ibrāhīm b. Ḥasan Shabistarī, sometimes known as "the second Sībawayh" on account of his surpassing command of Arabic grammar. He is credited with a commentary on the first twelve *sūra*s of the Qur'ān; *Anbiyā'-nāma,* a narrative poem on the lives of the prophets; and *Nihāyat al-Bahja,* an exposition in verse of Arabic grammar. In 917/1511–12 Shabistarī left Iran to go on the hajj and possibly to escape Safavid persecution as well. But while still inside Safavid territory he had the misfortune near Erzincan to encounter followers of Şahkulu, leader of an abortive pro-Safavid uprising in Anatolia, as they fled eastward to escape the wrath of the Ottomans.[87] They killed him on the spot, either as a straightforward act of banditry or for reasons of sectarian hatred. Nothing is known of Ibrāhīm Shabistarī's lineage in the Naqshbandiyya, and there is no reason to assume that he transmitted the *ṭarīqa* to anyone, except possibly his son Niyāzī Ibrāhīm Efendi (d. 936/1529), who did succeed in migrating.[88]

An 'Abd al-Vahhāb Hamadānī—entirely distinct from the identically named person discussed in detail above—was a *murīd* in Herat of Maulānā Ghiyāṣ al-Dīn Aḥmad (d. 957/1550), son and *khalīfa* of Maulānā 'Alā' al-Dīn Maktabdār. When Shah Ismā'īl took the city in 916/1510, this 'Abd al-Vahhāb Hamadānī traveled first to Arabia before settling in the Ṣāliḥiyya quarter of

Damascus near the tomb of Ibn ʿArabī, dying there in 954/1547; he wrote poetry under the pen-name Vahhābī.[89] There is no evidence that ʿAbd al-Vahhāb Hamadānī belonged to a well-rooted Naqshbandī tradition in Hamadan or that he attempted to propagate the *ṭarīqa* after leaving Herat.

Some slight evidence of a Naqshbandī presence in Hamadan is, however, provided by the biography of yet another ʿAbd al-Vahhāb Hamadānī, who died coincidentally in the same year as the refugee from Herat. Known also as ʿAbd al-Vahhāb al-Ṣābūnī ("the soapmaker"), presumably with reference to his trade, he is said to have been initiated into the Naqshbandiyya by his father, Khwāja Jalāl, in Hamadan and to have fled the city sometime during the reign of Shah Ṭahmāsp. His travels brought him to Cairo, where he acquired a Mevlevî affiliation and resided for a while in the Mevlevîhane before choosing a life of seclusion in Medina, where he passed away in 954/1547. His written legacy consists of *Ṣavāqib al-Manāqib,* a synopsis of *Manāqib al-ʿĀrifīn* (Aḥmad Aflākī's celebrated collection of Mevlevî biographies), completed in 947/1540, with elements that Hamadānī deemed repugnant to the *sharīʿa* deleted; a collection of riddles (*muʿammā*); and a small amount of Turkish verse signed with the pen-name Abdî.[90] Clearly, this third ʿAbd al-Vahhāb Hamadānī's original Naqshbandī affiliation was superseded by the Mevlevî loyalties he acquired after leaving Iran, and there is no indication that he did anything to propagate the Naqshbandiyya in Egypt or the Hijaz.

THE NAQSHBANDĪS OF HERAT

Herat had been a far more important focus of Naqshbandī activity in pre-Safavid times than either Tabriz or Qazvin.[91] By the middle of the ninth/fifteenth century, the city had become the third principal center of the Naqshbandiyya, after Bukhara and Samarqand. This development was due principally to Saʿd al-Dīn Kāshgharī (d. 860/1456), who, shunning the option of *khānaqāh* life, resided in the Madrasa-yi Ghiyāṣiyya and met with his numerous devotees in the adjacent Masjid-i Jāmiʿ.[92] The most prominent follower of Kāshgharī was, of course, ʿAbd al-Raḥmān Jāmī, whose eminence in the scholarly and political life of Herat helped enhance the luster of the order; he also devoted a number of his lesser works to the exposition of its principles.[93] It was no doubt in acknowledgment of these accomplishments that Kāshgharī declared himself to have been favored by God with the entry of Jāmī into his circle of devotees.[94] Ever reluctant to assume the burdens of spiritual preceptorship, Jāmī did not, however, emerge as formal leader of the Naqshbandī congregation of Herat when his master died in 860/1456. Instead, he encouraged Kāshgharī's followers to gather around Maulānā Shams al-Dīn Muḥammad Rūjī (d. 904/1499).[95] While thoroughly devoted to Kāshgharī, Jāmī also enjoyed close and mutually respectful relations with Khwāja 'Ubaydullāh Aḥrār; the two men exchanged visits and correspondence.[96] Jāmī thus served *inter alia* as a link between the two most vital branches of the Naqshbandiyya in his age.

The efflorescence of the Naqshbandiyya in Herat came to an end with the Safavid conquest of the city in 916/1510. For reasons that will soon become apparent, the fairly recently deceased 'Abd al-Raḥmān Jāmī was, and for long remained, a particular target of Safavid wrath. Mīrzā Makhdūm Sharīfī informs us that his name was the most recent on a list of ninety prominent Sunnis singled out by Shah Ṭahmāsp for permanent and quasi-ritual execration.[97] Devotees of Jāmī, correctly anticipating that the Safavids would attempt to exhume and scatter his remains, prudently removed them for temporary burial outside the city before the arrival of Shah Ismā'īl's army.[98] Several Naqshbandīs fled. Ḍiyā' al-Dīn Jāmī, third son of Jāmī and one of his few *khalīfa*s in the Naqshbandī order, was imprisoned in the citadel of Herat by the first Safavid governor but managed to escape to Arp, a village in the remote region of Ūbah, some fifteen *farsakh*s from the city. He died there, apparently without leaving any initiatic descendants.[99] Another of Jāmī's disciples, Maulānā Shahīdī Qummī, deciding to place a much greater distance between himself and the Safavids, migrated to Gujarat.[100] Two *khalīfa*s of Shams al-Dīn Rūjī sought refuge in Bukhara with the Shibanids. One was Muḥammad Ṣalāḥ Hiravī, who died in roughly 960/1553 and was buried next to the tomb of Khwāja Bahā' al-Dīn Naqshband himself.[101] The other was Maulānā Jalāl Hiravī, to whom the Uzbek ruler 'Abd al-'Azīz Khān is said to have been so devoted that he would not sit down in his presence without his permission. In addition to continuing his preceptorial activities in Bukhara, Maulānā Jalāl Hiravī wrote a brief treatise on the *ṭarīqa* and made a synopsis of Jāmī's *Nafaḥāt al-Uns*. He died in either 957/1550 or 976/1568.[102]

By contrast, Fakhr al-Dīn 'Alī Ṣafī, author of the *Rashaḥāt-i 'Ayn al-Ḥayāt*, the most important source for the early history of the Naqshbandiyya, did not take the opportunity to seek refuge with the Uzbeks that was provided by their year-long siege of Herat in 939/1532–33. Instead, as soon as it was lifted, he made for Ūbah in the remote region of Gharjistān that was for a while beyond the reach of both Uzbeks and Safavids. When the forces of Shah Ṭahmāsp threatened this refuge, he decided to return to Herat but collapsed and died before he could enter the city, possibly in the same year he had left it. His body, however, was brought back for burial near the citadel in Herat.[103]

Another Naqshbandī who found it necessary to quit the Herat region was Maulānā Zayn al-Dīn Qavvās (or Kamāngar), variously described as a *murīd* of Nūrullāh Isfandānī, a *khalīfa* of Sa'd al-Dīn Kāshgharī, and as a *murīd* of Maulānā Ghiyāṣ al-Dīn, son and successor of 'Alā' al-Dīn Maktabdār. Originally from the village of Bihdādin near Khwāf, he migrated to Qandahar in 961/1554 and died there six years later. One of his *khalīfas*, Shaykh Mu'īn Miskīn (d. 995/1587), apparently stayed in Qandahar, while two others, Maulānā Muḥammad Amīn and Maulānā Khwāja, migrated to Lahore.[104]

Like their colleagues from the Iranian northwest who migrated to the Ottoman lands, these stray migrants who went from Khurasan to Qandahar, Bukhara, and India were unable to perpetuate their lineages effectively.

THE NAQSHBANDĪS: A SPECIAL TARGET OF SAFAVID HOSTILITY?

The Naqshbandīs were by no means the only order to suffer from the bitter enmity of the Safavids. The destruction of the Sufi orders appears to have been an article of policy, especially for Shah Ismā'īl, not only because in most cases as Sunnis they were the bearers of an ideology at variance with his own but also because of their actual or potential influence on society. Summarizing the situation, Ibn al-Karbalā'ī reports that Shah Ismā'īl "uprooted and eradicated most of the lineages of *sayyids* and shaykhs" and "crushed all the *silsilas*, destroying the graves of their ancestors, not to mention what befell their successors."[105] The Kubravī line Ibn al-Karbalā'ī had inherited from his grandfather, Badr al-Dīn Aḥmad Lālā'ī, quickly vanished from Tabriz. With the departure of Ibrahim Gülşenî from Tabriz for Diyarbekir, Jerusalem, and Cairo, soon after Shah Ismā'īl's conquest of the city, the Khalvatiyya effectively disappeared from the Safavid territories.[106] In some cases, the possibility of timely flight did not exist. When Shah Ismā'īl conquered Fars in 909/1503, the Kāzarūnī (also known as Isḥāqī) *ṭarīqa* was extirpated in the course of a massacre of some 4,000 people, and the tomb of its founder, Abū Isḥāq Kāzarūnī (d. 426/1035), was desecrated.[107]

Sufi orders with an affiliation to Shi'ism were able, it is true, to survive somewhat longer by collaborating with the Safavids. Thus Shah Qāsim Fayḍbakhsh, son of Sayyid Muḥammad Nūrbakhsh (d. 869/1464), was rewarded for his loyalty to Shah Ismā'īl with an enlargement of the family lands near Rayy; but Shah Qavām al-Dīn, the grandson of Fayḍbakhsh, was put to death by Ṭahmāsp, who had grounds to suspect him of planning an insurrection.[108] The Ni'matullāhīs similarly went from favor to disfavor, albeit over a longer period. A descendant of Shah Ni'matullāh Valī (d. 834/1430–31) was brought from Yazd and appointed *ṣadr* by Shah Ismā'īl in 917/1511; and other members of the family contracted marriages with the Safavid house during the following reign. The relations of the Ni'matullāhīs with the monarchy soured, however, in the time of Shah 'Abbās, and all *ṭarīqa* activity on their part came to an end at the latest by the middle of the eleventh/seventeenth century.[109] Only the Ḏahabī offshoot of the Kubraviyya was able to remain active throughout the Safavid period. Despite occasional harassment by the Shi'ite *'ulamā'*, it encountered no significant hostility from rulers until the time of Shah Sulṭān Ḥusayn (r. 1105–35/1694–1722).[110]

Despite this general suppression of the Sufi orders, there are indications that the Naqshbandiyya may have been a special target of Safavid hostility. Mīrzā Makhdūm Sharīfī (d. 994/1586), a Sunni notable who fled Iran after the death of Shah Ismā'īl II in 986/1577 to seek refuge with the Ottomans, wrote in his *al-Nawāqiḍ li Bunyān al-Rawāfiḍ* (a polemic against Shi'ism) that "whenever they suspect anyone of engaging in contemplation [*murāqaba*], they say, 'he is a Naqshbandī,' and deem it necessary to kill him."[111] This might be dismissed as hyperbolic propaganda, particularly if we bear in mind that the only Naqshbandī known by name definitely to have been killed by the Safavids was Shaykh 'Alī Kurdī of Qazvin and that traces of the Naqshbandiyya persisted in both Tabriz and Qazvin for several decades after the foundation of the Safavid state. An equally energetic polemicist from the opposing camp, however, Qāḍī Nūrullāh Shushtarī (d. 1019/1610), responded to Mīrzā Makhdūm Sharīfī by proudly confirming that Naqshbandī blood had indeed been shed.[112]

The reasons for particularly acute hostility to the Naqshbandiyya—if its existence can indeed be deduced from this exchange—are not immediately apparent. The order does not seem to have been widespread or well rooted enough, especially in central and northwestern Iran, to have presented a major threat to the religious policies of the Safavids. Only Ṣun'ullāh Kūzakunānī in Tabriz and the line of 'Alī Kurdī in Qazvin are credited with significant followings, although it is conceivable that other Naqshbandī groups existed of which no historical record has survived. The ties of the Naqshbandiyya with the two major external foes of the Safavids, the Ottomans and the Shibanids, may, of course, have played a role in inciting a special hostility to the order.[113] It is more likely, however, that in early Safavid times, when the mass propagation of Shi'ism was far from complete, the Naqshbandiyya was seen as especially repugnant because of its quintessentially Sunni nature. The accusation of Naqshbandī allegiance might have been a popular mode of undiscriminating denunciation of all recalcitrant Sunnis, whether Naqshbandī or not. Early Naqshbandī attitudes to Shi'ism deserve, therefore, to be examined in some detail.

EARLY NAQSHBANDĪ ATTITUDES TO SHI'ISM

A distinctive feature of the Naqshbandiyya from the time of its first emergence has been a claim to initiatic descent from Abū Bakr. This view of its spiritual ancestry certainly barred any embrace of Shiʿism analogous to the choice made by the originally Sunni Niʿmatullāhiyya and the Nūrbakhshī and Ḏahabī offshoots of the Kubraviyya.[114] It also prevented Shushtarī, that voracious appropriator of Sufi lineages on behalf of Shiʿism, from claiming the Naqshbandiyya as an essentially Shiʿite phenomenon.[115] It did not, however, necessitate in itself any marked hostility to Shiʿism, and the invocation of the *bakrī* lineage was, in any event, balanced by awareness of a separate line of spiritual descent from ʿAlī, the standard *silsila* for almost all Sufi orders.[116] In addition, Shiʿism had only the most marginal of presences in Central Asia at the time when the Naqshbandiyya came into being. It is true that Amīr Kulāl (d. 770/1368), one of the preceptors of Bahā' al-Dīn Naqshband, has been credited with persuading Tīmūr to expel Shah Niʿmatullāh Valī from Transoxiana because of proto-Shiʿite tendencies he allegedly perceived in him; but the story rests in large part on a confusion between Amīr Kulāl and Shams Kulāl, a figure whose links with the Naqshbandiyya are far from certain.[117]

As for Khwāja ʿUbaydullāh Aḥrār, with whom the real expansion of the order begins, he seems not to have nourished any particularly venomous dislike of Shiʿism. When Fakhr al-Dīn ʿAlī Ṣafī introduced himself to Aḥrār as a native of Sabzavār, Aḥrār responded jocularly with the story of how a quick-witted Sunni of Sabzavār escaped retribution for stabbing a Shiʿite who had written the names of Abū Bakr and ʿUmar on the soles of his feet. In somewhat more serious mode, he went on to tell of a shaykh whose followers had wished to chastise a Shiʿite for vilifying Abū Bakr. He forbade them to do so, saying that "they [the Shiʿites] do not vilify our Abū Bakr; they have a different Abū Bakr from ours. They curse an imaginary Abū Bakr who usurped the caliphate and was at odds with the Messenger—peace and blessings be upon him—and his Ahl al-Bayt—may God be pleased with them. We too curse and denounce such an Abū Bakr." On hearing this, the Shiʿite in question repented of his error.[118]

Naqshbandī attitudes to Shiʿism appear to have sharpened with the expansion of the order to Herat at a time when the city was becoming an arena of bitter conflict between Sunnis and Shiʿites. ʿAbd al-Raḥmān Jāmī clearly took a leading role in combating Shiʿism, on both the political and theological planes. Together with Mīr ʿAlī Shīr Navāʾī, also a Naqshbandī initiate, he was able to dissuade Ḥusayn Mīrzā Bāyqarā (r. 875–912/1470–1506) from openly embracing Shiʿism at the outset of his reign.[119] Jāmī's clashes with Shiʿites were not limited to Herat; he found himself debating them in Baghdad in the presence of the Ḥanafī and Shāfiʿī *muftī*s of Baghdad, while en route to the hajj in 877/1472.[120] His clearest written condemnation of Shiʿism came in the *Silsilat al-Ẕahab*, a didactic *maṣnavī* completed in roughly 875/1470 and dedicated to Ḥusayn Mīrzā Bāyqarā. There he asserts that "the evil of rafḍ [Shiʿism] comes from its hatred of the people of fidelity [i.e., the Companions of the Prophet]" and that "whoever has a disposition to rafḍ is worthless as a rag [*khalaq*]; he's a source of shame to the whole of creation [*mā khalaq*]."[121]

Less formal but perhaps more revealing remarks in the condemnation of Shi'ism are to be found in a biography of Jāmī written by one of his most intimate companions, 'Abd al-Vāsi' Niẓāmī Bākharzī. There Jāmī is recorded, for example, to have complained that the Shi'ites of his time had become unduly assertive and discourteous; rejoiced in the enmity they showed him as an indication of his own rectitude; claimed that *all* Shi'ites were effectively bastards because they did not regard the unintentional utterance of a formula of divorce as legally binding; looked forward to the advent of the Twelfth Imam because—far from vindicating the cause of the Shī'a—he would extirpate them together with all unbelievers; and asserted that throughout their history they had only two scholars worth mentioning, Sayyid Sharīf Raḍī (d. 406/1015) and Ibn Muṭahhar al-Ḥillī (d. 726/1325). One day, confronted by a preacher of "corrupt belief" from Qā'in, Jāmī even declared that the repeated failure of Shi'ites to gain lasting and substantial political power was a further proof of the emptiness of their creed, an argument that was soon to be invalidated in the most palpable of ways.[122]

The crudity and vehemence of these arguments is at first sight surprising, in view of Jāmī's undoubted profundity as a mystic and subtlety as a poet. They should nonetheless be placed in the context of the heightened confessional strife that characterized the period. It is significant that Jāmī speaks specifically of "the Rāfiḍīs of our age [*Ravāfiḍ-i vaqt*]" as "abandoning courtesy so far as to call Sunnis Kharijites" and that he denounces as "lacking any basis those followers of Shi'ism that have come to my attention; I know not what path their predecessors followed."[123] This emphasis on the turpitude of contemporary Shi'ites may be taken as an indication that—in the view of Jāmī and like-minded persons—Shi'ism had taken a decided turn for the worse in his time. The same can be deduced from his outrage that Shi'ites had extended the practice of cursing Yazīd—reasonable enough in itself—to include Abū Bakr and 'Umar.[124]

Still more significant, however, is that for all his hostility to Shi'ism, Jāmī insists on his own reverence for the Twelve Imams and even denies that any connection ever existed between them and Shi'ism:

> We are firmly convinced that the Ahl al-Bayt of the Messenger, consisting of the Twelve Imams—may peace and blessings be upon him and upon them—never held this impure belief. By God Exalted and Almighty, if I were convinced that this was the creed and belief of the immaculate progeny of the Prophet, I would be the first to accept it. [What happened was rather that] a handful of ignorant Jews, wishing to cast doubt on the very bases of religion, concocted some nonsense and slanderously attributed it

to those pure and immaculate ones, although they were never aware of any part of it.[125]

According to Jāmī, the claim of Shiʿites that Imam Jaʿfar al-Ṣādiq originated their school of jurisprudence was wholly without merit, for his *madhhab* was "nothing other than the straight path of [the people of] the Sunna and the Community [*jādda-yi sunnat va jamāʿat*]."[126] The Twelve Imams are thus presented by Jāmī as proponents of Sunni Islam, with the practical result that their spiritual prestige becomes an object of contest between Sunnis and Shiʿites.[127]

It should not be thought, however, that Jāmī was simply improvising, in the heat of confessional dispute, a transparently farfetched and polemical argument against Shiʿism. His condemnation of Shiʿism in *Silsilat al-Ẕahab* is preceded by a passionate declaration of love for the Ahl al-Bayt ("this is not Rafḍ; it is the essence of faith, the established custom of the people of gnosis") and followed by a disquisition on the *āyat al-taṭhīr* (Qur'ān, 33:33) that corresponds fully to the Shiʿite understanding of the verse as conferring sinlessness on the Twelve Imams.[128] In his *Shavāhid al-Nubuvva,* a work recounting miracles attributed to the Prophet, his Companions, and his progeny, each of the Twelve Imams is mentioned in turn, in detail, and with palpably sincere veneration. Particularly striking is the fact that ʿAlī is listed not as the fourth of the Rightly Guided Caliphs of Sunni belief but as the first of the Imams.[129]

Among Jāmī's own contemporaries in Herat, the two Kāshifīs, father and son, manifested similar devotion to the Twelve Imams. The father, Ḥusayn Vāʿiẓ-i Kāshifī (d. 906/1500–1501 or 910/1504–5), initiated into the Naqshbandī path by Jāmī himself, numbered among his many works the *Rauḍat al-Shuhadā',* one of the most celebrated of all books written in Persian on the martyrs of the Ahl al-Bayt.[130] The son, Fakhr al-Dīn ʿAlī Ṣafī Kāshifī, accords the Twelve Imams an entire section in his *Laṭā'if al-Ṭavā'if* (a book of amusing or edifying anecdotes) and refers in the same work to ʿAlī as the *vaṣī* (legatee) of the Prophet, a designation not commonly encountered in Sunni writings. Kāshifī the younger also wrote *Ḥirz al-Amān min Fitan al-Zamān,* a book on the properties of the letters of the Arabic alphabet and other arcane matters, which he declared to be within the exclusive preserve of the Imams of the Ahl al-Bayt.[131]

It is said of Kāshifī the elder that he was viewed with hostility as a Sunni when in Sabzavār and suspected of Shiʿism when in Herat; and of Kāshifī the younger (Fakhr al-Dīn ʿAlī Ṣafī) that when preaching in Herat he refused to identify himself as either Sunni or Shiʿite.[132] But it would be wrong to conclude that this seemingly ambiguous or even contradictory combination of Sunni identity with veneration of the Twelve Imams first arose among Naqshbandīs in late Timurid Khurasan. For in his *Faṣl al-Khiṭāb,* Khwāja Muḥammad Pārsā (d. 822/1419)—a leading scholar of Bukhara and a direct successor to Khwāja Bahā' al-Dīn Naqshband—first emphasizes in accordance with Sunni tradition that all of the Companions of the Prophet are beyond reproach but then stresses with equal vigor the necessity of loving the Twelve Imams, each of whose lives he recounts in some detail.[133]

Particularly remarkable in the books of Pārsā, Jāmī, and Ṣafī Kāshifī is that the Twelfth Imam is identified as the Mahdī, in complete accord with Shi'ite doctrine.[134] Indeed, the details of his birth and early life are taken with explicit acknowledgment from Shi'ite sources, even by the sharply antagonistic Jāmī, if for no other reason than the lack of any alternative source. The Shi'ite doctrine of the Twelfth Imam's occultation (*ghayba*), however, is mentioned by Pārsā without either endorsement or refutation.[135] Jāmī for his part similarly mentions the *ghayba* as a specifically Shi'ite belief while also citing the view of the Kubravī 'Alā' al-Daula Samnānī (d. 736/1335) that the Twelfth Imam died after inheriting the function of *quṭb* (the head of the unseen spiritual hierarchy in which Sufis believe) from a certain 'Alī b. Ḥusayn Baghdādī and exercising it for a period of nineteen years, at the end of which he was buried in Medina by his successor, 'Uthmān b. Ya'qūb Juvaynī.[136] The discussion of the Twelfth Imam by these Naqshbandīs illustrates well what might be called a syncretist view of the Twelve Imams: a professed veneration for the Ahl al-Bayt that includes an acknowledgment of the Twelfth Imam—a figure for whom Shi'ite traditions provided the only source available—and a polemical insistence on denying his predecessors any role in the origins and development of Shi'ite Islam. In brief, Pārsā, Jāmī, and the two Kāshifīs may be counted among those whom the late Muḥammad Ja'far Maḥjūb has felicitously termed "Twelver Sunnis" (*sunnīān-i davāzdah-imāmī*).[137]

SUFI PROTO-SHI'ISM AS PREPARATION FOR SAFAVID SHI'ISM?

With the exception of the *tafsīr* and brief treatises surviving from Bābā Ni'matullāh Nakhchivānī and the learned works of Ibrāhīm Shabistarī, no writings are extant from the Naqshbandīs present in northwestern Iran in the ninth/fifteenth and tenth/sixteenth centuries. It cannot therefore be assumed that their attitudes to Shi'ism and the Twelve Imams were identical with those outlined above. It is, however, probable that they were; Ṣun'ullāh Kūzakunānī was, after all, an associate of Jāmī and a product of the same milieu in Herat, and he presumably transmitted a similar amalgam of beliefs to his own following. As for Muḥammad Bādāmyārī, we have seen that he claimed direct authority from Imam Ja'far al-Ṣādiq for his own rejection of Shi'ism.[138]

The question of Naqshbandī attitudes to Shiʿism and the Twelve Imams has some relevance to the problem of the genesis of Shiʿism as the quasi-national creed of Iran. Scholars such as Henry Corbin, Marijan Molé, Sayyed Hossein Nasr, and Abdoldjavad Falaturi have propounded the thesis that a heightened and reverential awareness of the Twelve Imams on the part of the Sufi orders active in post-Mongol times helped prepare the way for the acceptance of Shiʿism under the Safavids.[139] In somewhat similar vein, Jean Aubin has suggested that while "the Iranian Muslim community" was certainly not prepared for "the brutal and bloody shock of Türkmen messianism," it was "gradually impregnating itself with Twelver Shiʿism" and therefore getting ready to welcome it in more thoroughgoing fashion.[140]

There is in general no firm evidence that a pacific evolution toward Shiʿism was underway that sooner or later would have reached its natural conclusion and that all the Safavids contributed was a coercive acceleration. In particular, the case of the Naqshbandiyya casts considerable doubt on the notion of allegedly proto-Shiʿite Sufi orders preparing the way for the mass acceptance of Shiʿism in Iran. For it is evident that neither in Herat nor in the Iranian northwest did the devotion of the Naqshbandīs to the Twelve Imams predispose them in the least to the acceptance of Shiʿism; on the contrary, they proclaimed themselves convinced that Shiʿism was an erroneous doctrine slanderously ascribed to the Twelve Imams by its adherents. The same pattern continued long after the Safavid assumption of power, although no longer in Iran. Especially in India, Naqshbandīs continued to express veneration for the Twelve Imams—albeit less frequently than before—while plunging with great enthusiasm into the polemical struggle against Shiʿism.[141]

CONCLUSION

Whether the Naqshbandiyya would have been able to put down lasting roots in Iran had it not been for the advent of the Safavids is naturally a matter of pure speculation. It seems, however, unlikely that the order would have to come to flourish there as it did, for example, in the Ottoman realm: Mollâ Abdullah Ilâhî (d. 896/1491) and Shaykh Aḥmad Bukhārī (d. 922/1516), both disciples of Aḥrār and contemporaries of Kūzakunānī, had an incomparably greater impact in Istanbul than Kūzakunānī did in Tabriz. It may be significant, in fact, that Kūzakunānī's *khalīfa*s came from the rural hinterland of Tabriz, not from the city itself. None of the Naqshbandīs who left Iran for the Ottoman domains were able to transplant their lineages, with the sole exception of Şeyh Aziz from Urūmiya, and even in his case the line died out in a few generations. It may, then, not be entirely due to the hostile policies of the

Safavids that no lasting memory of the Naqshbandīs of Tabriz and Qazvin was preserved by later generations.[142]

What is certain is that by the time of the celebrated Shiʿite traditionist Mullā Muḥammad Bāqir Majlisī (d. 1111/1700) the Naqshbandīs had been so long absent from the central Safavid domains that he was able to criticize Jāmī for including in his *Nafaḥāt al-Uns* mention of Naqshbandīs who were "unknown to all but the ignorant Uzbeks."[143] In times of peace, Central Asian Naqshbandīs were able to pass through Iran without encountering sectarian harassment, and in some cases they were even received with great honor.[144] But it was not until the rise of the Khālidī branch of the order in the early thirteenth/nineteenth century that any substantial Naqshbandī presence was reestablished in Iran, and then only in Sunni-inhabited borderlands such as Kurdistan and Tālish. By contrast, the Naqshbandiyya flourished continuously in the three great domains that adjoined the Safavid realm—the Ottoman, the Uzbek, and the Mughal; these came to constitute a triangle of spiritual and intellectual exchange in which Naqshbandīs played an active and significant role. The Naqshbandiyya may thus be counted as part of the legacy of the Sunnism of the broader Iranian world that was inherited more fully by the neighbors of Iran than by Iran herself. It is important not to exaggerate the consistency or the pervasiveness of the sectarian antagonism that undoubtedly followed in the wake of the Safavid promotion of Shiʿism. Moreover, there can be little doubt that Iran did not become as culturally isolated from her neighbors as has been sometimes assumed. Nonetheless, the disappearance of the Naqshbandiyya from Iranian territory—limited as the potential of the order may have been there—was one indication among many others that under the auspices of the Safavids Islamic Iran had taken a new and largely unprecedented direction.

NOTES

1. For detailed examinations of the early history and geographic distribution of the Khwājagān and the early Naqshbandiyya, see Jürgen Paul, *Die politische und soziale Bedeutung der Naqšbandiyya in Mittelasien im 15. Jahrhundert* (Berlin and New York: W. de Gruyter, 1991) and Necdet Tosun, *Bahâeddin Nakşbend: Hayatı, Görüşleri, Tarikatı* (Istanbul: İnsan Yayınları, 2002).

2. Fakhr al-Dīn ʿAlī b. Ḥusayn Vāʿiẓ Kāshifī (Ṣafī), *Rashaḥāt-i ʿAyn al-Ḥayāt,* ed. ʿAlī Aṣghar Muʿīniyān, 2 vols. (Tehran: Bunyād-i Nīkūkārī-yi Nūrīānī, 2536 imperial/1977), 1:158–60, 168–72; ʿAbd al-Raḥmān Jāmī, *Nafaḥāt al-Uns,* ed. Maḥmūd ʿĀbidī (Tehran: Iṭṭilāʿāt, 1370 Sh./1991), pp. 401–2, 407–8. Neither of these sources provides any biographical information on ʿAbdullāh Imāmī Iṣfahānī; and there is certainly no reason to assume that he propagated the Naqshbandī path in Isfahan. It may be, however, that the repute of the order had reached Isfahan, causing him to leave his homeland and join the circle of

'Aṭṭār in Chaghāniān. Two brief treatises are attributed to him: *Risāla dar Bayān-i Kayfiyyat-i Masghūlī-yi Khwājagān,* MS Süleymaniye, Hamidiye 1457, fols. 138a–41a; and *Kalimāt-i Qudsiyya-yi 'Abdullāh Imāmī Iṣfahānī,* MS Süleymaniye, Tahir Ağa Tekkesi 276, fols. 36a–36b.

3. They are completely absent from the collection of hagiographical texts published by 'Ārif Naushāhī under the title *Aḥvāl va Sukhanāb-i Khwāja 'Ubaydullāh Aḥrār* (Tehran: Markaz-i Nashr-i Dānishgāhī, 1380 Sh./2001), which would seem to confirm their lack of close involvement with Aḥrār.

4. This Kubravī *khānaqāh* appears to have functioned as a gathering place for many of the Sufis of Tabriz, irrespective of *ṭarīqa* affiliations; it was frequented by at least one other Naqshbandī, Ṣun'ullāh Kūzakunānī, as well as by the Khalvatī Dede 'Umar Raushanī. See Ḥāfiẓ Ḥusayn Karbalā'ī Tabrīzī, known as Ibn al-Karbalā'ī, *Rauḍāt al-Jinān va Jannāt al-Janān,* ed. Ja'far Sulṭān al-Qurrā'ī, 2 vols. (Tehran: Bungāh-i Tarjuma va Nashr-i Kitāb, 1344 Sh./1965), 2:151.

5. This is the first indication of coalescence or at least compatibility with the Kubraviyya (and even its heretical offshoot, the Nūrbakhshiyya) on the part of these early Naqshbandīs. See also the section "Ṣun'ullāh Kūzakunānī and His Descendants" below.

6. Ibn al-Karbalā'ī, *Rauḍāt al-Jinān,* 1:416; Muḥammad b. Ḥusayn Qazvīnī, *Silsila-nāma-yi Khwājagān-i Naqshband,* MS Bibliothèque Nationale, supplément persan 1418, fol. 18a. It is worth noting that a Bulghārī belonging to the initiatic ancestry of the Naqshbandiyya may also have spent his last days in Tabriz. This is Ḥasan Bulghārī, a native of Ganja in Azerbayjan, who acquired the designation Bulghārī because of lengthy residence among the Volga Bulghārs before coming to Bukhara and joining the following of Khwāja Gharīb. He is commonly held to have been buried in Bukhara, but a variant tradition reports him to have been laid to rest in Tabriz on his death in 699/1299. See Şehabeddin Mercani, *Müstefâdü 'l-Ahbâr fi Ahval-i Kazan ve Bulgar,* 2 vols. (Kazan: Tipografiya B. L. Donbrovskago, 1897), 1:83.

7. Nakhchivānī is listed as a *murīd* of Aḥrār in anonymous, *Silsilat al-Ṭuruq fi 'l-Taṣawwuf,* MS Süleymaniye, Esad Efendi 3680, fol. 60b. Tosun (*Bahâeddin Nakşbend,* p. 284) discounts this testimony as late and unsupported by other sources; he suggests that Nakhchivānī may instead have been a disciple of Ṣun'ullāh Kūzakunānī, which is unlikely, given that the *khalīfa*s of Kūzakunānī are all known by name (see the section "Ṣun'ullāh Kūzakunānī and His Descendants" below). In any event, Taşköprüzade precedes his notice of Nakhchivānī with an entry on Shaykh Ismā'īl Shirvānī (d. 933/1527 in Mecca) and follows it with an entry on Shaykh Muḥammad Amīn Badakhshī (d. 923/1517 in Damascus), both of whom were indubitably *murīd*s of Aḥrār (*al-Shaqā'iq al-Nu'māniyya* [Beirut: Dār al-Kitāb al-'Arabī, 1395/1975], p. 214); the context thus suggests the same of Nakhchivānī.

8. Taşköprüzade, *al-Shaqā'iq al-Nu'māniyya,* pp. 160–61.

9. The *tafsīr* was published at Istanbul in 1326/1908 under the auspices of the Shaykh al-Ḥaram of Medina, with an introduction by Mehmed Şükrü Ankaravî. It was republished by Dār Rikābī of Cairo in 1999 under the title *al-Tafsīr al-Ṣūfī al-Kāmil li 'l-Qur'ān al-Karīm.*

10. Concerning this *tafsīr,* see Süleyman Ateş, *Işârî Tefsir Okulu* (Ankara: İlahiyat Fakültesi, 1974), pp. 225–30; and M. Ayāzī, *al-Mufassirūn: Ḥayātuhum wa Manhajuhum* (Tehran: n.p., 1373 Sh./1994), pp. 563–66.

11. Taşköprüzade, *al-Shaqā'iq al-Nu'māniyya,* p. 214.

12. Ibid., p. 161. Apart from his own commentary on the Qur'ān, Nakhchivānī is credited with glosses on the *tafsīr* of Bayḍāwī; commentaries on Fakhr al-Dīn 'Irāqī's *Lama'āt*

(MS Süleymaniye, Tevfik Paşa 1521/3, fols. 33b–73a), Ibn 'Arabī's *Fuṣūṣ al-Ḥikam,* and Shabistarī's *Gulshan-ı Rāz* (MS Süleymaniye, Lala Ismail 168, fols. 2a–246b); a treatise on being (MS Nuruosmaniye 2386, fols. 1a–78a); and a general treatise on Sufism called *Hadiyat* [or *Hidāyat*] *al-Ikhwān.* See Lamiî Çelebi, *Nefehat Tercemesi* (reprint, Istanbul: Marifet Yayınları, 1980), p. 576; Muḥammad 'Ali Tarbiyat, *Dānishmandān-i Āẕarbāyjān* (Tehran: Maṭba'a-yi Majlis, 1314 Sh./1935), pp. 61–62; and Tosun, *Bahâeddin Nakşbend,* p. 284. Reşat Öngören (*Osmanlılarda Tasavvuf: Anadolu'da Sufiler, Devlet ve Ulemâ* [Istanbul: Iz Yayıncılık, 2000], p. 143) is of the opinion that at least some of these works should more correctly be ascribed to Shāh Ni'matullāh Valī (d. 834/1431), eponym of the Ni'matullāhiyya.

13. There is, however, one reference to him in *Rashaḥāt-i 'Ayn al-Ḥayāt* (2:569–70) as "Mīr 'Abd al-Vahhāb, the Shaykh al-Islām of Iraq"; while in Samarqand, the author tells us, 'Abd al-Vahhāb Hamadānī would repeatedly tell how he had once described Aḥrār to the Sufis of Mecca, only to discover that he was already well known to the people of the Sacred City thanks to the frequent visits he paid them, miraculously enough while he was known by others to be simultaneously present elsewhere. The wording of this passage suggests that Hamadānī was genuinely devoted to Aḥrār and also that he spent enough time in Samarqand to be a familiar figure to Fakhr al-Dīn 'Alī Ṣafī. It appears, too, that Hamadānī remained in touch with Aḥrār after his departure from Samarqand and retained his goodwill. When Hamadānī sent some of his relatives to Samarqand to sell the property he had left behind and to collect a copy of the *Ṣaḥīḥ* of Bukhārī that he had ordered from Herat, Aḥrār provided them with letters of recommendation to facilitate their tasks. See Jo-Ann Gross and Asom Urunbaev, *The Letters of Khwāja 'Ubayd Allāh Aḥrār and His Associates* (Leiden: E. J. Brill, 2002), pp. 106–7.

14. Ibn al-Karbalā'ī, *Rauḍat al-Jinān,* 1:215.

15. Muhyi Gülşenî, *Menâkıb-ı Ibrahim Gülşenî,* ed. Tahsin Yazıcı (Ankara: Türk Tarih Kurumu, 1982), pp. 104–6. The qadi mentioned by Muhyi Gülşenî appears to be Qāḍī Ḥusayn b. Mu'īn al-Dīn Maybudī, whose collected correspondence includes a letter to 'Abd al-Vahhāb denouncing the corruption and impiety of government officials in Yazd (*Munsha'āt-i Maybudi,* ed. Nuṣratullāh Furūhar [Tehran: Nuqṭa, 1376 Sh./1997], pp. 81–82). The same collection includes a letter to Khwāja Yaḥyā, a son of Aḥrār, from the text of which it may be deduced that Maybudī's request for affiliation to the *ṭarīqa* had been denied (*Munsha'āt,* pp. 196–97). This suggests in turn that Maybudī was acquainted with Aḥrār himself and may have been drawn to 'Abd al-Vahhāb in part by a shared reverence for him. He also seems to have had some interest in the Nūrbakhshiyya; see *Munsha'āt,* pp. 118–9.

16. Gülşenî, *Menâkıb-ı Ibrahim Gülşenî,* pp. 227–29.

17. Ibid., pp. 228–36.

18. Ibid., pp. 253–54. The story that 'Abd al-Vahhāb was himself the originator of the distinctive Qizilbash turban, designing it according to instructions received in a dream from Imam 'Alī and then recommending it to Shah Ismā'īl, must be dismissed as apocryphal for a variety of obvious reasons. See Jean Aubin, "L'Avènement des Safavides reconsidéré," *Moyen Orient et Océan Indien* 5 (1988): 99–100.

19. Ibn al-Karbalā'ī, *Rauḍāt al-Jinān,* 1:216. This detail is revealing in that it may betray an uneasy awareness on the part of Shah Ismā'īl that he was less qualified to espouse the cause of the Imams of the Ahl al-Bayt than the *sayyids*, often of Sunni affiliation, who were popularly acknowledged as their heirs.

20. Text of the letter in Feridun Bey, *Münşeâtü 's-Selâtîn,* 2 vols. (Istanbul: n.p.,

1274/1858), 1:391. See also ʻAbd al-Ḥusayn Navāʼī, *Shāh Ismāʻīl Ṣafavī: Asnād va Mukātabāt-i Tārīkhī* (Tehran: Bunyād-i Farhang-i Īrān, 1347 Sh./1968), pp. 232–33 (Navāʼī speculates that Selim may have thought ʻAbd al-Vahhāb still loyal at heart to the Aqqoyunlus and therefore capable of being detached from the Safavids); and Jean-Louis Bacqué-Grammont, *Les Ottomans, les Safavides et leurs voisins* (Istanbul and Leiden: Nederlands Historisch-Archaeologisch Institut te Istanbul, 1987), p. 82.

21. For the text of the letter that ʻAbd al-Vahhāb was to deliver to Selim, see Feridun Bey, *Münşeâtü 's-Selâtîn* 1:413–14. Selim had given Tājlū Khānum in marriage to the *kadıasker* Tacizade Cafer Çelebi, an act that could be justified with reference to the several *fatvā*s that had declared the Qizilbash heretics and their marriages null and void. It nonetheless aroused widespread disapproval among the Ottoman *ʻulamā*ʼ; see Saʻdüddin, *Tâcü 't-Tevârîh,* 2 vols. (Istanbul: Tabʻhane-i Âmire, 1280/1863), 2:275. The assertion of Mīrzā ʻAbdullāh Afandī Iṣfahānī (d. 1130/1718) in his *Riyāḍ al-ʻUlamā*ʼ (6 vols. [Qum: Maktabat Āyatillāh al-Marʻashī al-ʻĀmma, 1401/1980], 3:287) that ʻAbd al-Vahhāb (whom he calls "al-Sayyid al-Amīr ʻAbd al-Vahhāb al-Tabrīzī") was a contemporary of Shah Ṭahmāsp and that it was he who sent him on a diplomatic mission to Istanbul after Kânûnî Süleyman's occupation of Tabriz in 941/1534 (not Shah Ismāʻīl after Selim's occupation of the city in 920/1514) appears to rest on a misreading of the relevant passage of Iskandar Munshī's *Tārīkh-i ʻĀlam-ārā-yi ʻAbbāsī* (ed. Īraj Afshār, 2 vols. [Tehran: Amīr Kabīr, 1350 Sh./1971], p. 153; English translation by Roger Savory: Eskandar Monshi, *History of Shah ʻAbbas,* 3 vols. [Boulder: Westview Press, 1978], 1:244) and a confusion of ʻAbd al-Vahhāb with one of his sons, Sayyid Ḥasan.

22. Bacqué-Grammont, *Les Ottomans, les Safavides et leurs voisins,* pp. 75–76.

23. Ibn al-Karbalāʼī gives the date of death as 927/1521, which would make sense in view of the wish expressed by ʻAbd al-Vahhāb in his testament to be reunited with his sons in Tabriz; evidently death overtook him before he could make arrangements to leave (*Rauḍāt al-Jinān,* 1: 216, 221). The date of death is given erroneously by Bacqué-Grammont (*Les Ottomans, les Safavides et leurs voisins,* p. 83) as 930/1524 because of his misreading of Khwāndmīr, who in fact says that "he [ʻAbd al-Vahhāb] is apparently still alive in the present year, which is 930" (*Ḥabīb al-Siyar,* ed. Jalāl Humāʼī and Muḥammad Dabīr Siyāqī, 4 vols. [Tehran: Kitābkhāna-yi Khayyām, 1333 Sh./1954], 4:609). Ḥājī Mīrzā Muḥammad ʻAlī Qāḍī Ṭabātabāʼī, a recent descendant of ʻAbd al-Vahhāb Hamadānī, has asserted on the basis of unnamed contemporary and near-contemporary sources that his ancestor died in captivity as early as 922/1516–17; see ʻAbd al-ʻAlī Kārang, *Āṣār-i Bāstānī-yi Āẕarbāyjān* (Tehran: Anjuman-i Āṣār-i Millī, 1351 Sh./1973), p. 669.

24. On the prestige enjoyed by *sayyid* families in several regions of pre-Safavid Iran, see Jean Aubin, "Šāh Ismāʻīl et les notables de l'Iraq persan," *Journal of the Social and Economic History of the Orient* 2 (1959): 40–42.

25. Khwāndmīr, *Ḥabīb al-Siyar,* 4:608–9.

26. See note 20 above.

27. Navāʼī, *Shāh Ismāʻīl Ṣafavī,* p. 232.

28. Saʻdüddin, *Tâcü 't-Tevârîh,* 2:274–75. See also Bacqué-Grammont, *Les Ottomans, les Safavides et leurs voisins,* pp. 83–86.

29. Bacqué-Grammont, *Les Ottomans, les Safavides et leurs voisins,* p. 86. Bacqué-Grammont (p. 83, n. 231) raises the possibility that the entire Safavid delegation was composed of Sunnis, given the fact that Maulānā Shukrullāh Mughānī, one of its members

imprisoned together with 'Abd al-Vahhāb Hamadānī but later released, was among thirty Sunni notables executed in the reign of Shah Ṭahmāsp. Maria Szuppe characterizes the conduct of 'Abd al-Vahhāb in the service of Shah Ismā'īl as that of a crypto-Sunni (*Entre Timourides, Uzbeks et Safavides* [Paris: Association pour l'Avancement des Etudes Iraniennes, 1992], p. 125).

30. Ibn al-Karbalā'ī, *Rauḍāt al-Jinān,* 1:221.

31. See, for example, the discussion below of Fakhr al-Dīn 'Alī Ṣafī, a figure whose Naqshbandī identity was far more marked than that of 'Abd al-Vahhāb Hamadānī. Aubin remarks perceptively of 'Abd al-Vahhāb: "His career epitomizes the enigma of those members of the Iranian élite who rallied to the Safavids" ("L'Avènement des Safavides reconsidéré," p. 100).

32. Even more remarkable than 'Abd al-Vahhāb's ability to pass with relative ease from the service of one dynasty to the next has been the lasting prominence of his descendants, principally in Tabriz, as scholars, qadis, and Shaykhs al-Islām. Their record of unbroken continuity from Aqqoyunlu times through the Safavid, Qajar, and Pahlavi periods into the era of the Islamic Republic is probably unequaled by any other scholarly lineage in Iran, despite the frequent occurrence of hereditarily transmitted religious eminence. The late 'Allāma Muḥammad Ḥusayn Ṭabāṭabā'ī (d. 1981), author of *Tafsīr al-Mīzān,* the most outstanding commentary on the Qur'ān to appear in the twentieth century, was a descendant of 'Abd al-Vahhāb Hamadānī in the thirteenth generation; for the complete genealogy, see Muḥammad al-Ḥusayni, *al-Shams al-Sāṭi'a* (Beirut: Dār al-Maḥajjat al-Bayḍā, 1417/1997), pp. 31–32. Concerning the successive generations of the "'Abd al-Vahhābī *sayyids* of Tabriz," see Iskandar Beg Munshī, *Tārīkh-i 'Ālam-ārā-yi 'Abbāsī,* 1:153 (Eskandar Monshi, *The History of Shah 'Abbas,* 1:244); Nādir Mīrzā, *Tārīkh va Jughrāfiyā-yi Dār al-Salṭana-yi Tabrīz* (Tehran: n.p., 1325/1907), pp. 222–31; Muḥammad 'Alī Tarbiyat, *Dānishmandān-i Āẕarbāyjān,* p. 268; and Muḥammad Sharīf Rāzī, *Ganjīna-yi Dānishmandān,* 7 vols. (Tehran: Kitābfurūshī-yi Islāmiya, 1352 Sh./1973), 3:322–25.

33. Bābā Mardūkh Rūḥānī makes of Ṣun'ullāh a Kurdish scholar and Sufi, despite the fact that he was born close to Tabriz, and attributes to him a period of study in "Kurdish-inhabited areas of Iran and Iraq" (*Tārīkh-i Mashāhīr-i Kurd,* 3 vols. [Tehran: Surūsh, 1364 Sh./1985], 1:141). These statements are not confirmed by the only source he cites, 'Alī Mınıq's *al-'Iqd al-Manẓūm fī Dhikr Afāḍil al-Rūm* (in margins of Ibn Khallikān, *Wafāyāt al-A'yān* [Būlāq: al-Maṭba'at al-'Āmira, 1310/1892–93], 2:252–53).

34. Ibn al-Karbalā'ī, *Rauḍāt al-Jinān,* 1:98–99; Qazvīnī, *Silsila-nāma-yi Khwājagān,* fol. 18b. On Maktabdār, see Tosun, *Bahâeddin Nakşbend,* pp. 141–42. Mardūkh Rūḥānī writes that Ṣun'ullāh not only traveled with Jāmī to Samarqand to meet with Aḥrār but also was initiated there by him (*Tārīkh-i Mashāhīr-i Kurd,* 1:141); this statement is unsupported and conflicts with all other accounts.

35. Ibn al-Karbalā'ī, *Rauḍāt al-Jinān,* 1:102–3. Ghijduvānī (d. 575/1179 or 617/1220) counts as the ancestor of the Khwājagān and is often designated in Naqshbandī literature as *sar-silsila-yi khwājagān* ("the first link in the chain of the Khwājagān"), given his role in formulating the distinctive principles of what was to become the Naqshbandiyya (see Hamid Algar, "Hâcegân," in *Türkiye Diyanet Vakfi Islam Ansiklopedisi,* 14:431). Ṣun'ullāh's mention of him rather than Bahā' al-Dīn suggests that even at this relatively advanced date the perception that a significant new development had been inaugurated by Bahā' al-Dīn was not yet universal among Naqshbandīs.

36. Khwāndmīr, *Ḥabīb al-Siyar,* 4:609.

37. Ibn al-Karbalā'ī, *Rauḍāt al-Jinān,* 1:102–3; Nevîzade Ataî, *Hadâikü 'l-Hakâik fî Tekmileti 'ş-Şekâik* (reprint, Istanbul: Çağrı Yayınları, 1989), p. 207; 'Alī Mınıq, *al-'Iqd al-Manẓūm fi Dhikr Afāḍil al-Rūm,* in margins of Ibn Khallikān, *Wafāyāt al-A'yān,* 2:252–53. Mardūkh Rūḥānī claims (without adducing evidence) that, after the audience with Shah Ismā'īl, Ṣun'ullāh was kept under close surveillance, compelled to abandon teaching, and ultimately died in grief-stricken isolation (*Tārīkh-i Mashāhīr-i Kurd,* 1:142).

38. Ibn al-Karbalā'ī, *Rauḍāt al-Jinān,* 2:71; Qazvīnī, *Silsila-nāma-yi Khwājagān-i Naqshband,* fol. 19a. The occurrence in Khusraushāhī's full designation of *akhi* (member of an urban sodality, usually in Anatolia) may also be a trace of his Kubravī connection; see Franz Taeschner, "Spuren für das Vorkommens des Achitums ausserhalb von Anatolien," in *Proceedings of the Twenty-second Congress of Orientalists (Istanbul, 1951),* 5 vols. (Leiden: E. J. Brill, 1954), 2:275–77.

39. Qazvīnī, *Silsila-nāma-yi Khwājagān-i Naqshband,* fol. 19a; Tosun, *Bahâeddin Nakşbend,* p. 282, citing Açıkbaş Mahmud Efendi, *Risâle-i Nurbahşiyye.*

40. See the section "The Shaykh from Urūmiya" below.

41. This fusion is most notably exemplified by Ḥazēnī, a Sufi of triple Naqshbandī, Yasavī, and Kubravī affiliation who came to Istanbul in the reign of Sultan Selim. See his *Cevâhiru 'l-Ebrâr min Emvâc-ı Bihâr,* ed. Cihan Okuyucu (Kayseri: Erciyes Üniversitesi, 1995).

42. Qazvīnī, *Silsila-nāma-yi Khwājagān-i Naqshband,* fol. 19a.

43. Mustafa b. Hayrettin, *Silsilenâme-i Hâcegân-i Nakşibend* (Turkish translation of Qazvīnī's *Silsila-nāma* with supplementary information), MS Süleymaniye, Hüsrev Paşa 408, fol. 15a.

44. At least one Naqshbandī fleeing Safavid oppression did in fact make his way to India. This was Maulānā Shahīdī Qummī, a disciple of 'Abd al-Raḥmān Jāmī in Herat, who found refuge in Gujarat. See Qazvīnī, *Silsila-nāma-yi Khwājagān-i Naqshband,* fol. 16a. He is said by Khwāndmīr to have been a poet of jovial temperament (*Ḥabīb al-Siyar,* 4:611).

45. See Ḥājī Khalīfa, *Kashf al-Ẓunūn,* ed. Şerefeddin Yaltkaya and Rıfat Bilge, 2 vols. (Istanbul: Milli Eğitim Basımevi, 1971), 2:col. 1107.

46. Nevîzade Ataî, *Hadâikü 'l-Hakâik,* pp. 207–8; 'Alī Mınıq, *al-'Iqd al-Manẓūm fī Dhikr Afāḍil al-Rūm,* pp. 253–56; Mehmed Süreyya, *Sicill-i Osmanî* (Istanbul: Matba'a-i Âmire, 1308/1890), 1:186–87; Mürsel Öztürk, "Ebû Said-i Sânî," in *Türkiye Diyanet Vakfi Islam Ansiklopedisi,* 10:225.

47. According to Muḥammad b. Ḥusayn Qazvīnī (the author of the *Silsila-nāma-yi Khwājagān-i Naqshband*), who knew Sayyid Muḥammad Bādāmyārī and esteemed him highly, some Shi'ites attending Bādāmyārī's gatherings in Urūmiya sought to explain to him that "the *mujtahid* of our *madhhab* is Imam Ja'far al-Ṣādiq." After they left, Bādāmyārī declared to his followers that, while the Shi'ites were speaking, Imam Ja'far al-Ṣādiq had appeared to him and told him: "I know nothing of what they say; they are slandering me" (fol. 19b). Part of the explanation for this claim to supernatural communication with Imam Ja'far al-Ṣādiq is that he is the fifth link in the initiatic chain of the Naqshbandīs and that they therefore were—and still are now—reluctant to forfeit his spiritual patronage to the Shi'ites. Dina Le Gall's attribution to Qazvīnī of a report that Bādāmyārī's family lineage caused him sometimes to be taken for a Shi'ite is incorrect and seems to rest on a misreading of this anecdote of supernatural communication ("The Ottoman Naqshbandiyya in the

Pre-Mujaddidī Phase: A Study in Islamic Religious Culture and Its Transmission" [Ph.D. dissertation, Princeton, 1992], p. 29).

48. Tosun, *Bahâeddin Nakşbend,* p. 280. Tosun's assertion earlier in his work (p. 143) that Muḥammad Bādāmyārī ultimately escaped Safavid oppression by fleeing to Sayrām in Central Asia, taking all his family and followers with him and dying there in 970/1562, seems incompatible with this continuation of the family line in Urūmiya.

49. Concerning the identity of Sayyid Aḥmad Bādāmyārī with Koçağa Sultan, see ibid., p. 226; and Martin van Bruinessen, "The Naqshbandī Order in 17th Century Kurdistan," in *Naqshbandis: Cheminements et situation actuelle d'un ordre mystique musulman,* ed. Marc Gaborieau, Alexandre Popovic, and Thierry Zarcone (Istanbul and Paris: Editions Isis, 1990), p. 351. Van Bruinessen cites a *silsila* from Mustafa b. Hayrettin's *Silsile-nâme-i Hâcegân-i Nakşibend* (fol. 15b), which erroneously makes of Ilyās Bādāmyārī a *khalīfa* of 'Alī-jān Bādāmyārī rather than of Darvīsh Akhī Khusraushāhī. The correct lineage appears to be that cited by Dina Le Gall from anonymous, *Şerâit ve Nasâih-i Meşayih* (MS Fatih 2658, fol. 73b); see "The Ottoman Naqshbandiyya," p. 198.

50. The allusion is, of course, to the divine preservation of Abraham from the fire into which the idolaters had cast him, as described in Qur'ān 21:69. Van Bruinessen ("The Naqshbandī Order in 17th Century Kurdistan," p. 349) interprets the phrase *ma'sum-ı pak* ("innocent and pure") used by Evliyâ Çelebi to describe the state of Koçağa Sultan's disinterred body to mean "young child," which does not at all follow from the text as a whole; earlier in the same passage Evliyâ Çelebi describes the body as "pure white, brilliant as crystal, fresh and soft like cotton."

51. Evliyâ Çelebi, *Seyahatname,* 10 vols. (Istanbul: Ikdam Matba'ası, 1314/1895), 4:304–5.

52. Tosun, *Bahâeddin Nakşbend,* p. 291, n. 65; Le Gall, "The Ottoman Naqshbandiyya," p. 198.

53. Mustafa Naîmâ, *Tarih,* 6 vols. (Istanbul: Matba'a-i Âmire, 1281–83/1864–66), 3:385.

54. Ibrahim Peçevi, *Tarih,* 2 vols. (Istanbul: Matba'a-i Âmire, 1281–83/1864–66), 2:462. The sense of *el-mülkü 'akîm fehvasınca sebeb-i gayz-ı padişahi olmuştu* ("as if the kingdom were bereft of a ruler, thus arousing the monarch's anger") has been mistranslated by van Bruinessen as "bearing complaints to the effect that their lands were barren, which caused the sultan's anger" and adduced by him as proof that Şeyh Aziz's lower-class following was composed largely of angry and impoverished peasants, thus giving the whole affair an aspect of social rebellion that it does not seem to have had ("The Naqshbandī Order in 17th Century Kurdistan," pp. 343–44).

55. *Hünkâr* is most probably an abbreviation of Persian *khudāvandigār* ("ruler," "lord," "master") that entered Turkish by way of Arabic; see Muḥammad Ḥusayn Tabrīzī, *Burhān-i Qāṭi',* ed. Muḥammad Mu'īn, 4 vols. (Tehran: Kitābkhāna-yi Zuvvār, 1330 Sh./1951), 2:719. But insofar as bloodshed was viewed as the essential business of rulers, it was natural that the first syllable should be popularly interpreted as *khūn* ("blood").

56. Martin van Bruinessen and Hendrik Boeschoten, *Evliyâ Çelebi in Diyarbekir* (Leiden: E. J. Brill, 1988), pp. 184–87 (relevant section of the *Seyahatname* together with translation and commentary).

57. Şeyhî Mehmed Efendi, *Vekâyi'ü 'l-Fudalâ',* ed. Abdülkadir Özcan, 2 vols. (Istanbul: Çağrı Yayınları, 1989), 1:68, adds the interesting and entirely plausible detail that the intriguers suggested to Murad that Şeyh Aziz wished to emulate the example of "Sakarya *şeyhi*" (the shaykh of Sakarya), who had led a revolt earlier in his reign. Concerning this

rebel, see Kâtib Çelebi, *Fezleke,* 2 vols. in 1 (Istanbul: Ceride-i Havadis, 1286–87/1869–70), 2:295–97.

58. Van Bruinessen and Boeschoten, *Evliyâ Çelebi in Diyarbekir,* pp. 188–89. A somewhat different twist is given to the alchemical aspect of the episode in an account reported with some skepticism by Naîmâ (*Tarih,* 3:387–89). Şeyh Aziz supposedly assured Sultan Murad that his Druze houseguest was indeed able to produce large quantities of gold, so he agreed to finance her activities. On his return from the Baghdad campaign, it became apparent that she had managed to manufacture only an inferior yellowish metal, so Murad ordered that she be put to death and, for good measure, the shaykh as well. For illustrations of the room where Şeyh Aziz was put to death, a chest containing the bloodstained garments in which he met his end, and possessions such as a walking staff and seal that have been preserved in Diyabekir down to the present, see M. Şefik Korkusuz, *Tezkire-i Meşâyih-i Amid (Diyabekir Velileri)* (Istanbul: n.p., 1997), pp. 96–98.

59. Peçevî, *Tarih,* 2:462. The story reminded Peçevî of the killing of Shaykh Majd al-Dīn Baghdādī in 616/1219 by Sultan Muḥammad Khwārazmshāh, in that the earlier execution also arose from a shaykh's dealings with a lady of the royal house.

60. Van Bruinessen and Boeschoten, *Evliyâ Çelebi in Diyarbekir,* pp. 190–91.

61. Peçevî, *Tarih,* 2:462.

62. Van Bruinessen and Boeschoten, *Evliyâ Çelebi in Diyarbekir,* p. 149.

63. This book, *Baba Kelamı,* was evidently begun by Şeyh Aziz and completed by various of his successors. See Kenan Erdoğan, "Seyyid Aziz Mahmud Urmevî, Urmevîlik ve Bilinmeyen bir Eseri: Baba Kelâmı," *Bir* 9–10 (1998): 211–25.

64. Evliyâ Çelebi's wording at this point, *bunda olan tevhid ü tezkir-i sübhani bir diyara mahsus değildir* (van Bruinessen and Boeschoten, *Evliyâ Çelebi in Diyarbekir,* pp. 144, 146), is admittedly somewhat ambiguous; but if it does refer to the unique character of the *dhikr* that Evliyâ Çelebi witnessed, some Kubravī-inspired deviation from Naqshbandī norms may have been what caught his attention.

65. Ibid., pp. 158–61; Korkusuz, *Tezkire-i Meşâyih-i Amid,* p. 145; Ali Emiri, *Tezkire-i Şu'arâ-yi Amid* (Istanbul: Matba'a-i Âmire, 1327/1909), pp. 20–21.

66. Korkusuz, *Tezkire-i Meşâyih-i Amid,* p. 73.

67. The *tekke* in question is known as "Atîk" (ancient) in order to distinguish it from the Nakşibendî-i Cedid Dergahı (the New Naqshbandī Tekke), founded about a century later by Cizyedarzade Hacı Hüseyin Ağa, concerning which see Mustafa Kara, *Bursa'da Tarikatlar ve Tekkeler* (Bursa: Sır Yayıncılık, 2001), pp. 237–38.

68. These works are in MS Süleymaniye, Hayri Abdullah Efendi 146, fols. 112b–17a and 52b–111a. See also Tosun, *Bahâeddin Nakşbend,* p. 282; and Mustafa Kara, *Bursa'da Tarikatlar ve Tekkeler,* p. 234. It may be due to the influence of Açıkbaş Mahmud Efendi or his predecessors in this particular line of Naqshbandī tradition that the *Aurād-i Fatḥiyya* are still commonly recited by Naqshbandīs in Turkey and the Balkans, for the practice seems to be unknown among members of the *ṭarīqa* elsewhere.

69. See Mehmed Tahir, *Osmanlı Müellifleri,* 3 vols. (Istanbul: Matba'a-i Âmire, 1333/1915), 1:14.

70. Şeyhî, *Vekâyi'ü 'l-Fudalâ,* 1:562; Ismail Beliğ Bursevî, *Güldeste-i Riyaz-ı Irfan* (Bursa: Hudâvendigâr Vilâyeti Matba'ası, 1302/1884), pp. 154–59; Tosun, *Bahâeddin Nakşbend,* pp. 281–82; Mustafa Kara, *Bursa'da Tarikatlar ve Tekkeler,* pp. 235–36; Hasan Kâmil Yılmaz, "Açıkbaş Mahmud Efendi," in *Türkiye Diyanet Vakfı Islam Ansiklopedisi,* 1:332.

71. Şeyhî, *Vekâyi'ü 'l-Fudalâ,* 1:573–74; Bursevi, *Güldeste-i Riyaz-ı Irfan,* pp. 159–60; Mustafa Kara, *Bursa'da Tarikatlar ve Tekkeler,* p. 236.

72. Kara, *Bursa'da Tarikatlar ve Tekkeler,* p. 236.

73. For a complete list of all *postnişins* down to 1925, see ibid. The transfer of the direction of a *tekke* from one branch of the *ṭarīqa* to another was a fairly common phenomenon in the history of the Ottoman Naqshbandiyya.

74. Mustafa b. Hayrettin, *Silsile-nâme-i Hâcegân-i Nakşibend,* fol. 7a.

75. Tosun, *Bahâeddin Nakşbend,* p. 281.

76. Qazvīnī, *Silsila-nāma-yi Khwājagān-i Naqshband,* fol. 20b.

77. See Jean Aubin, "Šāh Ismā'īl et les notables de l'Iraq persan," p. 58, n. 3.

78. Evidence for the resilience of Sunnism in Qazvin, three-quarters of a century after the foundation of the Safavid state, is provided by the fact that many of its citizens qualified for the reward offered by Shah Ismā'īl II (r. 984–86/1576–77), to all those who had steadfastly refused to curse the first three caliphs. See Shohreh Golsorkhi, "Ismail II and Mirza Makhdum Sharifi," *International Journal of Middle East Studies* 26:3 (August 1994): 479, 481. The strength of Sunnism in Qazvin has also been noted by Jean Aubin ("Šāh Ismā'īl et les notables de l'Iraq persan," p. 58, n. 6).

79. Qazvīnī, *Silsila-nāma-yi Khwājagān-i Naqshband,* fol. 19b.

80. Ibid., fol. 20a. Shaykh Zāhid Gīlānī was, of course, the spiritual preceptor of Shaykh Ṣafī al-Dīn, the progenitor of the Safavids; but it is important to note that other Sufi lineages also descended from him. See Mahmud Cemaleddin el-Hulvî, *Lemezât-ı Hulviyye,* ed. Mehmet Serhan Tayşi (Istanbul: Marmara Üniversitesi, 1993), pp. 319–34.

81. Qazvīnī, *Silsila-nāma-yi Khwājagān-i Naqshband,* fol. 20a.

82. Ibid., fol. 20a. This should not be taken to imply that he had a secondary affiliation to a Malāmatī order; in this context, "Malāmatī" implies a spiritual temperament (*mashrab*), not an initiatic affiliation. On the general congruity of Malāmatī principles with the Naqshbandī path as expounded in the earliest period, see Hamid Algar, "Eléments de provenance Malâmatî dans la tradition primitive Naqshbandî," in *Melamis-Bayramis: Etudes sur trois mouvements mystiques musulmans,* ed. Nathalie Clayer, Alexandre Popovic, and Thierry Zarcone (Istanbul: Les Editions Isis, 1998), pp. 27–36.

83. Qazvīnī, *Silsila-nāma-yi Khwājagān-i Naqshband,* fol. 20b. On the trans-sectarian appeal of Shāhzāda Ḥusayn, the tomb of Ḥusayn b. 'Alī al-Riḍā, see 'Abd al-Jalīl Qazvīnī, *Kitāb-i Naqḍ,* ed. Muhaddiṣ Urmavī (Tehran: Anjuman-i Āṣār-i Millī, 1358 Sh./1979), p. 589; and on its general history, see Ḥusayn Mudarrisī Ṭabāṭabā'ī, *Bargī az Tārīkh-i Qazvīn* (Qum: n.p., 1361 Sh./1982).

84. Qazvīnī, *Silsila-nāma-yi Khwājagān-i Naqshband,* fol. 20b.

85. Ibid., fol. 21a. This expression, a sarcastic reversal of the oft-repeated Qur'ānic injunction to "command the good and forbide the evil," may of course be general in scope; but it is possible that Qazvīnī intends particularly the cursing of the first three caliphs that was frequently demanded by the Safavids as a token of the abandonment of Sunnism.

86. Ibid., fols. 16a, 21a. For evidence that Damascus was in general a favored place of refuge for Sunnis fleeing Iran, see Abdul-Rahim Abu Husayn, "The Shiites in Lebanon and the Ottomans in the 16th and 17th Centuries," in *La Shî'a nell' Impero Ottomano* (Rome: Academia Nazionale dei Lincei, 1993), p. 119.

87. Muḥammad 'Alī Tarbiyat, *Dānishmandān-i Āẕarbāyjān,* p. 16; Muḥammad 'Alī Mudarris, *Rayḥānat al-Adab,* 2nd ed., 8 vols. (Tabriz: Khayyām, n.d.), 3:111; Hanna Sohrweide, "Der Sieg der Safawiden und seine Rückwirkungen auf die Schiiten Anatoliens im

16. Jahrhundert," *Der Islam* 41 (1965): 155–56; and Jean Aubin, "L'Avènement des Safavides reconsidéré," pp. 90–91. Dates given for Shabistarī's death other than 917/1511–12 are either too early or too late, considering that he was killed in the immediate aftermath of Şahkulu's defeat near Sivas in July 1511. On the works of Shabistarī, see Süleyman Ateş, *Işârî Tefsir Okulu,* p. 225; Ḥājī Khalīfa, *Kashf al-Ẓunūn,* 1:col. 172 and 2:col. 1987; and Ismā'īl Paşa Baghdādī, *Īdāḥ al-Maknūn,* 2 vols. (Istanbul: Milli Eğitim Bakanlığı, 1972), 1:col. 308.

88. This son settled in Istanbul, where he gained an appointment as *müderris.* In addition to his learned works, he composed poetry, including a *qaṣīda* congratulating Kânûnî Süleyman on the conquest of Rhodes. See *Türk Dili ve Edebiyatı Ansiklopedisi,* 8 vols. (Istanbul: Deragh Yayınları, 1990), 7:67.

89. Qazvīnī, *Silsila-nāma-yi Khwājagān-i Naqshband,* fol. 18b.

90. See Abdülbaki Gölpınarlı, *Mevlânâ'dan Sonra Mevlevîlik,* 2nd ed. (Istanbul: Inkılap ve Aka Kitabevleri, 1983), p. 15; Ali Alparslan, "Abdülvehhâb es-Sâbûnî," in *Türkiye Diyanet Vakfi Islam Ansiklopedisi,* 1:286–87; and Cemal Kurnaz, *Anadolu'da Orta Asyalı Şairler* (Ankara: Kültür Bakanlığı, 1997), pp. 89–90.

91. The significance of the Naqshbandiyya in pre-Safavid Herat is such that it deserves separate monographic treatment; it is the contrasting sparseness of the record concerning the Naqshbandīs of Tabriz, Qazvin, and Urūmiya that has made possible the exhaustive coverage of them attempted in this article.

92. Hamid Algar, "Sa'd al-Dīn Kāshgharī," in *Encyclopaedia of Islam,* 2nd ed., 9:110–11. For a listing of Kāshgharī's followers, see Qazvīnī, *Silsila-nāma-yi Khwājagān-i Naqshband,* fols. 14b–18a.

93. Concerning Jāmī's devotion to the Naqshbandiyya and to Kāshgharī in particular, see Kāshifī, *Rashaḥāt-i 'Ayn al-Ḥayāt,* 1:233–86; and 'Abd al-Vāsi' Bākharzī, *Maqāmāt-i Jāmī,* ed. Najīb Māyil Hiravī (Tehran: Nashr-i Nay, 1371 Sh./1992), pp. 87–88. It was no doubt due to his friendship with Jāmī that 'Alī Shīr Navā'ī entered the Naqshbandiyya; for evidence of his Naqshbandī affiliations, see his *Khamsa,* ed. Porso Shamsiev (Tashkent: UZSSR Fanlar Akademiiasi Nashriyati, 1958), pp. 71–74. Principal among Jāmī's writings devoted to the Naqshbandiyya is the treatise *Sar-rishta-yi Ṭarīq-i Khwājagān,* ed. 'Abd al-Ḥayy Ḥabībī (Kabul: Anjuman-i Jāmī, 1343 Sh./1964). References to the order are also to be found scattered in a number of other works, especially *Silsilat al-Ẕahab* and *Tuḥfat al-Aḥrār.*

94. Bākharzī, *Maqāmāt-i Jāmī,* p. 88.

95. Jāmī's own disciples seem to have been restricted to three: Raḍī al-Dīn 'Abd al-Ghafūr Lārī (d. 912/1506), well known for his supplement to Jāmī's *Nafaḥāt al-Uns* (*Takmila-yi Nafaḥāt al-Uns,* ed. 'Alī Aṣghar Bashīr Hiravī [Kabul: Anjuman-i Jāmī, 1343 Sh./1964]); his own son, Khwāja Ḍiyā' al-Dīn Yūsuf; and Maulānā Shahīdī Qummī. See Qazvīnī, *Silsila-nāma-yi Khwājagān-i Naqshband,* fols. 15b–16a.

96. Bākharzī, *Maqāmāt-i Jāmī,* pp. 114–15, 123, 142, 200.

97. Cited in Gholsorkhi, "Ismail II and Mirza Makhdum Sharifi," p. 481.

98. 'Alī Aṣghar Ḥikmat, *Jāmī* (Tehran: Tūs, 1363 Sh./1984), p. 51; Fikrī Saljūqī, *Khiābān* (Kabul: n.p., 1343 Sh./1964), p. 94.

99. Qazvīnī, *Silsila-nāma-yi Khwājagān-i Naqshband,* fol. 15b; Fikrī Saljūqī's addenda to three works on the tombs of Herat, published together under the title *Mazārāt-i Harāt* (Kabul: Publishing Institute, 1346 Sh./1967), p. 153.

100. Qazvīnī, *Silsila-nāma-yi Khwājagān-i Naqshband,* fol. 16a.

101. Ibid., fol. 16b; Tosun, *Bahâeddin Nakşbend,* p. 144.

102. Qazvīnī, *Silsila-nāma-yi Khwājagān-i Naqshband,* fol. 15b, Tosun, *Bahâeddin Nakşbend,* p. 144. Maulānā Jalāl's treatise *Risāla-yi Rāhnamā-yi 'Uqda-gushāy* was published by Marijan Molé in *Farhang-i Īrān-zamīn,* 6:4 (1337 Sh./1958): 285–93. 'Abd al-'Azīz Khān was simultaneously devoted—at least for a time—to another Naqshbandī, Khwāja Muḥammad Islām Jūybārī (d. 971/1563), progenitor of the influential Jūybārī shaykhs of Bukhara; see Yuri Bregel, "'Abd al-'Azīz Solṭān," in *Encyclopaedia Iranica,* 1:101–2.

103. Qazvīnī, *Silsila-nāma-yi Khwājagān-i Naqshband,* fol. 19a. Qazvīnī remarks that Kāshifī suffered greatly at the hands of the "Ravāfiḍ," but this may refer to tribulations endured not in Herat but in his native city of Sabzavār, a major bastion of Shi'ism in pre-Safavid Khurasan. Fikrī Saljūqī is, however, of the opinion that the "one year's imprisonment" to which Fakhr al-Dīn 'Alī Ṣafī refers in the introduction to his *Laṭā'if al-Ṭavā'if* (ed. Aḥmad Gulchīn-i Ma'ānī [Tehran: Iqbāl, 1336 Sh./1957], p. 1) is to be taken literally as relating to a year's confinement in the citadel of Herat (shared with Ḍiyā' al-Dīn Jāmī) ordered by the Safavid governor of the city (Saljūqī's addenda to *Mazārāt-i Harāt,* pp. 13–15).

104. Qazvīnī, *Silsila-nāma-yi Khwājagān-i Naqshband,* fol. 18a; Tosun, *Bahâeddin Nakşbend,* p. 145. The dicta of Zayn al-Dīn Maḥmūd Kamāngar have been published by 'Ārif Naushāhī under the title "Malfūẓāt-i Bihdādinī Khwāfī," in *Barg-i Bībargī,* ed. Najīb Māyil Hiravī (Tehran: Ṭarḥ-i Nau, 1378 Sh./1999), pp. 435–517.

105. Ibn al-Karbalā'ī, *Rauḍāt al-Jinān,* 2:159, 491. On the Safavid suppression of Sufism in general, see Said Amir Arjomand, *The Shadow of God and the Hidden Imam* (Chicago: University of Chicago Press, 1984), pp. 112–19.

106. See Gülşenî, *Menâkıb-i Ibrahim Gülşenî,* p. 248.

107. Aubin, "Šāh Ismā'īl et les notables de l'Iraq persan," p. 58.

108. Hamid Algar, "Nūrbakhshiyya," in *Encyclopaedia of Islam,* 2nd ed., 8:135.

109. Hamid Algar, "Ni'mat-Allāhiyya," in *Encyclopaedia of Islam,* 2nd ed., 8:46.

110. Hamid Algar, "Dahabiyya," in *Encyclopaedia Iranica,* 6:579–80.

111. Mīrzā Makhdūm Sharīfī, *al-Nawāqiḍ li Bunyān al-Rawāfiḍ,* MS British Library, or. 7991, fol. 96a. Elke Eberhard misunderstands this passage in Mīrzā Makhdūm's work to refer to the killing of only a single Naqshbandī (*Osmanische Polemik gegen die Safawiden im 16. Jahrhundert nach arabischen Handschriften* [Freiburg i. Br.: Klaus Schwarz, 1970], p. 187).

112. Nūrullāh Shushtarī, *Maṣā'ib al-Nawāṣib,* MS Majlis library 2036, section 4, subsection 14, cited by Arjomand, *The Shadow of God and the Hidden Imam,* pp. 113, 297.

113. On the introduction of the Naqshbandiyya to Ottoman Turkey, see Le Gall, "The Ottoman Naqshbandiyya"; and on Naqshbandī relations with the first Uzbek khans, see Bakhtiyar Babajanov, "La Naqshbandiyya sous les premiers Sheybanides," in Maria Szuppe, ed., *L'Héritage timouride, Iran—Asie Centrale—Inde, XVème–XVIIIème siècles* (Tashkent and Aix-en-Provence: Institut Français d'Etudes sur l'Asie Centrale, 1997), pp. 69–90. The influence exerted by the Naqshbandī shaykhs of Transoxiana on the Shibanids came directly to the notice of Shah Ismā'īl during one of his campaigns against 'Ubaydullāh Khān. Deciding to sue for peace, the Uzbek ruler dispatched to Shah Ismā'īl's camp a certain Khwāja 'Abd al-Raḥīm Naqshbandī, a lineal descendant of Khwāja Bahā' al-Dīn Naqshband himself, who was allegedly 130 years old and could remember the days of Sultan Abū Sa'īd the Timurid (r. 855–73/1451–69). The *khwāja* pledged to Shah Ismā'īl that he would personally ensure observance of peace on the part of the Uzbeks; for, according to the anonymous Safavid chronicler, "the rulers of Turkistan would not dare to drink a drop of water without first obtaining his consent" (anonymous, *'Ālam-ārā-yi Ṣafavī,* ed. Yadullāh Shukrī, 2nd ed.

[Tehran: Iṭṭilā'āt, 1363 Sh./1984], pp. 446–52). A similar role of mediation was played many years later by another Naqshbandī named 'Abd al-Raḥīm, a shaykh of the Jūybārī line. In 1030/1621 he accompanied an Uzbek mission to Isfahan in order to plead with Shah 'Abbās that he forego a planned punitive expedition against Transoxiana. The shah is said to have treated him hospitably and respectfully. See 'Abd al-Ḥusayn Navā'ī, ed., *Shāh 'Abbās: Asnād va Mukātabāt-i Tārīkhī*, 2 vols. (Tehran: Bunyād-i Farhang-i Īrān, 1352 Sh./1973), 1:178–79.

114. Zayn al-'Ābidīn Shirvānī (d. 1253/1838), a widely traveled and open-minded Ni'matullāhī, reported that he had never encountered more than two or three Shi'ite Naqshbandīs (*Riyāḍ al-Siyāḥa*, ed. Aṣghar Ḥāmid Rabbānī [Tehran: Sa'dī, 1339 Sh./1960], p. 482). I have heard rumors of Shi'ite Naqshbandīs existing in present-day Tabriz but have not had the opportunity to investigate.

115. In his *Majālis al-Mu'minīn* (Tehran: Kitābfurūshī-yi Islāmiya, n.d.), p. 259, Shushtarī assails the *bakrī* lineage cited by the Naqshbandiyya as a deliberate and malicious forgery.

116. See, for example, Khwāja Muḥammad Pārsā, *Risāla-yi Qudsiyya*, ed. Muḥammad Ṭāhir 'Irāqī (Tehran: Taḥūri, 1354 Sh./1975), pp. 9–13; and Ṣafī, *Rashaḥāt-i 'Ayn al-Ḥayāt*, 1:11–13.

117. Jean Aubin, *Matériaux pour la biographie de Shâh Ni'matullâh Walî Kermânî* (Tehran and Paris: Institut Français d'Iranologie, 1956), pp. 13–14. See also Jürgen Paul, "Scheiche und Herrscher im Khanat Çağatay," *Der Islam* 67:2 (1990): 291–94, 309–10. The clearly deliberate omission of Shah Ni'matullāh Valī by 'Abd al-Raḥmān Jāmī from his *Nafaḥat al-Uns*, however, may indeed reflect a distaste for the founder of the Ni'matullāhiyya inherited from earlier generations of Naqshbandīs.

118. Ṣafī, *Rashaḥāt-i 'Ayn al-Ḥayāt*, 2:489–90. The origin of Aḥrār's anecdote appears to be an incident related of Shaykh Abū Sa'īd b. Abī 'l-Khayr; see Muḥammad b. Munavvar, *Asrār al-Tauḥīd fī Maqāmāt al-Shaykh Abū Sa'īd*, ed. Muḥammad Riḍā Shafī'ī Kadkanī, 2 vols. (Tehran: Āgāh, 1366 Sh./1987), 1:93.

119. A. A. Semenov, "Vzaimootnosheniia Alishera Navoi i Sultana Khusein-Mirzy," in *Issledovaniia po istorii kul'tury narodov vostoka: Sbornik v chest' Akademika I. A. Orbeli* (Moscow and Leningrad: Izdatel'stvo Akademii Nauk SSSR, 1960), p. 243.

120. Fakhr al-Dīn 'Alī Ṣafī, *Rashaḥāt-i 'Ayn al-Ḥayāt*, 1:254–60.

121. Jāmī, *Haft Aurang*, ed. Murtaḍā Mudarris Gīlānī (Tehran: Sa'dī, 1361 Sh./1982), pp. 146–47.

122. Bākharzī, *Maqāmāt-i Jāmī*, pp. 155–58.

123. Ibid., pp. 155–56. There is, of course, a certain irony in Jāmī's objection to the designation of Sunnis as Kharijites, for he freely indulges in the application of the pejorative term "Rāfiḍīs" to the Shi'ites.

124. Ibid., p. 157. In an incident that was probably not unique, some two to three years after the death of Jāmī, a certain Ḥasan 'Alī Maddāḥ was executed in Herat for cursing one of the Companions; see Zayn al-Dīn Vāṣifī, *Badāyi' al-Vaqāyi'*, ed. A. N. Boldyrev, 2 vols. (Moscow: Izdatel'stvo Vostochnoi Literatury, 1961), 2:1056. The fact that the execrator was a *maddāḥ*—one who extolled the virtues of the Ahl al-Bayt—is one indication among others that even in pre-Safavid times praise of the Imams was often accompanied by the cursing of those regarded by Shi'ites as their enemies. Indeed, *maddāḥ* appears sometimes to have been used interchangeably with *tabarrā'ī*, the appellation of a semiprofessional execrator (and, in Safavid times, one who compelled others to execrate); see Jean Calmard, "Les rituels shiites

et le pouvoir: L'imposition du shiisme safavide, eulogies et malédictions canoniques," in *Etudes Safavides,* ed. Jean Calmard (Paris and Tehran: Institut Français de Recherche en Iran, 1993), pp. 130, 134, 144.

125. Bākharzī, *Maqāmāt-i Jāmī,* p. 157. The reference to "a handful of ignorant Jews" echoes, no doubt, a stock theme of anti-Shi'ite polemics: that a certain 'Abdullāh b. Saba' made an insincere conversion from Judaism to Islam in order to spread among Muslims the false doctrines that subsequently became the foundation of Shi'ism. In all likelihood, such a person never existed; see Murtaḍā al-'Askarī, *Usṭūrat 'Abdillāh b. Saba'* (Beirut: n.p., n.d.).

126. Bākharzī, *Maqāmāt-i Jāmī,* pp. 155–56.

127. Jāmī's endorsement of the alleged tomb of 'Alī b. Abī Ṭālib discovered at Mazār-i Sharīf near Balkh as authentic no doubt belongs in the same context of claiming the Twelve Imams for Sunni Islam. It is significant that his biographer, Bākharzī, effectively describes its discovery as a divine response to the numerous, allegedly inauthentic *imāmzāda*s being established by Shi'ites in the region of Herat in the same period (see *Maqāmāt-i Jāmī,* pp. 190, 231–32). It is nonetheless difficult to reconcile Jāmī's approval of the claims made for Mazār-i Sharīf with the fervent *qaṣīda* he composed at Najaf, the commonly accepted site of 'Alī's burial (*Dīvān,* ed. Shams Brelvī [Tehran: Hidāyat, 1362 Sh./1983], pp. 25–26). The explanation may be simply that the tomb in Mazār-i Sharīf was not discovered until 885/1480, about five years after Jāmī had returned from the journey in the course of which he had visited Najaf; see Mu'īn al-Dīn Muḥammad Isfizārī, *Rauḍāt al-Jannāt fī Auṣāf Madīnat Hirāt,* ed. Muḥammad Isḥāq, 2 vols. (Aligarh: Aligarh Muslim University, 1961), 1:. In addition, it is worth noting that the first miraculous discovery of the alleged tomb had taken place as early as 530/1135 and was reported by the Andalusian traveler Abū Ḥāmid al-Gharnāṭī in an account of which 'Abd al-Ghafūr Lārī, one of Jāmī's leading disciples, was apparently aware; see Lārī, *Tārīkhcha-yi Mazār-i Sharīf,* ed. Māyil Hiravī (Kabul: Anjuman-i Tārīkh va Adab, 1350 Sh./1971), pp. 19–21. For more on the origins of the shrine at Mazār-i Sharīf, see Robert McChesney, *Waqf in Central Asia: Four Hundred Years in the History of a Muslim Shrine, 1480–1889* (Princeton: Princeton University Press, 1991), pp. 27–36.

128. Jāmī, *Haft Aurang,* pp. 145–46, 148–49.

129. Jāmī, *Shavāhid al-Nubuvva* (Istanbul: Hakikat Kitabevi, 1995), pp. 210–82. That Jāmī is determined to divorce the Imams from Shi'ism can be seen from his use of the formula "may God be pleased with him" (*raḍiya 'llāhu 'anh*) after the mention of each of their names instead of the invocation of peace (*'alayhi 'l-salām*) made by Shi'ites. On Jāmī's attitude to Shi'ism, see further Najīb Māyil Hiravī, *Shaykh 'Abd al-Raḥmān Jāmī* (Tehran: Ṭarḥ-i Nau, 1377 Sh./1998), pp. 114–22.

130. From one point of view, Sa'd al-Dīn Kāshgharī might be viewed as the initiator of Ḥusayn Vā'iẓ-i Kāshifī, for Kāshgharī—whom he had never seen before—invited him in a dream swiftly to join him at the station he had reached (*zūd bāsh khudrā ba manzil-i mā birasān*). This dream coincided, however, with the death of Kāshgharī, so it was Jāmī who, as one of Kāshgharī's successors, agreed with some reluctance to assume responsibility for Kāshifī's spiritual training. Insofar as Kāshifī dreamed of Kāshgharī while making a pilgrimage to the shrine of Imam Riḍā in Mashhad, it may also be suggested that his entry to the Naqshbandī path took place under the auspices of the Imam. See Fakhr al-Dīn 'Alī Ṣafī, *Rashaḥāt-i 'Ayn al-Ḥayāt,* 1:252–54; and Riḍā Jalālī-Nā'īnī, introduction to Ḥusayn Vā'iẓ-i Kāshifī, *Mavāhib-i 'Aliyya yā Tafsīr-i Ḥusaynī,* 4 vols. (Tehran: Iqbāl, 1317–29 Sh./1938–50), 1:8–9. Aḥrār was also aware of Kāshifī the elder and esteemed him; Kāshifī the younger

reports him as saying, "I have heard much of him; they say he has many virtues and accomplishments and his preaching is appreciated by the high and the low" (*Rashaḥāt-i 'Ayn al-Ḥayāt,* 2:491).

131. Gulchīn-i Ma'ānī cites the opening paragraph of this still unpublished work in his introduction to *Laṭā'if al-Ṭavā'if,* p. xi.

132. Muḥammad 'Alī Mudarris, *Rayḥānat al-Adab,* 5:29; Gulchīn-i Ma'ānī, introduction to *Laṭā'if al-Ṭavā'if,* p. x; Jalālī-Nā'īnī, introduction to *Mavāhib-i 'Aliyya,* 1:13–17. The *Mavāhib-i 'Aliyya,* Ḥusayn Vā'iẓ-i Kāshifī's commentary on the Qur'ān, does not cite any of the well-known Shi'ite *tafsīrs*, which must surely count as an indication of his Sunni identity. Jalālī-Nā'īnī's suggestion (introduction, p. 17) that he was practicing *taqiya* out of fear of Jāmī and Navā'ī must be discounted as arbitrary and implausible.

133. Khwāja Muḥammad Pārsā, *Faṣl al-Khiṭāb* (Tashkent: Litografiya Gulam Khasandzhanova, 1331/1913), pp. 402–43.

134. Ibid., p. 443; Jāmī, *Shavāhid al-Nubuvva,* pp. 276–82; Fakhr al-Dīn 'Alī Ṣafī, *Laṭā'if al-Ṭavā'if,* pp. 61–65. For lists of other Sunni authorities who regarded the Twelfth Imam, the son of Ḥasan al-'Askarī, as the Mahdī, see Najm al-Dīn Ja'far b. Muḥammad al-'Askarī, *al-Mahdī al-Mau'ūd 'inda 'Ulamā' Ahl al-Sunna wa 'l-Imāmiyya,* 2 vols. (Beirut: al-A'lamī, 1397/1977), 1:182–226; and Luṭfullāh al-Ṣāfī al-Gulpāyagānī, *Muntakhab al-Athar fī 'l-Imām al-Thānī-'ashar* (Qum: Maktabat al-Ṣadr, n.d.), pp. 322–41. It is probable, however, that most if not all of these figures regarded him as having been a Mahdī in a somewhat limited sense, not as the salvific figure who will come at the End of Time.

135. Pārsā, *Faṣl al-Khiṭāb,* p. 443.

136. Jāmī, *Shavāhid al-Nubuvva,* pp. 277, 281. Samnānī's account of the matter, replete with all manner of fantastic detail, is to be found in his *al-'Urwa li Ahl al-Khalwa wa 'l-Jalwa,* ed. Najīb Māyil Hiravī (Tehran: Mawla, 1362 Sh./1983), p. 367. It was also taken up by the Khalvatī author Mahmud Cemaleddin el-Hulvî, in his *Lemezât-ı Hulviyye* (p. 132).

137. Maḥjūb, "Az faḍā'il- va manāqib-khwānī tā rauḍakhwānī," *Iran Nameh* 2/3 (1984): 414.

138. See note 47 above.

139. See Henry Corbin, *En Islam Iranien,* 4 vols. (Paris: Gallimard, 1971), 1:1–38; Marijan Molé, "Les Kubrawiya entre Sunnisme et Shiisme aux huitième et neuvième siècles de l'hégire," *Revue des Etudes Islamiques* 29 (1961): 61–142 (especially pp. 61–65); Sayyed Hossein Nasr, "Shi'ism and Sufism: Their Relationship in Essence and History," in Sayyed Hossein Nasr, *Sufi Essays* (London: Allen and Unwin, 1972), pp. 117–18; idem, "Religion in Safavid Persia," *Iranian Studies* 7:1–2 (Winter–Spring 1974): 271–72; Abdoldjavad Falaturi, "Die Vorbereitung des iranischen Volkes für die Annahme der Schia zu Beginn der Safawiden-Zeit," in *Die islamische Welt zwischen Mittelalter und Neuzeit: Festschrift für Hans Robert Roemer zum 65. Geburtstag* (Beirut and Wiesbaden: in Kommission bei F. Steiner, 1979), pp. 140–45. For preliminary refutations of the view that the Kubraviyya was in its entirety a proto-Shi'ite order—a view on which the thesis of Sufi preparation for Shi'ism is largely based—see Hamid Algar, "Some Observations on Religion in Safavid Persia," *Iranian Studies* 7:1–2 (Winter–Spring 1974): 287–90; and Devin DeWeese, "The Eclipse of the Kubraviyah in Central Asia," *Iranian Studies* 21:1–2 (1988): 45–83 (especially pp. 81–83).

140. Jean Aubin, "La politique religieuse des Safavides," in *Le Shiisme Imamite,* ed. Taufic Fahd (Paris: Presses Universitaires de la France, 1970), p. 238.

141. We find that even biological as well as spiritual descent from Imam Ja'far al-Ṣādiq came to be attributed to Bahā' al-Dīn Naqshband, something of which there is no hint in

the earliest Naqshbandī sources; see Shāh Ghulām ʿAlī Dihlavī, *Makātīb-i Sharīfa* (Madras: Matbaʿ-i ʿAzīzī, 1335/1916), pp. 79–80; and Ghulām Sarvar Lāhūrī, *Khazīnat al-Aṣfiyā'*, 2 vols. (Kanpur: Naval Kishore, 1914), 1:549. Shaykh Aḥmad Sirhindī (d. 1033/1624), founder of the Mujaddidī branch of the *ṭarīqa*, described the Twelve Imams as the leaders of those who approach the divine presence by means of sainthood (*vilāyat;* see *Maktūbāt* [Lucknow: Naval Kishore, 1307/1889], 3:247–48), but he also directed a brief and bitter treatise against Shiʿism (*Kavā'if-i Shīʿa* [reprint, Istanbul: Hakikat Kitabevi, 1384/1965]). When passing through Mashhad, Maulānā Khālid Baghdādī (d. 1242/1827), originator of the Khālidī branch of the order, wrote one poem in praise of Imam Riḍā and another in condemnation of the Shiʿite *ʿulamā'* resident at his shrine (*Dīvān* [Būlāq: al-Maṭbaʿat al-ʿĀmiriyya, 1260/1844], pp. 41–42, 68). Another Naqshbandī, the celebrated Shah Valīullāh Dihlavī (d. 1176/1763), wrote the *Tuḥfa-yi Iṣnāʿasharī*, a polemic that in the Arabic synopsis prepared by Shihāb al-Dīn al-Alūsī (d. 1270/1854) is a favorite text among Naqshbandīs in Turkey and some Arab countries who still warm to the task of sectarian dispute.

Somewhat by contrast, another Naqshbandī, Shaykh Sulaymān Qundūzī (or Balkhī; d. 1294/1877), compiled the *Yanābīʿ al-Mawadda*, a compendium of edifying anecdotes concerning all the Imams of the Ahl al-Bayt, including the Twelfth. In the case of Qundūzī, it is relevant to note that after his migration to Istanbul he acquired a secondary affiliation to the Melâmiye, which may indeed be designated as an order permeated by Shiʿism while remaining nominally Sunni in creedal matters; see Abdülbaki Gölpınarlı, *Melâmîlik ve Melâmîler* (Istanbul: Devlet Matbaası, 1931), pp. 197–99. Moreover, while the *Tuḥfa-yi Iṣnāʿasharī* is regularly reprinted in Pakistan and Turkey (and its Arabic synopsis in Syria and Turkey), the *Yanābīʿ al-Mawadda* is a favorite of Shiʿite publishing houses in Beirut and Qum.

As for the general problem of the antecedents of early Safavid Shiʿism, it might be more profitable to pay greater attention to developments in Anatolia, the region from which a majority of the Qizilbash were recruited; see Faruk Sümer, *Safevî Devletinin Kuruluşu ve Gelişmesinde Anadolu Türklerinin Rolü* (Ankara: Güven Matbaası, 1976).

142. The information contained in Qazvīnī's *Silsila-nāma-yi Khwājagān-i Naqshband* was, however, reproduced in ʿAbd al-Majīd al-Khānī's *al-Ḥadā'iq al-Wardiyya fī Ḥaqā'iq al-Ajillā' al-Naqsbabandiyya* (Cairo: Dār al-Ṭibāʿa al-ʿĀmira, 1308/1890), pp. 154 and 172–73, and a still later work based explicitly on that of al-Khānī, Muḥammad al-Rakhāwī's *al-Anwār al-Qudsiyya fī Manāqib al-Sādāt al-Naqshabandiyya* (Cairo: Maṭbaʿat al-Saʿāda, 1344/1924), pp. 155 and 173–74. It may be that al-Khānī had access to the *Silsila-nāma-yi Khwājagān-i Naqshband*, which was after all drawn up in Syria. In both works, the term "Qizilbash" has been erroneously replaced with "al-Ūzbak."

143. Quoted in Rasūl Jaʿfariān, "Rūyārū'ī-yi Faqīhān va Ṣūfiān dar Aṣr-i Ṣafaviyya," *Kayhān-i Andīsha* 23 (Āẕar-Day, 1369/November–December 1990): 123. It has been correctly observed by Dina Le Gall ("The Ottoman Naqshbandiyya," p. 23, n. 38) that the existence of Naqshbandī lineages in post-Safavid Herat does not necessarily indicate their continued presence in the city while it was under Safavid rule. Nonetheless, the mere fact that Herat remained a predominantly Sunni city and that it stayed in contact, however sporadically, with the Central Asian khanates makes it likely that the disappearance of the Naqshbandiyya was never as complete in Herat as it was in Tabriz and Qazvin. The history of the Sufi orders in Afghanistan as a whole remains to be investigated. For a preliminary survey, see Bo Utas, "Notes on Afghan Sufi Orders and Khanaqahs," *Afghanistan Journal* 7:2 (1980): 60–67; and for a survey of Naqshbandīs active in Herat shortly before the overthrow

of Dā'ūd Khān's regime, see the same author's "The Naqshbandiyya of Afghanistan on the Eve of the 1978 Coup d'Etat," in *Naqshbandis in Western and Central Asia,* ed. Elisabeth Özdalga (Istanbul: Swedish Research Institute, 1999), pp. 121–24.

144. As early as 1006/1598, a Naqshbandī *khwāja* by the name of Mīrzā Beg accompanied an Uzbek ambassador to Isfahan while en route to the hajj and was treated with "great respect" by Shah 'Abbās (Iskandar Beg Munshī, *Tārīkh-i 'Ālam-ārā-yi 'Abbāsī,* 1:76; English translation by Savory: Eskandar Monshi, *History of Shah 'Abbas,* 2:727; this pattern was repeated in later years as well; see n. 113 above). About a century and a half later, 'Abdullāh Nidā'ī (d. 1174/1760), a Naqshbandī of the Kāsānī branch, did not encounter any problems when he visited Mashhad, Isfahan, and Shiraz in the course of his long migratory journey from Kashghar to Istanbul; see Hamid Algar, "From Kashghar to Eyüp: The Lineages and Legacy of Şeyh Abdullah Nidâî," in *Naqshbandis in Western and Central Asia,* ed. Özdalga, pp. 1–15. On the danger of assuming that Safavid Iran was at all times forbidden or perilous territory for Sunnis from Central Asia and elsewhere, see R. D. McChesney, "'Barrier of Heterodoxy'?: Rethinking the Ties between Iran and Central Asia in the 17th Century," in *Safavid Persia,* ed. Charles Melville (London: I. B. Tauris, 1996), pp. 231–67.

2

The Imagined Embrace

Gender, Identity, and Iranian Ethnicity in Jahangiri Paintings

Juan R. I. Cole

It is well known that Emperor Jahangir had several fantastic paintings done in the late teens of the seventeenth century depicting imaginary meetings between him and Shah 'Abbas I of Iran. Much speculation has swirled around the meaning of these paintings, which (it has been suggested by Milo Beach) were influenced by contemporary English allegory and symbolism, introduced to the Mughal court by British envoy Thomas Roe. That is, the pictorial equivalents of Edmund Spenser's *Faerie Queene* suggested to Jahangir and his painters the possibilities for symbolist encounters with foreign monarchs. While the tracing of influences, which tends to preoccupy art historians, can help us understand how certain techniques and motifs might have been introduced, they do not resolve the question of motivation or local meaning.

There is clear evidence that monarchs such as Jahangir took a lively interest in shaping their ateliers, following the work of individual authors, and setting basic themes as well as larger projects, so that painters were quite dependent on the monarch. Asok Kumar Das observes that

> at the time of Jahangir the dependence was carried to the extreme as the paintings were required to be modelled on the standard arbitrarily set by the emperor. When the painter worked according to the emperor's set ideas, he was likely to receive proper attention; otherwise he was destined to incur his displeasure. The paintings produced in Jahangir's studio are essentially products of his specific demands.[1]

Despite the ways in which the paintings therefore shed light on Jahangir's personality, the import of these works of representation for the construction of the self has tended to be ignored.

In this essay I wish to appeal in a general way to the "psychoanalytic idea of fantasy, with its ability to describe how the subject participates in and restages a scenario in which crucial questions about desire, knowledge, and identity can be posed and in which the subject can hold a number of identificatory positions."[2] I ask why Jahangir wished to meet Shah 'Abbas in the album and what drove him to request such fantasies from his stable of artists. I wish to argue that the symbolism of sex, gender, ethnicity, and status hierarchy is at the heart of the matter: that Jahangir's own fears of emasculation are sublimated in the Shah 'Abbas series by means of a homoerotic reassertion of his masculinity in the face of Iranian threats to it.

I begin by positing certain ambiguities of cultural identity in Mughal India. The Mughal Empire's elite was remarkable in many ways. First, it was extremely wealthy, although it almost certainly did not come close to realizing the claim it made on fifty percent of the country's agricultural production. The top Mughals were the equivalent then of our billionaires today. Although they did provide some security and saw to the irrigation canals, laying the basis for prosperity, they did so at a far higher cost than most contemporary states. As Walter Benjamin might have observed had he turned his gaze to the subcontinent, all Mughal art and architecture is a testament to the ruthless exploitation of the Indian peasantry. In addition, this ruling elite was strikingly multicultural, drawn from Iranians, Central Asian Turkic peoples of various sorts, Afghans, Indian Muslims, Rajputs, and Marathas, among others. Each of these ethnic groupings provided troops and officers to the military and could be mobilized on ethnic grounds on occasion.[3] Of course, these ethnicities within the Mughal power elite, whatever linguistic or religious bases they may have had, were continually constructed and reconstructed.

The "Iranian" had a number of potential meanings in court culture. Clearly, the Iranian can be heroic.[4] Here we can instance Rustam and other heroes of the fantastic who occupied such a central position in Mughal storytelling at Akbar's court. While Jahangir went on to be rather less interested in epics such as the *Shahnamah* or the *Mahabharata* than the mythologically minded Akbar had been, his atelier did not entirely forsake the legendary or fantastic. His painters reached a compromise with a sort of royal magical realism in the fantastic scenes of Jahangir's imaginary meetings with historical and contemporary religious and political figures, wherein the fabulous heroes of Iran were supplanted by Jahangir himself.

Among the Mughal elite the Iranis came to be the wealthiest faction, with the highest salaries, below only the Chaghatai ruling family of Timurids itself.

They knew and took pride in the way Shah Tahmasp had provided Humayun, the second Mughal ruler, with the arms and materiel to make a second assault on India, thus in effect bearing responsibility for the establishment of the Mughal Empire as an ongoing concern as opposed to Babur's mere adventure. Given this debt, Mughal India would always be in some sense subsidiary to Iran, from whence much of Indian court culture, language, and arts would also derive.

But the Iranian male can also be effeminate.[5] The princes, courtiers, poets, artists, and hangers-on who flocked to India in the Mughal period are often depicted in art as slender and lacking in manly qualities. The hedonic tradition in some Persian poetry, celebrating drink and decadence, could only add to this image of some Iranians as lacking the seriousness of the virile, clear-minded soldier. A painting done for Shah Isma'il's *Divan* illustrated the verses "I have never seen anyone so beautiful as you on earth, / never in this world anyone so gorgeous as you" with a depiction of five slender young men in a landscape, and the homoerotic overtones are palpable.[6] In Iranian and Mughal court culture, as in ancient Greece, the virile male was defined as the one who penetrated the bodies of others, whether male or female; and sex with a youth was not considered shameful or deviant for a powerful man, though being penetrated by another man did detract from the masculinity of the one who was penetrated. In India, Iranian youths were prized, like Iranian women, for their fairness of skin.

The Iranian can be an embodiment of wisdom, whether sober or ecstatic. Elite Mughals learned their ethics from Iranian poets, and their mysticism from Iranian Sufis.[7] Akbar had a particular fondness for Rumi, Jahangir for Sa'di. Indeed, Jahangir had a painting made of an imaginary audience between himself and the great ethical poet.[8] In turn, the ecstatic tradition of Persian mysticism evoked a different sort of drunkenness than that attained in Hafiz's taverns, though Sufis would read the latter as allegorical as well. As illustrated in the painting from Rumi's *Mathnavi,* the dancing of Sufis in the presence of the pir could form a visual analogue to the revelry of courtiers in the presence of the shah.[9] On a different level, in India these God-intoxicated male adepts formed a homoerotic analogue to the frolicking, love-struck gopis or cow-girls around the god Krishna.

Finally, the Iranian as female can embody the highest ideals of female beauty, fair-skinned as a *pari,* rose-cheeked, with a rosebud mouth, able to inspire an obsessive and self-destructive love as Layli did to Majnun.[10] (Although Layli is technically an Arab, Indians received the story through Nizami and his imitators, lending it a Persian aura.) Or she can represent the ecstasies of the erotic, as Shirin does in a Jahangiri painting of the teens, when Khusrau comes upon her naked and bathing (in a waterhole that itself represents the vagina, as

Hindu mythology—which sees all apertures in the earth as yoni or genitalia of the goddesses—also would acknowledge).[11] By the seventeenth century younger princes were dismissing these Iranian love stories, however, as hackneyed chestnuts. Das observes that the "Poet Nawi relates in his *Suz-u-Gudaz* . . . that Salim's [Jahangir's] brother Daniyal (d. 1604) told him: 'The love story of Farhad and Shirin has grown old; if we read at all let it be what we have ourselves seen and heard.'"[12] Things Iranian here are associated with the ersatz, with the medieval and the hoary, in contrast to the humanist sensibilities of many at court in seventeenth-century Mughal India, who wished to focus upon direct experience. A concern with naturalism and experiencing things for oneself is also characteristic of Jahangir's memoirs.

Now we come to Jahangir. Surely, for him, the "Iranian" inescapably had overtones of his relationship with his wife Nur Jahan, a Tehrani whom he married in 1611. Although counted among the "great Mughals," he certainly was the least of them. Brought up to wealth and luxury, he did not have to struggle simply to establish a kingdom, as his three hardened forebears had, but instead inherited one. He gradually sank into an alcoholic and drug-induced stupor that made it more and more difficult for him to actually rule the empire. Increasingly, his queen, Nur Jahan, took the reins of rule into her capable hands as well as aiding a process begun sometime earlier whereby her relatives gained a large number of important posts.[13]

As a pampered prince, Jahangir could indulge in sensual pleasures to his heart's content, as the paintings of his indefatigable cavorting with an evergrowing bevy of Hindu and Muslim wives and concubines suggest.[14] But reality did impinge on his life occasionally. He was denied the throne until his mid-thirties and was circumscribed by his father's policies and greatness. He even briefly went into rebellion against Akbar. Jahangir's cultivation of a state of alcohol- or opium-induced stupor may be seen as an attempt to deal with his unresolved conflicts with his father by regressing to a childlike, dependent state that predated them. And Ellison Banks Findly and others have pointed out that his middle-aged marriage to a middle-aged Nur Jahan appears to have represented at least in part a search for a nurturing mother figure who could manage his life, given his regression.[15]

Jahangir's drug-dependent state and his surrender to Nur Jahan as a surrogate mother were unsuccessful strategies insofar as they allowed him to avoid coming to terms with his troubled relationship with his very formidable father and therefore with his own manhood, thus stunting his growth as an individual and as a man. Unlike his three forebears, Jahangir virtually never led his troops into a major war, and his reign was not notable for any truly significant conquests (those that were accomplished against the Rajputs and in the Deccan were mainly the work of his third son, Khurram, later Shah Jahan). With

Figure 2.1. *Jahangir and Prince Khurram feasted by Nur Jahan*, India, ca. 1617. Freer Gallery of Art.

Nur Jahan's advent he is said to have lost interest in other women; and if we accept the maternal nature of her relationship to him, he was hardly by this time the stallion he had been in his youth. Among the few "masculine" activities he took part in was hunting, which he pursued with skill and alacrity when young. But he had taken a vow at sixteen not to kill animals in the hunt when he reached age fifty, and he attempted to honor the oath (although he was inconsistent about it). Whatever the origins of this vow—whether Akbar's "Divine Faith" (*din-i ilahi*) or Jahangir's personal psychology—it did deprive him in his later years of one of the last unambiguously male public roles left to him, leaving him even more emasculated in the terms of chivalric, courtly codes of masculinity.

These cultural symbols have implications for understanding the depiction of gender at the Mughal court, of course. But they are also imbricated in conceptions of ethnicity and cultural geography. Iran comes to be a symbol for the mother figure not only via the Iranian Nur Jahan but also because Tahmasp had played a key role in enabling Humayun to reconquer India, thus making Iran in some sense a "mother" of the Mughal Empire.

Despite Jahangir's love for Nur Jahan and gratitude to her for caring for him, it is impossible that he did not also at times feel threatened by the aggressive way she stepped in to play a major role in running his empire, most often through her brother, Asaf Khan; her father, I'timad ad-Dawlah; and the far-flung Tehrani clan in general. In the terms of the typical depictions of gender roles at the Mughal court, Jahangir's drugged passivity surely feminized him, while Nur Jahan's vigorous interventions in policy masculinized her.

Even at court, despite Jahangir's halo of authority, Nur Jahan was capable of reducing him to a guest in his own palace. Findly explicates the painting *Jahangir and Prince Khurram Feasted by Nur Jahan:*[16]

> An album painting depicts the festivities hosted by Nur Jahan for Jahangir and his son Prince Khurram in honor of the latter's conquests in the Deccan. The party took place in October 1617 in Mandu . . . although Jahangir is still the dominant figure . . . he now shares the viewer's attention with Nur Jahan, who is not only clearly in charge but supported as well by an army of women. While they do not intimidate, their numbers and their confident demeanor celebrate an autonomous environment of pleasure in which Jahangir and Khurram are still, decidedly, guests. Moreover, the cups of wine, the luxurious textures of cloth and stone, and the open necklines and midriffs indicate something new has happened to the lives of zanana women.

The management skills needed by a royal wife, who oversaw some 5,000 concubines in the harem and supervised many aspects of the running of the palace, no doubt prepared Nur Jahan for her interventions in wider imperial affairs.

The phallicization of Nur Jahan is apparent in her carrying a musket for hunting, in her sharp-shooting prowess, and in the way she substitutes herself for the emperor in 1619. In his memoirs, Jahangir writes:

> My huntsmen reported to me that there was in the neighborhood [of Mathura] a tiger, which greatly distressed the inhabitants. I ordered his retreat to be closely surrounded with a number of elephants. Towards evening I and my attendants mounted and went out. As I had made a vow not to kill any animal with my own hands, I told Nur Jahan to fire my musket. The smell of the tiger made the elephant very restless, and he would not stand still, and to take good aim from a howda is a very difficult feat. Mirza Rustam, who after me has no equal as a marksman, had fired three or four shots from an elephant's back without effect. Nur Jahan, however, killed this tiger with the first shot.[17]

The episode, a masculinization of Nur Jahan, was made possible both by her own initiative and previous target practice and by Jahangir's vow (which he may have honored on this occasion simply to mask the trembling hands of an alcoholic and opium addict). Even in a pre-Freudian culture the musket surely bore a phallic connotation, more especially in a largely Hindu society, which was often explicit about such symbols. Here the masculinization also strongly implies an emasculation of Jahangir (she uses his own musket!). A painting survives of Nur Jahan hunting, holding her musket upright.[18] It might be objected that this depiction of Nur Jahan must have been at the emperor's own instance. The story about how Jahangir shaped the works of his atelier, however, must be modified by the plausible assertion by Pratapaditya Pal and Ellison Findly that Nur Jahan also commissioned paintings and had an influence on subjects chosen by artists at court, especially in the new attention to the depiction of women as agents that characterizes the paintings of the Jahangir period.

Other paintings depict Nur Jahan's Tehrani relatives who held high office, such as Asaf Khan, her brother, attending Jahangir.[19] Jahangir was cognizant of the way in which Iranians both bordered his empire as neighbors and constituted a distinct ethnicity among his own nobles, transcending and transgressing the boundaries of self and other. The Tehranis constituted a network of supporters on whom he could rely, and he likewise viewed the external Iranians as allies. The depictions of Jahangir with his brother-in-law and father-in-law pose something of a difficulty for my analysis, since they show the emperor as darker in complexion than some Iranians at court. Yet there is evidence in other paintings that light complexion is used as a status marker (influenced, perhaps, both by the light blue skin of Hindu gods in the Rajput tradition and by the Persian aesthetic tradition of equating fair skin with celestial bodies such as the moon). The only explanation I can proffer at the moment is that Nur Jahan's fairness reflected well on the emperor's own status and therefore could be admitted in her and in her close relatives.

What of the Iranians without? Jahangir continually refers to Shah 'Abbas as his "brother" in his memoirs, at least until the 1622 Iranian reconquest of Qandahar. He even notes, when he forbids tobacco, that "his brother" Shah 'Abbas had taken the same step. This diction accords with the general "family romance" of Iranians in which Jahangir was entangled. If Safavid Iran had in some sense given birth to Humayun's Mughal Empire, and if the Iranian Nur Jahan was a surrogate mother for Jahangir, then the symbolic position of the Safavid emperor as Jahangir's brother takes on more than merely rhetorical resonance. In 1611 an embassy arrived in India from Iran, bearing gifts as signals of goodwill. In 1613 Jahangir reciprocated with an embassy headed by Khan 'Alam to Isfahan in order to seek continued good relations with Iran. The artist Bishan Das accompanied the Mughal party and painted several portraits of the Safavid monarch, which he brought back to India. Some of the imaginary meetings between Jahangir and Shah 'Abbas appear to have been painted while that embassy was still abroad, so that the figure of Shah 'Abbas had to be retouched (once his actual likeness was better known) upon the artist's return. Bishan Das, distant from court and without direction from Jahangir, tended toward naturalism; he shows Shah 'Abbas's complexion as much lighter than Khan 'Alam's.[20] Or it may be that Bishan Das used complexion to denote status, allowing the Iranian monarch to be fairer than the Mughal ambassador in his own court. In a portrait of the shah himself, Bishan Das renders his complexion somewhat darker.[21]

Back in Agra, one of the first fantastic paintings produced by Jahangir's atelier in the middle of the teens shows the emperor standing upon the globe, shooting an arrow at the decapitated head of his nemesis in the Deccan, the Abyssinian general who was the mainstay of the Ahmednagar Nizam Shahs, Malik 'Ambar.[22] The painting, dated around 1615, is pure wish-fulfillment. Malik 'Ambar was chased from the Ahmednagar capital in 1616 by Prince Parvez and then defeated decisively by Prince Khurram a little while later; but in the early 1620s he renounced the terms of the treaty he had signed with the Mughals once more. Under Jahangir, Ahmednagar would not stay conquered. The painting restores to Jahangir a centrality and a masculine role, symbolized by the shooting of the arrow, of which his addictions and lack of martial vigor had robbed him. The motif is repeated in the 1620s in a painting showing the emperor vanquishing poverty with his bow. Poverty is symbolized by the very dark figure of a Hindu mendicant. The dark pigmentation of both Malik 'Ambar and the figure of poverty had hierarchical ethnic implications in an empire where the ruling class tended to be fairer than the Indian peasantry. In the scene where he shoots poverty, Jahangir is standing upon a globe within which lie a lion and a lamb, symbols of peace that may be drawn from Christian iconography.

Another fantastic scene is a diptych in which the emperor is depicted receiving the ethical poet and mystic Sa'di at his court.[23] It seems to me that in this period Jahangir attempted to reinterpret his drug-induced stupor, which mortified him throughout his life, as a sort of *ḥāl* or mystical state of nearness to the divine. Iran was associated in the mind of the Mughal elite with Sufi and ethical teachings such as those of Sa'di, so that Jahangir's dependent passivity is recast not as effeminate and decadent but as the masculine role of a Sufi adept. Sa'di's *Bustan* and *Gulistan,* moreover, were very much associated with male education, reinforcing the legitimation of the emperor's manhood that the Iranian sage was made to provide.

Having met the Iranian Sa'di, master of the spiritual and ethical realms, Jahangir now proceeds to meet Shah 'Abbas, master of Iran itself. Here again, questions of gender symbolism enter in. Shah 'Abbas was hypermasculine in his activities, leading armies and making conquests. He took back Tabriz and Baghdad from the Ottomans and extended Iran's rule into Central Asia. He was as successful a conqueror for the Safavids as Akbar had been for the Mughals. In contrast, as we have seen, Jahangir added very little territory to the Mughal Empire during his reign, and his third son Khurram (later Shah Jahan)—ally of Nur Jahan—was mainly responsible for that. The motivation for the imaginary meetings with Shah 'Abbas appears to have been to associate himself with the machismo of the shah, making the point of his being an equal in power and masculinity despite the very different records of their reigns. Thus, the two monarchs are depicted sitting on a divan as equals, though Shah 'Abbas is given the slighter frame and is shown in three-quarters profile, whereas Jahangir is depicted as physically more prepossessing and is shown in pure profile, a regal pose in Mughal painting. Finally, the complexions are manipulated so that—in contrast to Bishan Das's contemporary paintings directly from the subject—Shah 'Abbas is shown as dark, whereas the half-Rajput Jahangir is shown as fair-skinned. They are waited upon by Asaf Khan, Jahangir's minister and an ethnic Iranian, the brother of Nur Jahan, suggesting the kindred nature of the Mughal's relationship to Iran.[24]

But the final fantastic image does not show equals at all. Jahangir and Shah 'Abbas are depicted astride the globe, Jahangir standing on a lion and the Safavid monarch on a lamb.[25] Shah 'Abbas is shown as even more slight of frame than in the portrait on the divan and is being dominated and encompassed by the bear hug of Jahangir. The pose recalls the attitude of Krishna

Figure 2.2. *Jahangir Welcoming Shah 'Abbas,* Abu'l-Hasan, ca. 1618. Freer Gallery of Art.

with Radha common in Rajput paintings of the time. Shah 'Abbas's slender body recalls the Iranian young men used as catamites by nobles, and Jahangir appears to be stretching his hand toward the shah's crotch. The image has the effect of reducing Shah 'Abbas from a ferocious, hypermasculine world-conqueror on the Mongol model to a willowy and seductive youth on lamb-skin. Jahangir is promoted from passivity, the effeminate dandy castrated by a domineering Nur Jahan, to a cosmic chieftain with the lion as his hypermasculine totem—his realm bigger than that of Shah 'Abbas, who is subjected by the homosocial embrace of the Mughal ruler. Here again, Jahangir is fair-skinned while the Iranian is depicted as dark.

Although the fantastic images were ostensibly aimed at celebrating the alliance between Iran and the Mughal Empire, they actually functioned as wish-fulfillment for the besotted Jahangir. By their means he recovered in the miniature painting the masculinity he feared he had lost to Nur Jahan and her clique of Iranians within his court and his empire. The elements of ethnicity, gender, and status hierarchy are all in play here. Jahangir is larger and fairer, emphasizing his higher status. Shah 'Abbas is forced into a feminine pose of erotic subjection.

A parallelism of pose and atmosphere exists between these fantastic paintings of Jahangir with Shah 'Abbas and a depiction of Jahangir with Nur Jahan. After the emperor's death, a painting was done in 1632 (attributed to Govardhan) of Jahangir with Nur Jahan as a dominating lover, larger than she is, wrapped around her. Was Shah Jahan attempting to restore his father to masculine supremacy over his wife's feisty aunt?[26] Ironically, this painting of the deceased emperor embracing his wife, who is depicted as petite, submissive, and loving, appears to be modeled on the homoerotic embrace that Jahangir bestowed upon Shah 'Abbas in Abu'l-Hasan's earlier fantasies of the late teens.

The Irani was a recognizable ethnicity in Mughal politics and culture, and Jahangir's atelier invested Iranianness with multiple meanings. The Iranian was mystic, sage, and teacher; and in his fabulous miniatures Jahangir could be shown giving a royal audience to a figure like Sa'di. The Iranian youth could be a ravishing catamite. Iranian courtiers were depicted as respectful and loyal servants. Shah 'Abbas, Jahangir's "brother," was a bosom buddy. In the real world that these fantasies were meant to deal with, of course, the Iranian could pose a dire threat to the monarch. Irani clans like the Tehranis, to which his queen belonged, could usurp royal prerogatives and arrogate to themselves enormous power in the kingdom. Nur Jahan and her relatives had vastly disproportionate control over Mughal resources, and the queen appears to have engaged in policy-making. Safavid Iran could be rival as well as ally, as in the conflict over Qandahar. The effeminate, drug-addicted libertine Jahangir was in reality no match for the lithe world-conquering Shah 'Abbas.

In these paintings the half-Chaghatai, half-Rajput Jahangir has by means of his intense masculinity pulled the Iranians around him, within and without, into a posture of erotic submission, turning them into analogues of the Rajput princesses with whom he frolicked on Holi. In the psychic struggles waged in Jahangir's picture albums between the Iranian as supportive (as mother, brother, lover, even Self) and the Iranian as symbol of the Other, of domination or even castration, the latter won out in the real world. Nur Jahan had great influence over the running of Jahangir's empire when his health collapsed in 1619; and then the armies of Shah 'Abbas recaptured Qandahar in 1622. But the fantasies of desire, knowledge, and identity generated by Jahangir and his atelier remain recorded in the miniatures. Here in the alternate dimension of the album, Jahangir's own fears of emasculation are sublimated in the Shah 'Abbas series by means of a homoerotic reassertion of his dominant masculinity in the face of Iranian threats to it. This pose even appears to resurface after his death, with Govardhan's substitution of Nur Jahan for Shah 'Abbas. Jahangir's fantasies allowed for many subject-positions with regard to the Iranians in his life; but in the album, unlike real life, he always maintained his imperial dignity in these encounters.

NOTES

1. Asok Kumar Das, *Mughal Painting during Jahangir's Time* (Calcutta: Asiatic Society, 1978), p. 107.

2. Constance Penley, "Feminism, Psychoanalysis and the Study of Popular Culture," in Norman Bryson, Michael Ann Holly, and Keith Moxey, eds., *Visual Culture: Images and Interpretations* (Hanover, N.H.: Wesleyan University Press, 1995), p. 303.

3. The locus classicus for this discussion is Satish Chandra, *Parties and Politics at the Mughal Court, 1707–1740* (Aligarh: Dept. of History, Aligarh Muslim University, 1959).

4. *Chase Scene from the Shahnamah,* N. India, early 1500s, private collection, in Pratapaditya Pal, *Court Paintings of India, 16th–19th Centuries* (New York: Navin Kumar, 1983), p. 117; *The Birth of Rustam,* from a *Shahnamah* produced early in Jahangir's reign (ca. 1610), Rothschild Collection, in P. and D. Colnaghi Co., *Persian and Mughal Art* (London: Colnaghi, 1976), p. 175; Basawan, *The Flight of the Simurgh,* Imperial Mughal, ca. 1590, Prince Sadruddin Aga Khan Collection, M. 146, in Amina Okada, *Indian Miniatures of the Mughal Court* (New York: Harry N. Adams, 1992), plate 81.

5. *Youth Lounging with Wine Cup and Fruit,* Isfahan, ca. 1600, in Colnaghi, *Persian and Mughal Art,* p. 41.

6. *Five Youths,* illustration from earliest MS of Shah Isma'il's *Divan,* Tabriz, ca. 1520, in Glenn Lowry with Susan Nemazee, *A Jeweler's Eye* (Washington, D.C.: Arthur M. Sackler Gallery, Smithsonian Institution, in association with University of Washington Press, Seattle, 1988), p. 119.

7. *Iranian Dervish in Mughal India,* Imperial Mughal, early seventeenth century, private collection, in Pal, *Court Paintings,* p. 163.

8. *Sa'di in the Hindu Temple of Somnath,* after an original by Dharm Das, Imperial Mughal, ca. 1625, private collection, in Pal, *Court Paintings,* p. 177.

9. *Dervishes Dancing at a Prince's Enthronement,* illustration from a fifteenth-century Iranian Mathnavi MS, in Lowry with Nemazee, *A Jeweler's Eye,* p. 155; this painting makes a visual analogy between royal pastimes and mystical enlightenment, in the spirit of Rumi.

10. *Laila, Majnun and the Animal Kingdom,* attributed to Mishkin, Imperial Mughal, ca. 1605, private collection, in Pal, *Court Paintings,* p. 155.

11. *Prince Khusrau Comes Upon Shirin Bathing,* Mughal, ca. 1610–20, Rothschild Collection, in Colnaghi, *Persian and Mughal Art,* p. 202.

12. Das, *Mughal Painting,* p. 60; cf. *Death of Farhad,* Imperial Mughal, 1650 or earlier, private collection, in Pal, *Court Paintings,* p. 169.

13. Ellison Banks Findly, *Nur Jahan, Empress of Mughal India* (Oxford: Oxford University Press, 1993); see especially the work she cites by Irfan Habib on this issue.

14. *Jahangir Plays Holi with His Concubines,* ca. 1615–25, ascribed to Govardhan, a page from the Minto Album, Chester Beatty Library, Dublin, in Okada, *Indian Miniatures,* p. 191.

15. Findly, *Nur Jahan.*

16. *Jahangir and Prince Khurram Feasted by Nur Jahan,* India, ca. 1617; Freer Gallery of Art, in Ellison Banks Findly, "The Pleasures of Women," *Asian Art* 6, no. 2 (Spring 1993): 80.

17. Jahangir, *Memoirs of Jahangir,* trans. H. M. Elliot, ed. John Dowson (Lahore: Islamic Book Service, 1975 [1871]), p. 205. The Persian text is Jahangir, *Tuzuk-i Jahangiri,* ed. Muhammad Hashim (Tehran: Intisharat-i Bunyad-i Farhang-i Iran, 1982).

18. Abu'l-Hasan, *Nur Jahan with a Firearm, Hunting,* ca. 1612–15, Raza Library, Rampur, in Milo Beach, *Mughal and Rajput Painting* (New York: Cambridge University Press, 1992), p. 96.

19. *Nur Jahan's Brother, Asaf Khan, in Audience with Jahangir,* ca. 1650, Late Shahjahan Album, Vever Collection, Sackler, in Lowry with Nemazee, *A Jeweler's Eye,* p. 170; *Nur Jahan's Father, I'timad ad-Dawlah, in Audience with Jahangir,* Manohar, ca. 1615, Kevorkian Album, Metropolitan Museum of Art, New York, in Okada, *Indian Miniatures,* p. 146.

20. Bishan Das, *Shah Abbas Receives Khan 'Alam, Jahangir's Envoy,* Goloubew Collection, Museum of Fine Arts, Boston, no. 14, 665, in Okada, *Indian Miniatures,* p. 158.

21. Bishan Das, *Shah 'Abbas,* ca. 1620, in Colnaghi, *Persian and Mughal Art,* p. 191.

22. Abu'l-Hasan, *Jahangir Symbolically Killing Malik 'Ambar,* ca. 1615–20, Minto Album, Chester Beatty Library, Dublin, in Okada, *Indian Miniatures,* p. 47, fig. 48.

23. *Jahangir Receives the Poet Sa'di,* attributed to Abu'l-Hasan; Mughal, ca. 1615, in Beach, *Mughal and Rajput Painting,* pp. 102–3.

24. Abu'l-Hasan, *Jahangir Welcoming Shah 'Abbas,* ca. 1618, St. Petersburg Album, Freer Gallery of Art, in Okada, *Indian Miniatures,* p. 56, fig. 53.

25. Abu'l-Hasan, *Jahangir's Dream,* ca. 1618, St. Petersburg Album, Freer Gallery of Art, in Okada, *Indian Miniatures,* p. 56, fig. 54.

26. Govardhan(?), *Jahangir and Nur Jahan,* 1632, a page from the Kevorkian Album, Metropolitan Museum of Art, New York, in Okada, *Indian Miniatures,* p. 192.

3

A Safavid Poet in the Heart of Darkness

The Indian Poems of Ashraf Mazandarani

Stephen Frederic Dale

Har keh az Īrān beh Hind āyad tasavvūr mīkunad
Īn keh chūn kaukab beh shab dar Hind zar pāshīdeh ast.

Whoever comes from Iran to India imagines
That in India gold is scattered like stars in the evening sky.
—*Ashraf Mazandarani*

In his provocative work *The Continent of Circe,* the Anglicized Bengali writer Nirad Chaudhuri recasts the legend of Circe and Odysseus as a metaphor for India's relation to her "European" conquerors. In his version Aryan tribes who migrated into and/or invaded the Indian subcontinent in the second century B.C. were the first such conquerors to be ensnared by the allure of India's wealth. Once there, they utterly forgot their Eurasian homelands, abandoned their vigorous steppe culture, and degenerated into the colonized Hindus of whom Chaudhuri spoke with caustic contempt during the Indian nationalist movement in the twentieth century.

> They stood at the gate of the goddess with flowing tresses, and heard her, Circe, sweetly singing before her loom, as she walked to and fro weaving an imperishable web, gorgeous and dazzling, such as only goddesses can make.
>
> So she lived on the island of Aeaea, and so she has in India. Men have stood at her gate, and called to be admitted, and to all she has opened her shining doors. She has taken them in, given them seats, and served food.

> But with the food she has also mixed the drug which makes them want to forget their country. Then she has turned them into rude beasts.[1]

Chaudhuri observes of the Aryans/Hindus that "to forget is one thing, and to be happy is another.... They learned neither to tolerate their new environment nor to adapt to it. This, for a people who had no recollection of their original home, was a terrible destiny.... Even after living in the country for thousands of years the Hindus have never got used to the heat."[2] As Aryans they also continued to revere fair complexions among the predominantly dark-skinned population, a considerable irony in view of the even more pronounced racial consciousness of later conquerors.

As Chaudhuri demonstrates, subsequent invaders such as the Timurid-Mughuls and the British were condemned to what many would think to be a far worse fate.[3] Drawn seductively by the Indian Circe into her subcontinental lair, they were corrupted in its humid, fecund, overheated environment but condemned to be miserable precisely because they remembered their homelands but could not return.

Chaudhuri exaggerates for effect—the effect of irritating his fellow Hindus—but his metaphor of Odysseus's men aptly evokes the simultaneous attraction and dread that most foreign rulers have felt in India. Entranced by the subcontinent's wealth and exoticism, they were repulsed by its enervating climate and either bewildered or offended by indigenous religion and social customs. And they were intensely homesick. These feelings were not peculiar only to conquerors of India, however; they were shared by most voluntary émigrés to the subcontinent. One such man who experienced these conflicting emotions and recorded them with unusual clarity and subtlety was the late seventeenth century Iranian poet Ashraf Mazandarani (d. A.H. 1116/ A.D. 1704). His Indian poems represent one of the most artistically complete evocations of feelings the Indian Circe provoked, while they also exemplify a universal émigré phenomenon, the ambivalence of exile.

THE CARAVAN OF INDIA

Muhammad Sa'id Mazandarani, commonly known by his *takhallus* or penname Ashraf, was born in Isfahan sometime between A.H. 1030 and 1035 (A.D. 1620–25) into a family of *'alims* from Mazandaran. His father, Mulla Muhammad Saleh, had immigrated to Isfahan in search of education and employment and became a student of the prominent *'ālim* Mulla Muhammad Taqi Majlisi, whose daughter he eventually married.[4] Ashraf himself seems to have had a superb religious and cultural education. He studied in the *madrasas* of the Shaykh al-Islam of Isfahan, Mirza Hadi, and Aqa Husain Khwansari, who was also a prominent poet with the *takhallus* 'Asr. Not only was Ashraf well connected, therefore, in the religious circles of the Safavid capital, but he studied poetry with the eminent poet Muhammad 'Ali Tabrizi (known by his *takallus* Sa'ib), who had recently returned from India when Ashraf met him. His Indian connections also included his calligraphy teacher, 'Abd al-Rashid Dailami, who previously had served as a calligrapher at the Timurid-Mughul court of Shah Jahan.[5] It seems likely that Ashraf's connection with Sa'ib and/or Dailami explains why, when he decided to go to India in 1658/59, he entered the highest court circles and became the tutor to Zib al-Nisa, the daughter of the recently enthroned Timurid-Mughul emperor Aurungzeb (d. 1707). He remained in India for fourteen years; and after briefly returning to Iran in 1672, he served Aurungzeb's son Shah 'Alam, at the prince's household in Patna. He died in nearby Bengal, where his children remained. One son, Mirza Muhammad 'Ali, became a scholar and poet.

Ashraf's career exemplifies the emigration of Iranian literati to India throughout the Safavid period, many of whom wrote substantial collections of *diwans* of Persian poetry. The number of Iranians who composed Persian verse in India offers some idea of the size of this migration of Safavid writers. In his aptly titled book *Karvan-i Hind* (Caravan of India) Ahmad Golchin Ma'ani lists more than 700 Iranians who were known as poets in India—within Timurid-Mughul territories or at the court of the sultanates of the Deccan, including Shi'i Bijapur. These Safavid writers who gained literary reputations in India have sometimes been seen as a distinct class of professional poets, but most were not court panegyrists who primarily made their living by writing verse. Instead, like Ashraf, most worked in India as bureaucrats, teachers, and scholars and, like so many educated Iranians, wrote poetry as an avocation.[6]

Different reasons have been given for this stream of literati from Iran to the Indian subcontinent. Safavid Shi'i ideology has sometimes been seen as a major and even the principal cause. This argument is composed of three related elements. First, Safavid persecution of members of non-Safavid Sufi orders has often been cited as an obvious cause of the relatively poor quality of Safavid poetry when measured against the great writers of the previous five centuries. This argument is based on the fact that so many Sufis were also poets, or vice versa. The memory of the last great "classical" Persian poet, the Naqshbandi Sufi poet of Timurid Herat 'Abd al-Rahman Jami, may lie behind some of these assertions, as Shah Isma'il hounded the Sunni Naqshbandis from Iran during the first decade of the sixteenth century. Second, E. G. Browne long ago offered a related reason for the dearth of high-quality poetic talent in sixteenth- and seventeenth-century Iran. Citing the Iranian scholar Qazvini, he suggested that Safavid rulers inadequately patronized poets because they diverted their scarce resources to build Shi'i religious institutions and Shi'i '*ulamā'* that had not existed in Iran prior to the Safavid conquest of Tabriz in 1501.[7] The words of Kausari, a favorite poet of Shah 'Abbas I, offer anecdotal evidence for the lack of royal literary patronage—for whatever reasons—when he contrasts the welcome that Iranian poets received in Timurid-Mughul India with their treatment in their homeland. Prefaced by his title, "Complaint about the Lack of Interest of Iranians in Poetry," Kausari's first line reads:

> Dar īn keshvar kharīdār-ī sukhan nīst,
> Kasī sargarm-i bāzār-ī sukhan nīst.[8]
>
> In this country there is no buyer of speech,
> No one attends to the market of speech.

Finally, there is the related reason offered by the Safavid historian Iskandar Beg Munshi, who, when writing about poets during the reign of Shah Tahmasp (1524–76), said that in the latter part of his reign he grew too pious to support panegyric poets. Tahmasp felt these writers should be writing panegyric verse to the Caliph 'Ali.[9]

Safavid religious persecution certainly drove many Sufis from Iran, and some of them may have been poets, but Shi'i religious intolerance or preoccupation is not a sufficient explanation for the presence of such great numbers of Safavid Iranians who wrote Persian poetry in India. Nor does convincing evidence exist to show that Shah Tahmasp's later attitude typified all Safavid monarchs or that royal patronage of poets completely dried up. As the Indo-Muslim scholar Aziz Ahmad has observed, all Iranian shahs patronized poets; but they just did not match the scale of patronage in Mughul India and the other Muslim courts of the subcontinent.[10] The most persuasive reasons for the massive migration of Safavid-era Iranian literati to India are three: the economic disparity between the Iranian plateau and the Indian subcontinent, political relations between Timurid-Mughul and Safavid monarchs, and the cultural biases of the Indo-Muslim administrative and political elite.

As E. G. Browne and others have observed, the economic disparity between Iran and India was a major cause of Iranian migration. The relative poverty of the Iranian plateau and Central Asia compared to the great wealth of the Indian subcontinent has been a fundamental determinant of economic relations between these two regions through the millennia. This continued to be so in the Safavid-Mughul era. In 1600, for example, when Safavid power was at its height under Shah 'Abbas I, Timurid-Mughul India was one of the world's wealthiest states. Its fertile agricultural lands supported a population of perhaps 100 million people. These lands not only generated a vast agricultural surplus, including such export commodities as sugar and newly cultivated tobacco, but produced cotton cloth and other manufactures. Cotton cloth was India's premier export commodity; Indian spices were largely grown along the southwestern coast well beyond Mughul dominions. The combined sales of agricultural and manufactured products brought foreign currency flowing into Indian ports and border towns from Iran and the surrounding regions. Even the indefatigable Shah 'Abbas could not alter the reality of Iranian geography and the paucity of its natural resources. When compared to the lavish agrarian and human resources of Mughul India, Safavid Iran was a largely arid plateau with extremely modest resources, a thinly populated area with no more than 10 million people, and a perennial foreign trade deficit with India.[11] Just as British India is said to have represented an employment agency for the British middle class, Timurid-Mughul India offered similar employment opportunities for the Iranian educated and professional elite.

Apart from the economic imbalance between Safavid Iran and Timurid-Mughul India, there were political and cultural factors that encouraged the migration of Ashraf and other Iranians to South Asia. First, substantial numbers of Iranians accompanied Babur's son and heir, Humayun, when he recovered the South Asian empire in 1555 that he had so carelessly lost to Afghan forces fifteen years earlier. The Safavids had not only welcomed Humayun as a guest in Iran when Afghan forces had driven him from India fifteen years earlier but had also provided him with substantial military aid that enabled him to reconquer his father's empire. When he returned to Agra, his entourage included many Iranians. His alliance with the Safavids established a close relationship that endured through the life of both dynasties, largely unaffected by their Shi'i-Sunni sectarian differences and even by their struggle for the control of Qandahar. In India Humayun's son Akbar (r. 1556–1605) welcomed all faiths to his court, a policy proudly noted by his successor Jahangir (r. 1606–28), who pointed out that in Iran only Shi'as were welcome:

> The good qualities of my revered father are beyond the limit of approval and the bounds of praise.... The professors of various faiths had room in the broad expanse of his incomparable sway. This was different for the practice in other realms, for in Persia there is room for Shias only.... [In Akbar's realm] there was room for professors of opposite religions, and for beliefs good and bad.... Sunnis and Shias met in one mosque, Franks and Jews in one church, and observed their own forms of worship.[12]

Ashraf's court appointment illustrates how this relationship prospered in spite of the two regimes' contrasting religious and political interests. Indeed, his appointment is especially interesting in view of Aurungzeb's ostentatious Sunni piety.

Second, Iranians were especially valued in India because Humayun and his successors regarded the knowledge of Persian literature and Iranian administrative skills as normative for a civilized Islamic state. Persian, of course, had also been widely used in the various governments of the Delhi sultanate—and by historians, poets, and Sufis in India—several centuries prior to Mughul rule. Indo-Persian culture was the dominant aristocratic ethos of the later Timurids, including Zahir al-Din Muhammad Babur, the founder of the Timurid-Mughul Empire. His own maternal grandfather, the Mongol Yunas Khan, had spent many years in exile in Iran and returned to the Chaghatai *ulūs* in Central Asia with the attributes of an urbane Iranian courtier. As described by Babur's Mongol cousin, Mirza Haidar Dughlat, Yunas Khan was "[p]ossessed of splendid qualities.... He was skilled in enigmas, calligraphy, painting.... He was well trained in instrumental music and singing."[13] The prestige of Perso-Islamic values can partly be seen in the popularity of a Nasirean *akhlāq* manual known as the *Akhlāq-i Humāyūnī,* written by the chief *qāzī* of Husain Bāiqarā (d. 1506) of Herat and dedicated to Babur, whom the author met in Kabul. The treatise later became required reading among courtiers in Agra and Delhi.[14] Respect for the language and Persianate culture reached new heights, however, in the sixteenth and seventeenth centuries. Indeed, as Muzaffar Alam has pointed out, Akbar actively recruited Iranian literati in the late sixteenth century, making cultural preference into state policy.[15] Under his successor Jahangir, increased emigration was also partly a function of his marriage to the Iranian woman Nur Jahan, precipitating a deluge of relatives who poured into India after her. A final interesting point about this migration is that it was, apart from Indian merchants, almost entirely one way. Whereas many Iranians occupied high administrative/military posts and were sometimes recognized as poet laureates at the Timurid-Mughul court, no Persian-speaking Indian Muslims are known to have attained similar recognition in Safavid Iran. In economic and cultural terms, the relationship between Iran and India seems to have been similar to that between England and the United States in the late nineteenth century and early twentieth century.

ASHRAF MAZANDARANI: INDIAN VERSE

Most of the Iranians who wrote Persian poetry in India either made no allusion to their adopted home or denounced it. Writers who composed classically structured *ghazal*s and *rubā'i*s set in the abstracted rose garden of the imagination rarely hinted that they lived in a climate where roses withered and nightingales never sang. Others who mentioned India usually "had nothing but evil to say of the country."[16] Ashraf is exceptional, for he presents an unusually wide spectrum of reactions to Mughul India. Indeed, in his verse he depicts the country almost as the Circe of Nirad Chaudhuri's imagination, as a land whose riches seduced relatively impoverished Iranians who could not abstain from migrating but who once in India remained alienated and bitterly homesick. In his poems he manifests the exile experience: why Iranians migrated to India, his own reactions to the subcontinent, his reasons for returning home to Isfahan, and, most engagingly, his awareness of his complex, conflicting feelings for Iran and his voluntary Indian exile. The "Indian poems" represent only a small proportion of his verse, which include *qaṣīdas*, *rubā'iāt, masnavis*, and "fragments" on various subjects, including expressions of Shi'ite piety. Some of the poems Ashraf addressed to his family are particularly touching and offer additional autobiographical information on the poet's life. The "exile poems" represent merely an introduction to the cultural attitudes of this exceptionally interesting and influential émigré Indo-Persian poet.

Ashraf candidly explains in his verse why he and other Iranians abandoned their country for the subcontinent: they were driven from Iran by scarce opportunities and drawn to India by her wealth and the pleasures of Indian life. In these poems he repeatedly uses night—or darkness or henna—as the metaphor for India, employing stereotypical imagery that originated in Hellenistic times and was commonly used by Arab-Muslim writers and classical Perso-Islamic poets such as Rumi, Amir Khusrau, and Hafiz.[17] Ashraf sometimes makes this Indian "night" seem a necessary but distasteful exile; at other times, a benign, comforting refuge. In two poems he says that he himself and Iranians in general long for India to escape the nakedness of poverty:

> 1. Beh Hind-i tīreh bakhtī raftam az rāh-i parīshānī,
> Beh tārīkī kashīdam khwīshrā az sharm-i 'uryānī.[18]
>
> Melancholy drove me to this black-omened India,
> From the shame of nakedness I dragged myself into the darkness.
>
> 2. Dar Īrān nīst juz' Hind ārzū bīrūzgārānrā,
> Tamām-i rūz bāshad hasrat-i shab rūzeh dārānrā.[19]
>
> Among destitute Iranians there is nothing but desire for India.
> All day the fasting people long for night.

Contrasting these images of being forced by circumstance into the unknown and potentially ominous Indian darkness is another verse in which Ashraf makes the Indian "night" seem benign:

> Dar ū har lahzeh mīgardad chirāgh-i dīgarī raushan,
> Sawād-i Hind, shabhā-yi chirāghānast pindārī.[20]

At each moment another lamp is lit.
You might imagine India's darkness to be a night of lamps.

In another verse the darkness of the Indian night is entirely transformed into an entrancing spectacle, almost like the Timurid-Mughul miniatures picturing the annual diwali festival of lights.

Har keh az Īrān beh Hind āyad, tasavvūr mīkunad,
Īn keh chūn kaukab beh shab, dar Hind zar pāshīdeh ast.[21]

Whoever comes from Iran to India imagines,
That in India gold is scattered like stars in the night sky.

Given these attractions, it is scarcely surprising that Ashraf says in another verse:

Muflisī kard az zindān-i vatan āzādam,
Pāyam az pīsh badar raft u Hind uftādam.[22]

Indigence freed me from the prison of my homeland;
My feet going before, I left and stumbled into India.

While in these lines Ashraf conveys both his reluctance to leave Iran and his compelling reasons for choosing exile in India, in several others he speaks directly about his reaction to India. Some of these echo and anticipate the oft-repeated complaints of Central Asian, Iranian, and European exiles about India's oppressive heat, as in the following *rubāʿi:*

Dar Hind keh khāk u gard mīgardad garm,
Tā gumbad-i lājavard mīgardad garm,
Chūn tab keh natījeh-yi havā khurdagīst,
Ābesh zi nasīm-i sard mīgardad garm.[23]

In India where the soil and dust becomes hot,
Until heaven becomes hot,
Like fever that comes from a draft,
Its water is heated by a cold breeze.

Yet Ashraf does not dwell excessively on the weather, the often tedious subject of so many émigré memoirs and laments—Iranian, Turkish, or British. Indeed, like so many others who sought their fortunes in India, Ashraf prospered there. He did after all enjoy an exceptional position as a tutor to Aurungzeb's daughter. In one couplet and two *rubāʿis* he exalts Mughul India, and in all three verses he reworks the metaphor of *sawād* (darkness) and *shab* (night), transmuting the often unfavorable connotations into sometimes transcendent images. In one couplet *sawād* becomes the Persian poet's metaphorical rose garden:

Sawād-i Hind gulistān-i khwābrā mānad
Havā-yi shūreh-i ābesh sarābrā mānad,
Nazāreh-i but-i Hindī pas az butān-i Mughul,
Beh sāyeh dar shudan az āftābrā mānad.[24]

The Indian darkness resembles the rose garden of dreams.
The air of its marshy water seems a mirage.
Seeing the Indian idol, after the idols of the Mughuls,
Is like entering a shadow from the sun.

The next verse, a *rubā'i,* echoes Kausari's sentiment about the dearth of patronage in Iran, now with scholars, and presumably Ashraf himself among them, representing lights illuminating the night that is India:

Īrān nah ravāj bakhsh-i dānā bāshad,
Har chand keh asbāb muhaiyā bāshad,
Dar Hind būvad hunar ravānrā shuhrat,
Shab raushanī-yi chirāgh paidā bāshad.[25]

There is no currency for learned men in Iran,
Although the means may be found.
In India the talented are renowned.
A lantern will illumine the darkness.

In a second *rubā'i* the poet anticipates the title of a work of a later literary exile, Joseph Conrad: Ashraf takes the illumination theme one step further, arguing that God himself has blessed India's darkness. Although the phrase *dil-i shab* literally means "heart of night" or midnight, it is rendered here as "heart of darkness," arguably the most appropriate translation in view of Ashraf's repeated invocation of the metaphor:

Har chand khudā dar hameh jā dādgarast,
Khwān-i karamash kashīdeh dar bahr u barast,
Razzāqī-ye ū beh Hind zāhir gardad,
Faiz-i azalī dar dil-i shab bīshtarast.[26]

Although God is everywhere just,
Dispensing his blessing on sea and land,
His providence is manifest in India;
God's grace is greater in the heart of darkness.

Finally, in a fourth poem Ashraf seems to conclude his thought by observing that it is natural for Iranians in the darkness of sleep to long for India:

Rū beh sū-ye Hind shabhā dar vatan khwābideh ast,
Har keh 'aish u 'ishrat-i Hindūstānrā dīdeh ast.[27]

At night in his homeland he sleeps with his face toward India,
Whoever has seen the pleasures and delights of Hindustan.

Yet for all the poetically resonant reasons for leaving Iran and dwelling in Mughul India, Ashraf seems to have felt his émigré status with all the emotional force of a refugee. He is still homesick in the midst of his newly found prosperity, mournful for the friends he has left behind, and contemptuous of the inferior culture of his adopted home. The poet repeatedly expresses the conflicting emotions of a voluntary exile. In three separate lines he offers a classic émigré's lament; in the midst of prosperity he is inexplicably unhappy:

1. Dar keshvar-i Hind kasī cherā dārad gham,
Paivasteh dar ūst dard ū darmān bā ham.[28]

In India why should a person mourn?
Joined together in it are affliction and cure.

2. Man keh juz' gham nīst dar bāram, namīdānam cherā,
Chūn matā'-i 'aish dar Hindūstān uftādeh am.[29]

I do not know why there is naught in me but grief,
Since the means of happiness have fallen to me in India.

3. Har keh āmad bar umīd-i ni'mat-i alvān-i Hind,
Khurd chandān khūn-i dil kaz zindegānī sīr shud.[30]

Whoever has come in search of India's blessings,
He has suffered such heartache that he is tired of life.

Yet Ashraf seems to appreciate that he desires the impossible, the best of both worlds—the Indian and the Iranian. When in the following lines he mentions Iran's cold he may be alluding to Amir Khusrau's poem *Nuh Sipihr,* which favorably compares India's climate to that of frigid Iran:[31]

'Ālamī khwāham keh bāshad e'tidālish bar qarār,
Dād az Hindūstān garm u Īrān khunuk.[32]

I wish that a happy mean could be fixed in the world;
Remove heat from Hindustan and cold from Iran.

In some measure at least, Ashraf realizes he is suffering just the absence of friends and family:[33]

> Dar īn ghurbat shudam ghamgīn va ghamkhwārî namiāyad,
> Beh sarvaqtam zi yārān-i vatan yārī namiāyad.[34]

> I have become mournful in this exile and no sympathetic companion comes;
> No friend among the friends of my country comes to my chamber.

Yet Ashraf's melancholia has more profound causes. As he shows in two separate verses, he longs for Iran:

> 1. Gar beh sad zahmat man az Hindūstān āyam birūn,
> Khud begū az ʿuhdeh-i Īrān chisān āyam birūn.[35]

> If with great effort I shall leave Hindustan,
> Tell me how can I ever break my ties with Iran.

> 2. Ashraf az keshvar-i Īrān nakunī dil keh nihāl,
> Chūn ze jā kandeh shud az nushū u namā miuftad.[36]

> Ashraf, do not uproot your heart from Iran,
> For like a shoot wrenched from the ground, you will not thrive.

Ashraf's contradictory impulses seem genuine. Ultimately, however, he leaves little doubt where his heart really lies, making clear his preference for his homeland and his belief in its cultural superiority. How can you, he asks, really weigh one country against another? Iran is not only different but so superior as to be incomparable:

> Beh khāk-i Hind cheh sanjī diyār-i Īranīrā?
> Beh khāk-i tireh barābar makun gulistānrā!

> How can you compare the soil of Hind with the land of Iran?
> Do not equate black soil with a rose garden!

He expresses his feelings more baldly in two culinary comparisons in which Indians are said to be flat and uninteresting—saltless bread and saltless meat—while Iranians are portrayed as pure or uncorrupted—saltless water and saltless wine:

> Hindīst nān bīnamak, Īrāni āb bīnamak.
> Ān chūn kebābī bīnamak, în chūn sharâbī bīnamak.[37]

Indians are like saltless bread; Iranians like saltless water;
That one is like saltless kebab; this one like saltless wine.

Elsewhere Ashraf is brutally frank when he writes that India is a pale reflection of his homeland. In this instance he is playing on the variant meanings of *sawād,* which may mean copy as well as darkness:

Bā mulk-i Hind, nisbat Īrān cheh mīkunī?
Chūn e'tibār-i asl nabāshad sawādrā.[38]

How can you compare the Indian kingdom to Iran?
As the copy can never be equal to the original.

Iranians may well have felt that Timurid-Mughul India was a bad reproduction of Safavid Iran—and many culturally insecure Indian Muslims may have accepted their critique. Most "modern" literary historians of Persian believed until quite recently that Indo-Persian poetry (Sabk-i Hindi) was itself a debased form of Iranian-Persian poetry.[39] Nirad Chaudhuri might have nodded his head in agreement. Here was another example of Aryans going to seed in the subcontinent.

Ashraf arrived in India in 1658/59 just after Aurungzeb had won the war of succession against his brothers. He also imprisoned his father, Shah Jahan, in Agra fort, as he usurped the throne and proclaimed himself padshah. One of the poems Ashraf wrote appears to refer to these events. Alluding to a poem of the Ghaznavid poet Sana'i in which the "son of India" seems to refer to Mu'awiya, whose mother's name was Hind bint 'Utba, Ashraf writes:

Īnkeh az keshvar-i khūd jāneb-i Hind āmadeh-ī,
Dar vilāyat khabar-i Hind magar nashnīdī?
Ba'd az ān kih āmadî qasd-i eqāmat cheh kuni?
Qessehha-yi zarar-i Hind magar nashenīdī
Kīsehhā dukhteh bahr-i umīd-i zar wa sīm,
Bī-baqā'ī-yi zar-i Hind magar nashenīdī?
Zādeh-i Hind kamar-basteh-i qatl-i pedarast.
In sukhan dar safar-i Hind magar nashenīdī?
Kad-khudāī kunī īnjā zi barāyi farzand.
Dāstān-i pesar-i Hind magar nashnīdī?[40]

O you who have come from your country to India;
In your region have you not heard the news of India?
After arriving, why do you intend to stay?
Have you not heard tales of India's peril?
Purses sewn, hoping for gold and silver.

Have you not heard of the transience of India's gold?
The Indian-born intent on killing his father.
Have you not heard this story on your Indian journey?
You marry here for a child.
Have you not heard the story of the Indian son?

Ashraf became a tutor to Aurungzeb's daughter Zib al-Nisa, a religious scholar, poet, and patron who herself was imprisoned by Aurungzeb in January 1681 for aiding or at least sympathizing with her brother Akbar's rebellion against the emperor. Like Shah Jahan she remained a captive—but for more than twenty years—until she died in Delhi in May 1702.[41] Ashraf himself returned to Isfahan in 1672 and at an unknown later date returned to India, where he served a member of the royal family in Patna, later dying in Munger in Bihar in 1704. One of his more touching poems apart from those he addressed to his wife is a *qaṣīda* that he wrote to Zib al-Nisa, evidently after he decided to return to Iran in 1672. This is one of two poems in which he asks for her permission to depart. In some of its last lines Ashraf writes:

Yekbāreh az vatan natavān bar gereft del
Dar ghurbatam agarcheh fuzūn ast e'tebār.
Pīsh-i tū qurb va bu'd tafāvut namīkunad,
Gū khidmat-i huzūr nabāshad marā shi'ār
Nisbat chū bātenīst cheh Delhī cheh Isfahan
Dil pīsh-i tust tan cheh be Kābul cheh Qandahār.[42]

The heart cannot wholly renounce its country,
Although I have greater esteem in my exile.
It does not matter if I am near or far from you
Flattery is not in my character.
As our connection is a spiritual one,
What is Delhi or Isfahan?
My heart is with you,
Whether my body is in Kabul or Qandahar.

THE EMIGRÉ LAMENT

Ashraf's Indian verse is exceptionally evocative and honest; but as a manifestation of conflicted feelings it is also quite typical—both of other migrants to India and of émigré writers in general throughout the world. Zahir al-Din Muhammad Babur, the founder of the wealthy Mughul Empire that employed Ashraf, and Rudyard Kipling, whose family found employment in British India, expressed almost identical reactions to the Indian Circe. Babur wrote as frankly as anyone ever has about his reactions to the country he reluctantly conquered, having been expelled from his Central Asian homelands in the early sixteenth century. Writing in 1527 and 1528, he recalls his astonishment when he first rode from Kabul into the subcontinent in 1505: "A different world came into view—different plants, different trees, different wild animals and different birds, people and tribes with different manners and customs. It was astonishing, a truly astonishing place."[43]

Babur's astonishment, though, was composed of one part attraction and nine parts repulsion. "The pleasant aspect of Hindustan," he says, "is that it is a large country and is thick with gold and silver."[44] In every other way Babur disliked the country he conquered in 1526. The climate was awful. "He suffered," he writes, "from three things in Hindustan. One was its heat, another its fierce winds, and a third its dust."[45] Apart from these physical irritations, he despised Indian culture and society. "The people of Hindustan," he caustically remarks, "have no beauty, they have no convivial society, no social intercourse, no intellect or discernment, no urbanity, no nobility or chivalry."[46] Many of his Turco-Mongol nobles were so homesick that they abandoned Babur to return to Afghanistan or Central Asia immediately after victories near Delhi and Agra in 1526 and 1527. Babur's own sense of *ghurbat* or exile, the word repeatedly used by Ashraf, was intense. From the moment of his conquest he longed to return to Kabul, to the climate, society, and gardens that he loved. In lines from a Turki *ghazal* he probably wrote around 1529, a year before his death, he expresses almost exactly the same sentiments as Ashraf. Beginning with an allusion to his *ghurbat* in India during the month of Ramadan, Babur writes:

Ghurbattah ol ay hijrī meini pīr qilib tur
Hijrān bileh ghurbat menkā ta'sīr qilib tur.

In exile this month of abstinence ages me.
Separated from friends, exile has affected me.

After lines in which Babur rues his fate, he says he does not know whether he will remain on "that" or "this side," referring apparently to Kabul or his Ferghanah homeland versus India. Then, like Ashraf, he poignantly speaks about his love-hate feelings for India:

Bu Hind yeri hāsilidin kob köngül aldïm.
Ni sūd kih bu yer meini dilgîr qilib tur.
Sendin bu qadr qaldï yeraq olmadï Bābur
Ma'zūr tut ay yār ki taqsīr qilib tur.[47]

I deeply desired the riches of this Indian land.
What is the profit since this land oppresses me?

Left so far from you, Babur has not perished,
Excuse me, beloved, for this my error.

At just about the same time, Babur expressed similar feelings in prose. In a letter that he wrote to his longtime boon companion, Khwajah Kalan, who had fled from India's climate to return and govern Kabul, Babur said that he desperately hoped to join him after stabilizing his new Indian regime:

> We have an immense and unreserved desire to go there. Things in Hindustan have also reached a sort of conclusion. The hope is such that, with God most high, this current work will with God's grace quickly be finished. After this work has been arranged, immediately, if God determines, I shall set out.
>
> How can a person forget the pleasures of those regions, especially when one has thus repented and abstained [from wine]? How can a person banish from his mind the legal pleasures like melon and grapes? Thus considered, a melon was brought. Cutting and eating it had a strange effect. I broke down in tears.[48]

Rudyard Kipling reiterated both Babur's and Ashraf's reactions to the Indian climate and their homesickness in voluntary exile. In one of his short poems in the larger set titled, appropriately enough for a discussion of Iranian exile verse, "Certain Maxims of Hafiz," he made one of his many witty comments about the debilitating effect of the Indian climate:

The temper of chums, the love of your wife, and a new piano's tune—
Which of the three will you still trust at the end of an Indian June?[49]

In another verse from his poem "Christmas in India" he conveys the *Heimweh*/homesick feelings of all expatriates in India's Circe better than any other "Aryan" literary exile of the British period. Having come to India for "gold," they now, like Ashraf, realized the emotional consequences of abandoning their country:

High noon behind the tamarisks—the sun is hot above us—
As at home the Christmas Day is breaking wan.
They will drink our healths at dinner—those who tell us how they love us.
And forget us till another year be gone!
O the toil that knows no breaking! Oh the
Heimweh, ceaseless aching!
O the black dividing Sea and alien Plain!
Youth was cheap—wherefore we sold it.
Gold was good—we hoped to hold it,
And today we know the fullness of our gain.[50]

It is tempting to imagine a posthumous poetry recital, a *mushā'irah,* in which Kipling, Babur, and Ashraf would spontaneously compose verses playing off each other's Indian imagery. It would be even more fitting if they held the literary competition near Shah Jahan's confident inscription on Delhi's Red Fort:

> Agar firdaus bar rū-yi zamīn ast,
> Hamīn ast hamīn ast hamīn ast!
>
> If there is paradise on earth,
> It is this, it is this, it is this![51]

NOTES

I am indebted to my colleagues Dick Davis and Alam Payind, both poets and translators of poetry, for their help with the translations in this article. Professor Muzaffar Alam of the University of Chicago was also kind enough to read the entire manuscript and suggest changes, as did Paul Losensky of Indiana University. The anonymous readers of the manuscript for *Iranian Studies* were exceptionally meticulous and helpful in their critiques.

1. Nirad C. Chaudhuri, *The Continent of Circe* (New York: Oxford University Press, 1966), p. 306.

2. Ibid., p. 136.

3. The term "Timurid-Mughul" is used for the name of the dynasty usually identified as Mughul for two reasons. As is well known, Mughul means Mongol and thus fundamentally misrepresents this patrilineal Timurid dynasty. The founder of the dynasty, however, Zahir al-Din Muhammad Babur (1483–1530), was a matrilineal descendant of Chingiz Khan and respected and patronized his Chaghatai Chingizid relatives only second to those of Timurid descent. Therefore, "Timurid-Mughul" reflects this dual heritage and the respect Babur gave to both his patrilineal and matrilineal lines.

4. This was the father of Muhammad Baqir al-Majlisi, the well-known Safavid cleric. See S. H. Nasr, "Spiritual Movements, Philosophy and Theology in the Safavid Period," in *The Cambridge History of Iran, 6,* ed. Peter Jackson and Laurence Lockhart (Cambridge: Cambridge University Press, 1986), pp. 693–94.

5. For Mazandarani's early life, see Mahmud Hasan Sayyidan, ed., *Divān-i ash'ār Ashraf Māzandarānī* (Tehran: Bunyād-i mawqūfat-i Duktur Mahmūd Afshār Yazdī, 1374/1994), pp. 1–21.

6. Aziz Ahmad, "Safawid Poets and India," *Iran* 14 (1976): 129–31.

7. E. G. Browne, *A Literary History of Persia,* 4 vols. (Cambridge: Cambridge University Press, 1953), 4:26.

8. Muhammad Abdu'l Ghani, *A History of Persian Language and Literature at the Mughal Court* (Allahabad, India: Indian Press, repr. 1972), 2:168.

9. Quoted by S. Safa in "Persian Literature in the Safavid Period," in *Cambridge History of Iran,* ed. Jackson and Lockhart, p. 954.

10. Ahmad, "Safawid Poets and India," p. 118.

11. Stephen Frederic Dale, *Indian Merchants and Eurasian Trade, 1600–1750* (Cambridge: Cambridge University Press, 1994), chapter 2.

12. Alexander Rogers, trans., and Henry Beveridge, ed., *The Tūzuk-i Jahāngīrī, or Memoirs of Jahāngīr* (Delhi: Munshiram, repr. 1978 of 1909–14 edition), 1:37.

13. Mirza Haidar Dughlat, *Tarikh-i Rashidi,* ed. W. M. Thackston (Cambridge: Mass., Harvard University Press, 1996), fols. 61b–62.

14. See Muzaffar Alam, "Akhlāq-ī Norms and Mughal Governance," in *The Making of Indo-Persian Culture* by Françoise Nalini Delvoye and Marc Gaborieau (Delhi: Manohar, 2000), pp. 67–95.

15. Muzaffar Alam, "The Pursuit of Persian: Language in Mughal Politics," *Modern Asian Studies* 32, no. 2 (1998): 320–21.

16. Browne, *A Literary History of Persia,* 4:259. Browne is quoting the Urdu poet and literary critic Shiblī Nu'mānī, for whom see J. A. Haywood, "Shiblī Nu'mānī," in *The Encyclopaedia of Islam* by C. E. Bosworth et al., new ed. (Leiden: E. J. Brill, 1996), 9:433–34.

17. Annemarie Schimmel discusses this imagery with her typical erudition in "Turk and Hindu: A Poetical Image and Its Application to Historical Fact," in *Islam and Cultural Change in the Middle Ages,* ed. Spero Vryonis, Jr. (Wiesbaden: Harrassowitz, 1975), pp. 107–26.

18. Ma'ānī, *Kārvānī-I Hind,* 1:72.

19. Ibid., 1:71.

20. Ibid., 1:72.

21. Ibid., 1:71.

22. Ibid.

23. Ibid., 1:73–74.

24. Ibid., 1:71.

25. Ibid., 1:73.

26. Ibid.

27. Ibid., 1:70.

28. Ibid., 1:74.

29. Ibid., 1:72.

30. Ibid.

31. One of Amir Khusrau's favorable contrasts is between the cold of Khurasan and the warmth of Arabia and India. Muhammad Wazid Mirza edited the Persian text in his book *The Nuh Sipihr of Amir Khusrau* (London: Oxford University Press, 1949); and R. Nath and Faiyaz Gwaliori have published an annotated translation of the third section of the poem, in which Amir Khusrau praises India. See *India as Seen by Amir Khusrau in 1318* A.D. (Jaipur: Historical Research Documentation Centre, 1981).

32. Ma'ānī, *Kārvānī-I Hind,* 1:73.

33. See Mahmud Hasan Sayyidan's affecting discussion of Mazandarani's reasons for returning to Iran, including especially his separation from his family: *Divān-i ash'ār Ashraf Māzandarānī,* pp. 29–31.

34. Ma'ānī, *Kārvānī-i Hind,* 1:70.

35. Ibid., 1:71.

36. Ibid., 1:70.

37. Ibid., 1:73.

38. Ibid., 1:72.

39. Many Iranians still feel this way; but recent scholarly assessments of Indo-Persian verse have tried to examine the verse on its own terms, although not always without an implicit bias. That bias is evident in Ehsan Yarshater's essay "The Indian Style: Progress or De-

cline," in *Persian Literature,* ed. Ehsan Yarshater (Albany, N.Y.: Biblioteca Persica, 1988), pp. 405–21. Jan Marek offers a far more sympathetic assessment in "Persian Literature in India," in *History of Iranian Literature* by Jan Rypka (Dordrecht, Netherlands: D. Reidel, 1968), pp. 713–34. A fine study of an individual poet that makes this debate seem irrelevant is Paul E. Losensky's *Welcoming Fighānī, Imitation and Poetic Individuality in the Safavid-Mughal Ghazal* (Costa Mesa, Calif.: Mazda Publishers, 1998).

40. Ma'ānī, *Kārvānī-I Hind,* 1:73; and Fr. Buhl, "Hind bint 'Utba," in *Encylopaedia of Islam* by Bernard Lewis et al., new ed. (Leiden: E. J. Brill, 1971), 3:455.

41. Jadunath Sarkar, "The Romance of a Mughal Princess: Zeb-Un-Nisa," in *Studies in Aurungzeb's Reign* (Calcutta: Sangam Books, repr. 1989), pp. 90–98.

42. Ma'ānī, *Kārvānī-I Hind,* 1:62–63. The entire poem is given by Sayyidan, *Divān-i ash'ār Ashraf Māzandarānī,* pp. 95–100.

43. Eiji Mano, ed., *Bābur-Nāma (Vaqāyi')* (Kyoto: Syokado, 1995), fols. 145a–b.

44. Ibid., fol. 291a.

45. Ibid., fol. 300a.

46. Ibid., fol. 290b.

47. I. V. Stebleva, *Semantika Gazelei Babura* (Moscow: Nauka, 1982), no. 119. For a modern Turkish transcription of Babur's Chaghatai, see Bilal Yücel, *Bābür Dīvānï* (Ankara: Atatürk Kültür Merkezi, 1995), no. 124. For exile poetry of another kind and as a genre, see Sunil Sharma, *Persian Poetry at the Indian Frontier: Mas'ūd Sa'd Salmān of Lahore* (Delhi: Permanent Black, 2000), especially chapter 2.

48. Mano, *Bābur-Nāma (Vaqāyi'),* fol. 359a.

49. Rudyard Kipling, *Departmental Ditties and Barrack Room Ballads* (New York: Doubleday, 1912), p. 126.

50. Ibid., p. 114.

51. This is a literal verbal echo of a line in Amir Khusrau's poem *Nuh Sipihr* in which he describes India as an earthly paradise. See n. 31 above.

4

Muhammad Baqir Majlisi, Family Values, and the Safavids

Shireen Mahdavi

The subject of this essay is the influence of the works of Muhammad Baqir Majlisi (1627/28–1699/1700) on the position of women and the family in Iran. The following discussion examines the role of women in Iran prior to the impact of Majlisi's ideas, showing that his influence drastically changed the position of Iranian women up to the present.

When the Safavids declared Shi'ism the state religion of Persia in 1501, the majority of the population was still Sunni and many of the customs and institutions of the Timurid and Aqquyunlu periods still prevailed, including those related to the role of women. These Turkic dynasties shared many tribal ways in common with the Mongols, such as the high status of women. Women held a higher social position in the Turkic societies than within orthodox Islamic communities.[1] In her work on women during the Mongol period, Shireen Bayani also notes that women held a high position both politically and socially.[2] She attributes this to the predominance of tribal customs.

These customs were still prevailing at the beginning of the reign of the Safavids. There is some evidence of the relative freedom, independence, and influence of women in the early Safavid period.[3] Contemporary reports by Italian travelers and merchants indicate that, at the beginning of the Safavid reign, women were neither veiled nor secluded. In his account of the battle of Chaldiran in 1514 between the Ottoman Sultan Selim (r. 1512–20) and the first Safavid Shah Isma'il (r. 1501–24), Caterino Zeno says: "The Persian ladies themselves follow in arms the same fortunes as their husbands, and fight like men, in the same way as those ancient Amazons who performed such feats of arms in their time."[4] The popular Safavid histories provide further evidence of the physical prowess of the early Safavid women and their participation in the battle of Chaldiran. Tajlu Khanum, one of Shah Isma'il's wives and the mother of Shah Tahmasb, is reputed to have been an able fencer and wrestler who participated in the battle of Chaldiran.[5] Another royal woman, who actually led an army in 1578–79 against the Ottomans in the battle of Shirvan, was Khayir al-Nisa Bigum, the wife of Shah Muhammad Khudabanda.[6] An Italian merchant traveling in Persia during the reign of Shah Isma'il, in discussing taxes, reports the abundance of prostitution, which seems to have been officially recognized and even encouraged. He says: "Also the harlots, who frequent the public places, are bound to pay according to their beauty, as the prettier they are the more they will have to pay."[7]

According to Vincento d'Alessandri, Venetian ambassador to the court of Shah Tahmasb (r. 1524–76), the head-to-toe covering that became the custom during the later Safavid period and continued through the Qajar era did not exist in his time in Iran. D'Alessandri says: "The women are mostly ugly, though of fine features and noble dispositions, their costumes not being so refined as those of the Turkish ladies. They wear robes of silk, veils on their heads and show their faces openly. They have pearls and other jewels on their head."[8] This is further confirmed by the Venetian Michele Membre, who went on a mission to the court of Shah Tahmasb: ". . . the Shah's maidens pass on fine horses; and they ride like men and dress like men, except that on their heads they do not wear caps but white kerchiefs . . . and they were beautiful."[9] Although it appears that Membre and d'Alessandri disagree on the women's facial characteristics, the important fact is that these Europeans were permitted to see the women.

In the early Safavid period a number of royal women played important political roles. Tajlu Khanum, mentioned earlier, was eventually banished by her son, Shah Tahmasb, for her political activities. Pari Khan Khanum, the daughter of Shah Tahmasb, not only was an influential princess during her father's reign but also was involved in politics after her father's death. She was a kingmaker who was instrumental in the accession of two successive Safavid Shahs, Isma'il II and Muhammad Khudabanda, which eventually led to her murder.[10] Ironically it was another influential Safavid woman, Khayir al-Nisa Bigum, the wife of Muhammad Khudabanda, who was instrumental in her downfall and held the reigns of power after her death until her own assassination at the hands of the Qizilbash.[11]

Pre-Safavid and early Safavid miniatures and manuscript illustrations also bear witness to the fact that women were not totally secluded or veiled. These works of art depict women engaged in various activities and in front of men. There are examples of distinguished women without the veil meeting with free

Figure 4.1. *Man before a Princess with Attendants.* Miniature from Sadaqa b. Abi i-Qasim Shirazi, *Kitab-i Samak-i 'Ayyar.* Iran, Ingu style, 1330 to 1340. 11 × 11.4 cm. MS. Ouseley 379–81, vol. 1, fol. 119r. Courtesy of Bodleian Library, Oxford.

men who were not related to them, if not in public at least in their own domain. Other examples show women reigning, riding, hunting, fighting, and dancing. Although these miniatures are illustrations of literary texts, it must be assumed that the artists based their work on existing conditions familiar to them.[12]

Women played a part in politics in Iran during the post-Mongol period. A reigning princess is shown in a miniature from the first half of the fourteenth century (fig. 4.1). The fact that she is in a position of power is established by the crown she is wearing, the presence of the courtier kneeling in front of her, and the respectful pose of the two attendants behind her. Another miniature shows the wives, daughters, and attendants of Timur (r. 1370–1405) on horseback riding out to meet him (fig. 4.2). The princesses wear headdresses of white decorated cloth with plumes of heron feathers.

Figure 4.2. *Timur's Family Rides Out from Samarkand to Meet Him.* Miniature from Sharaf al-Din Yazdi, *Zafarnama.* Iran, Shiraz style, around 1533. 13 × 13 cm. Pers. Ms. Eth. 175 (I.O.137), fol. 368 v. Courtesy of India Office Library, British Library, London.

Figure 4.3. *Khusraw and Shirin Hunting.* From a manuscript of *Khusraw u Shirin* by Nizami (d. 9). Iran, Tabriz, early fifteenth century. Opaque watercolor, ink, and gold on paper. 21.7 × 15.8 cm. Courtesy of Freer Gallery of Art, Smithsonian Institution, Washington, D.C.

Figure 4.4. *Lovers Entertained by Musicians and Dancers.* Miniature from a *Divan* of Hafiz painted for Sam Mirza ca. 1527–33. 11⅜ × 7¼ inches. Courtesy of Fogg Museum of Art, Harvard University.

An early fifteenth century illustration of Nizami's *Khusraw and Shirin* shows Shirin in the upper half of the composition, hunting dressed in men's attire (fig. 4.3). She is riding her legendary horse Shabdiz and has just slain a lion with her sword. A more demure Khusraw is shown with a bow and arrow, hunting a gazelle. The interesting aspect of this painting is that all the action seems to be concentrated on Shirin in the top half of the painting rather than on Khusraw. Shirin's female attendants behind the hill wear tall conical hats and are also dressed in male clothing.[13]

A painting whose lyrical beauty illustrates both the mystic spirit of the poem and the spirit of early Safavid ethos as reflected in their painting style is one of the five miniatures of *Diwan-i Ḥafiz* painted for Sam Mirza (fig. 4.4).[14] This miniature is a *fête champêtre* that shows a flowering garden shaded by a beautifully ornamental canopy under which two lovers, possibly a prince and a princess, are seated on a carpet. In front of them are two dancing girls (one in red, the other in orange), who stand out in stark contrast against the dark green of the grass, swaying toward one another and playing castanets. They are dressed simply but colorfully in long robes that reveal their necks. Their faces can be seen openly, and their hair is covered only by a transparent material that is evidently more ornamental than practical. A cupbearer is serving wine, and musicians are sitting on either side. The woman on the carpet is obviously from a different social class: she not only wears a fine cloak but also has a bejeweled diadem in her hair. There is apparently no impediment to her appearing thus in front of male musicians and the cupbearer. This painting is attributed by Cary Welch to Sultan Muhammad, court painter to both Shah Isma'il and Shah Tahmasb, whom he calls the greatest artist of the Safavid period.[15] Sultan Muhammad was a Sufi, whose style of painting was a synthesis of Timurid and Turkoman art and whose works were imbued with the Sufi spiritual ideals.[16]

It is not only travelers' accounts that describe women as warriors; they are shown as such in many illustrations of Firdusi's epic *Shahnama.* Figure 4.5 depicts women on horseback fighting a male adversary. The combatants carry quivers full of arrows. The horses have beautiful ornamental saddlecloths.

More than a hundred years later, during the reign of Shah Sulayman (r. 1666–94), Sir John Chardin reported that Persian women were more closely guarded and secluded than their other Islamic counterparts. Their veiling is described thus: "Their head is very well cloath'd and over it they have a Vail that falls down to their Shoulders, and covers their Neck and Bosom before. When they go out, they put over all, a great White Vail, which covers them from Head to Foot, not suffering anything to appear in several Countries but the Balls of their Eyes. The Women wear four Vails in all; two of which they wear at Home, and two more when they go Abroad."[17]

Figure 4.5. *Sohrab Takes the Helmet Off Rudabeh Who Is Disguised as a Warrior.* Miniature from Firdusi, *Shahnama.* Iran, School of Isfahan, dated 1014/1605. 24.5 × 14 cm. MS Or. fol. 4251, f. 227r. Courtesy of Deutsche Staatsbibliothek, Berlin

There is thus a suggestion that, as the Safavids lost their revolutionary zeal and became more orthodox, a parallel development took place with regard to the position of women. The rise of orthodoxy under the Safavids was accompanied by the growing power of the *ʻulama,* culminating in the unprecedented political, social, and religious power of ʻAllama Muhammad Baqir Majlisi (1627?–1700?). The last Safavid, Shah Sultan Husayn (deposed 1722), was very much under the influence of the *ʻulama* in general and Majlisi in particular, as a result of which he enforced strict Shi'i orthodoxy. An aspect of the development of this orthodoxy was the fact that the Shi'i interpretations of the Islamic position on women superimposed themselves completely upon all past customs and traditions. The seclusion of women under Shah Sultan Husayn reached such a degree that when women of the royal harem made public outings the royal route had to be cleared of all males, including shopkeepers.[18]

The most prominent and influential Shi'i theologian of all time was 'Allama Muhammad Baqir Majlisi, whose work has had an enormous influence on subsequent generations of Shi'i *'ulama* down to the present day. His life spanned the reigns of the last five Safavid shahs. He was born in Isfahan at the end of the reign of Shah 'Abbas the Great (r. 1587–1629) and came to prominence in the reigns of Shah Sulayman (r. 1666–1694) and Shah Sultan Husayn (r. 1694–1722), during whose reign he died. Majlisi was descended from a long line of a distinguished clerical family. He was the son of another notable Shi'i theologian, Muhammad Taqi (generally referred to as Majlisi-yi Awwal), whose views differed radically from those of his son. Following his family tradition, Majlisi studied various Islamic sciences with both his father and many other prominent scholars of the period. Having attained great scholarship in all the Islamic sciences, he decided to abandon further study of those disciplines and dedicate himself to the study of the Prophetic traditions. He devoted the rest of his life to lecturing on Shi'ism and the collection of scattered and forgotten Shi'i *hadith*s.

Majlisi wrote more than sixty books, the most famous of which is *Bihar al-Anwar,* an encyclopedic collection of Shi'i *hadith*s in Arabic.[19] He also wrote books in Persian, some of which were translations of *Bihar al-Anwar,* although he was not an innovator in this realm. Prior to him, in the reign of Shah Isma'il, Kamal al-Din Husayn Ardabili, as E. G. Browne says, "was the first to compose books in Persian on matters connected with the Holy Law according to the doctrine of the Shi'a."[20] Majlisi's objective in writing in Persian was, in his own words, to make the Prophetic tradition accessible to the common people who could not read Arabic and thus engrain his own brand of Shi'ism in the people's psyche.[21] There is a dichotomy in Majlisi's thinking: in spite of his wish to acquaint the general public with his brand of Shi'ism, he wrote most of his works in Arabic.

Aside from his writing and scholarship, Majlisi held a number of government positions. In 1686 he was appointed Shaykh al-Islam and Imam Jum'a by Shah Sulayman. According to some sources, his title of Shaykh al-Islam changed to Mullabashi on the accession of Shah Sultan Husayn to the throne. It has also been argued, however, that the office of Mullabashi only came into being after Majlisi's death.[22] Whether Majlisi was just Shaykh al-Islam or Mullabashi, he not only held the highest religious office but had a carte blanche from Shah Sultan Husayn to institute whatever religious, political, and social policies he chose.[23] According to Abdul Hadi Ha'iri, for all intents and purposes he was the actual ruler of Persia.[24] His primary objective was to suppress any kind of belief that was tainted by heresy. This included the demolition of the Indian idols of Isfahan; suppression of Sufis, mystical philosophy, and Sunnis; and repudiation of any kind of innovation.[25] In their place he propagated a dogmatic form of Twelver Shi'ism through his numerous works, supported by Shi'i *hadiths* and made popular by a number being in Persian and accessible to the general public (although we do not know how many people were literate and who the readers were). In this way Majlisi put his mark on Shi'ism and at the same time sealed the position of women within that system for posterity.[26]

The book in which Majlisi discusses the role, duties, and upbringing of women and family life is *Hilyat al-Muttaqin* (The Ornament of the Pious),[27] a book in Persian on morals, ethics, example, conduct, and manners. This work consists of precepts on various aspects of everyday life, including hygiene, the etiquette of eating and drinking, remedies for various ailments, precepts of social behavior, rules regarding travel, household practices, property ownership, the rights of women, marriage and sexual intercourse, and almost every other aspect of human behavior, supported by *hadiths* attributed to the Prophet and the Imams. It is not easy to categorize *Hilyat al-Muttaqin* in the typology of Muslim works. This is not a book on laws; nor is it a discourse on Islamic duties and obligations as prescribed according to the five pillars. In his very short introduction Majlisi used the terms *makarim-i akhlaq* (good morals) and *mahasin-i adab* (good manners) to describe the contents of his work. Thus, the genre of the book falls into a classification somewhere between *adab* and *akhlaq* literature.[28] It differs from *adab* literature in that it lacks the anecdotes and lightness of style found, for instance, in the works of Sa'di. It differs from *akhlaq* literature in that it lacks the philosophical foundations upon which those works were based. The book is most similar to the Second Discourse of *Akhlaq-i Nasiri* by Nasir al-Din Tusi except that Tusi's precepts are not supported by *hadiths* and are more theoretical in nature (Majlisi's precepts are practical and deal with some actual circumstances).[29] It also differs from *Akhlaq-i Nasiri* in that it is directed at the common people.

In his brief introduction Majlisi states that all the *hadiths* quoted have come down from the Shi'i Imams and emphasizes that the objective of writing the book in Persian is to make the general public acquainted with its axioms. The book is divided into fourteen chapters (singular: *bab*) containing twelve sections (singular: *faṣl*) each and a concluding chapter covering miscellaneous questions. The fourth chapter is devoted to family matters and is entitled "An explanation of the virtues of matrimony, rules regarding sexual intercourse and association with women, and the methods of the upbringing of children and association with them."[30] This chapter may serve as an example of Majlisi's methodology and the light it throws on the position of women in Shi'ism today.

The first section is dedicated to the virtues of matrimony and the prohibition of celibacy. The *hadith*s brought forward in support of these two topics read like a paradise of epicurean delight for men. Three points are emphasized over and over again: the virtues of sweet smells, delicious food, and sexual intercourse with women. The prescription of all the *hadith*s in this section can be summarized in a *hadith* in which three women came to see the Prophet. One said that her husband did not eat meat; the other said that her husband did not smell sweet fragrances; and the third said that her husband did not have sexual intercourse with women. The Prophet became so angry at the state of things that he went to the pulpit and said: Why do some of my followers abstain from eating meat, from smelling sweet fragrances, and from having intercourse with women? I eat meat, I smell sweet fragrances, and I go to women. Those who do not follow my customs are not a part of me (p. 69). In another *hadith* attributed to the Prophet, he said: The worst men among you are the celibate ones. Whoever wants to follow my *sunna* must also want women, as that is part of my *sunna* (p. 68).

The second section discusses the commendable and contemptible qualities of the female species (pp. 69–72). In a *hadith* attributed to Imam Ja'far Sadiq it is stated that a woman is like a shackle that you put around your neck, so look well and see what kind of shackle you are acquiring (p. 69). In a number of *hadith*s attributed to the Prophet, he enjoins men to choose for their seed a woman who deserves to bear their children. They should want virgin women, whose mouths smell sweeter, whose uterus is cooler, whose breasts are more brimming with milk, and who will produce more children. A woman is admirable who produces the most children, who is a friend to her husband, who is chaste, who obeys whatever her husband says, and who when alone with her husband does not repudiate him but does not cling to him to force him into intercourse. The worst woman is one who dominates her husband, who is barren, who does not listen and obey her husband, and when in private denies him that which he desires. In a *hadith* attributed to Imam Ja'far Sadiq, he states that the worth of a woman consists in her *mahria* being large and her childbirth easy. The liability of a woman is that her *mahria* is small and her childbirth difficult (p. 71).

The third, fourth, and fifth sections are devoted to rules of marriage and sexual intercourse (pp. 72–80). These three sections constitute the greater body of the chapter, indicating an unusual preoccupation with sexual intercourse. In *hadith* after *hadith,* many attributed to the Prophet, detailed rules of days, time, and place when marriage or sexual intercourse is permitted are set out. Simultaneously, occasions when sexual intercourse is not permitted are specified. Specific parts of the female anatomy that may be touched or seen are designated as well as the state of dress or undress permitted. The rules applying to free women are different from those applicable to slave women, as more latitude is permitted in relationship with slaves. Noncompliance with these rules will be catastrophic for the conceived child and the female, resulting in various ailments or afflictions ranging from leprosy to blindness to mental retardation. The male partner who has participated in the act is spared from any of the consequences. For instance, Friday is the best day for the marriage ceremony to take place, and the marriage should be consummated at night. Wednesday is the worst day. Neither the ceremony nor the consummation should occur when the moon is in Scorpio, as the marriage will not last and the baby will be aborted. Sexual intercourse when the moon is in Scorpio is neither recommended nor disapproved but *makruh*. Intercourse in the bath is permitted but not in a boat. A man can sleep between two slave women but not two free women. These details continue ad infinitum. Particular Arabic prayers to be uttered before, during, and after intercourse are stipulated.

Section six covers the duties of husband and wife toward each other (pp. 80–83). This section begins with a *hadith* attributed to both Imam Muhammad Baqir and Imam Ja'far Sadiq. In this *hadith* it is stated that God created only men with a sense of honor (*ghayrat*) and that women do not possess honor. Consequently it is *halal* (permitted) for men to have four wives and as many temporary wives and slave women as they wish, while women can only have one husband (p. 80). The argument is that since women have no honor they do not suffer from jealousy, whereas men, possessing honor, are jealous. According to a *hadith* attributed to the Prophet, the primary duty of a wife is obedience to her husband, the fulfillment of all his desires, and obtaining his permission for all her acts, including disposal of her own property even for charitable purposes. The husband in return is obliged to have sexual intercourse with his wife every four months and to provide her with meat every three days, henna every six months, and four sets of clothes every year (two for the winter and two for the summer).

It is also the duty of the husband according to a *hadith* of the Prophet to prevent his wife from reading Surah 12: Yusuf of the Qur'an, which relates the passion of Potiphar's wife for Joseph. It is interesting that this surah is considered dangerous, because as it appears in the Qur'an it is a triumph of virtue over temptation.[31] The prohibition must be due to the belief that women might miss the point and behave to the contrary. But a husband should teach his wife Surah 24: al-Nur of the Qur'an, which praises chastity, modesty, and piety in women while prescribing punishments for adulteresses. The husband is enjoined in a *hadith* attributed to Imam Hasan never to consult with women, as their opinions are weak and their resolve infirm (p. 82). This is further supported by a *hadith* of the Prophet, who whenever he wanted to go to war consulted his wives and then did the contrary.

Section seven cites the virtues of having children and contains prayers for infertility to be uttered prior, during, and after intercourse. Muhammad prevented the burial of newborn girls and in many *hadith*s enjoins his followers not to be unhappy at the birth of a girl. It is the birth of a boy that is auspicious, however, and in one *hadith* he says: "Whoever has one daughter has a heavy burden, he who has two daughters needs help, he who has three daughters should be exempt from Jihad and religious duties, and he who has four daughters, O you believers, help him, lend him money, and have mercy on him" (p. 84).

Section eight contains prescriptions for the period of pregnancy, childbirth, and the naming of the child. In various *hadith*s suitable foods for pregnant women are cited, which contribute to the characteristics of the baby. For instance, it is recommended by Imam Ja'far Sadiq that a pregnant woman should eat quince so that the child will smell more pleasant and have a more transparent skin. The Prophet recommends that a pregnant woman should eat frankincense so that the child will have a strong stomach and much wisdom. If it is a boy, he will be brave; and if it is a girl, she will have big buttocks, which will endear her to her husband. This section also contains various prayers to prevent difficult childbirth or to ease the birth. As far as naming the child is concerned, the names of the Prophets and Imams are considered the most suitable (p. 89).

The ninth section is devoted to oblation (*'aqiqa*) for the newborn and shaving of the head. It deals with the times, the manner, and the type of animal suitable for sacrifice and who may partake of the sacrificial meat and the time when the head should be shaved. For instance, the animal for a girl should be female and that for a boy male. The parents of the child may not partake of the meat, and the meat should not be distributed uncooked. Various prayers suitable for the time of sacrifice are included (pp. 91–93).

The tenth section covers the customs regarding the circumcision of boys and girls and the piercing of ears. It begins by stating that it is customary for the circumcision of boys to take place by the seventh day, if not before maturity; otherwise it is the duty of the person himself. The piercing of the ears of boys is also customary. The circumcision of girls is customary and recommended, but only a little should be cut. It goes on to state nevertheless that the circumcision of boys is customary but that of girls not so. But what could be better than this practice, which endears the woman to her husband? In support of this a *hadith* attributed to 'Ali is quoted in which he says that girls should not be circumcised before the age of seven. It is further supported by a *hadith* attributed to the Prophet in which a female practitioner of circumcision approaches the Prophet to discover whether the practice should continue; he not only tells her that it is *halal* but also instructs her on how much should be cut so that the face will glow more: the color will become clearer and endear the woman more to her husband (p. 94).

The eleventh section concerns breast feeding and the education of children. It is suggested that breast feeding should not continue beyond the age of two. Some of the *'ulama* consider it compulsory that the mother should feed the child with the first milk that comes to the breast—otherwise the child will not have any strength. This is supported by a *hadith* attributed to 'Ali in which he says that the most nutritious and valuable milk for the child is that of the mother. In another *hadith* attributed to Imam Ja'far Sadiq it is stated that the mother should feed the child from both breasts: one constitutes food, the other water. The *hadith* goes on to enumerate the qualities of a wet nurse. It is permitted to employ Christian or Jewish wet nurses; but they must be prevented from eating those things such as wine and pork that are *haram* in Islam, and they cannot take the child to their homes. The milk of an adulteress is not permitted. The milk of a slave who has committed adultery is permitted if the owners of the slave make the milk *halal* (p. 96). 'Ali said that the nursemaid should have a good face and character, as the child will inherit her characteristics.

The number seven appears conspicuously in the upbringing of children. Both 'Ali and Sadiq prescribe that children should be left to play for seven years, educated for seven years, and taught *halal* and *haram* for another seven years. The child will grow until the age of twenty-three and gain wisdom until the age of thirty-five (p. 96). In a *hadith* attributed to the Prophet it is stated that boys should be taught the Qur'an, to shoot, and to swim, while girls should be prevented from reading Surah Yusuf but taught Surah Nur and married off as soon as possible (p. 97).

Section twelve treats the duty of children toward their parents. It begins by saying that respect for parents is one of the laws (*shari'a*) of religion. Offending parents or inflicting pain upon them is one of the major sins. In *hadith* after *hadith* attributed to the Prophet and the Imams this section advocates respect and obedience to both mother and father. In a *hadith* attributed to the Prophet, it is explained that even *jihad* is not incumbent upon an individual who has elderly parents who need care. In their lifetime parents should be supported in every way, financial and otherwise. After their death all their obligations fall upon their offspring, including debts as well as unfulfilled fasting and hajj, which should be undertaken on behalf of the parents.

Majlisi's style and methodology and the types of *hadith*s he uses in these sections are not consistent. He begins some sections immediately with a *hadith* that he classifies as *sahih, hasan,* or *mu'tabar;* or he simply says *manqul ast* (it is reported) or "the Prophet" or "one of the Imams said," in which case he does not qualify the type of *hadith.* For instance, in the second section, in which he discusses women, he starts by saying *az hazrat-i Sadiq manqul ast:* a woman is like a shackle round your neck. He goes on to illustrate his points by using sixteen *hadith*s in this section. Among these only one is *sahih,* attributed to Imam Muhammad Baqir. Six of the *hadith*s attributed to the Prophet and Imam Ja'far Sadiq are only qualified by *farmud* (said). The rest are qualified by *manqul ast* (reported).

In other sections Majlisi simply starts with a statement of his own, not necessarily then or later on supported by a *hadith.* For instance, he begins section three, entitled "Explanation of mores regarding consummation of marriage and intercourse," by saying: "[K]now that consummation when the moon is in Scorpio or in eclipse is *makruh* and intercourse inside a woman's vulva when a woman is menstruating or bleeding after childbirth is *haram.*" He does not support the above or the following statements with a *hadith,* however.

It is difficult to know whether in writing *Hilyat al-Muttaqin* Majlisi was reiterating familiar precepts already in practice or whether he became aware of what he considered to be a state of moral decline, necessitating a manual in which (through his vivid imagination) all possible transgressions were conceived to prevent the believers from committing them. For instance, he produces a saying of Imam Muhammad Baqir prohibiting intercourse with girls under nine years of age. Does this mean that such a practice was prevalent and Majlisi wished to prevent it or that this prohibition was observed and Majlisi was repeating an existing tenet? It is not known whether the *hadith*s supporting female circumcision were presented because this was not a Persian custom and Majlisi wished to propagate it for the greater enjoyment of men or whether it had already been adopted by the Persians from the Arabs.

Two factors throw a certain amount of light on Majlisi's motivation for writing *Hilyat al-Muttaqin.* One is the appearance of a manuscript during the last years of the reign of Shah Sulayman (r. 1666–94) entitled *'Aqa'id al-Nisa,* ascribed to a member of the *'ulama,* Aqa Jamal Khwansari.[32] Although it is written as a parody of the customs of Isfahani women, a close reading of the text reveals that the local customs practiced by the women did not strictly adhere to the injunctions of the *shari'a.* As an *'alim* the writer mocks these customs; yet he shows that women were more concerned with social aspirations than with religious practices and when convenient they would abandon the latter in favor of the former. They would appear unveiled in front of tradesmen, would go out alone, and had certain expectations of their husbands.[33] An edict promulgated by Shah Sultan Husayn in 1694 and signed by Muhammad

Baqir Majlisi as the Shaykh al-Islam of Isfahan bears witness to the fact that certain nonorthodox customs still survived at that time. Majlisi, who for all intent and purposes was in charge of the country during the reign of Shah Sultan Husayn, was determined to eradicate them. The edict prohibits the drinking of wine as well as music and dancing at weddings and prescribes the enforcement of veiling.[34] Another contemporary text, *Tuhfat al-'Alam,* by Mir Abu Talib Findiriski, confirms that non-*shar'i* customs prevailed. It relates that Shah Sultan Husayn ordered that women should not appear in public, whether shopping in the bazaar or strolling in gardens, without *shar'i* reasons or without their husbands.[35]

There are certainly precedents for some of Majlisi's beliefs and injunctions both in the Qur'an and its interpretations and in the *hadith*s; but there are no precedents for some others. For instance, a number of points regarding women made by Majlisi have precedents in the interpretation of Abu al-Futuh Razi (d. 538/1144) of Qur'an IV:34, the verse beginning *Ar-rijal qawwamun 'ala an-nisa* (Men are the maintainers of women). In his commentary on this verse, Razi reached the conclusion that men are superior; women are inferior beings who are deficient in reason and must therefore at all times obey men. It must be noted that there is a difference of opinion among the *'ulama* as to the exact translation of the word *qawwamun.* Different translations and interpretations of this verse portray man as manager, superior, or simply preferred by God. Razi, like Majlisi, considers *mut'a* (temporary marriage) permissible in his commentary on Qur'an IV:24, which includes the line *Fa-ma istamta'tum bi-hi minhunna, fa-a'tuhanna ujurahunna* (Those women whom you have enjoyed and who have given you pleasure [*tamattu*], give them their reward).[36] Once again there is a difference of opinion among the Shi'i *'ulama* themselves as well as with the Sunni *'ulama,* hinging on the meaning of the word *tamattu* in the interpretation of this verse and as to whether *mut'a* is permissible.

One century later Nasir al-Din Tusi in *Akhlaq-i Nasiri* also holds some precepts in common with Majlisi, although Tusi's injunctions are polished, urbane, and couched in a more reasonable style than those of Majlisi, which are crude and seem to promote superstition rather than morals. For instance, Tusi also holds the view that a virgin is preferable as a wife; but not, as Majlisi asserts, because her uterus is cooler and she will produce more children but because she is more malleable and can be trained as the husband wishes.[37] Tusi also warns against consulting women on important matters or confiding secrets to them or permitting them to read Surah 12: Yusuf.[38]

The precepts that do not appear to have precedents according to the Qur'an and its interpretations are those related to the manner and time of intercourse, which are said to result in tragic consequences and appear to have a more superstitious origin. Whether there were precedents for Majlisi's injunctions or not, he created a precedent himself to be followed by later *'ulama.*

In *Hilyat al-Muttaqin* Majlisi presents the image of woman as a lesser being, whose main function is childbearing and whose sexuality needs to be controlled while fulfilling that of the male. Great importance is attached in Islam to the family bond and the preservation of family unity and harmony; women are seen as a danger to that end and must be circumscribed in as many ways as possible. Due to the fact that Majlisi attributes his injunctions to the Prophet and Imams, they acquired great authority in the eyes of both men and women. This image drawn by Majlisi forms the foundation for later analysis of the position of women within Shi'ism down to the twentieth century. In earlier research on aspects of this topic, I have discussed the views of three modern Shi'i *mujtahids*: Ayatulla Shaykh Murtiza Mutahhiri (d. 1979), 'Allama Yahya Nuri (1932–), and 'Allama Sayyid Muhammad Husayn Tabataba'i (1903–82). These three *mujtahids* use different arguments and examples to reach the same conclusion as Majlisi regarding the position, role, and function of women within Shi'ism.[39] Aside from these works, it should be noted in conclusion that in the genre of *Tawzih al-Masa'il,* which continues to be written by modern *'ulama,* the influence of Majlisi can also be discerned, a subject that is well worth further study.

NOTES

1. For the high position of women within Turkic societies, see Maria Szuppe, "La participation des femmes de la famille royale à l'exercice du pouvoir in Iran Safavid au XVIe siècle," *Studia Iranica* 23 (1994): 211–58; 24 (1995): 61–122, 212–13, in which she holds not only that women were active politically but that they actually participated in battle as warriors and received war booty. 7

2. Shireen Bayani, *Zan dar 'Asr-i Mughul* (Tehran: Tehran University Press, 1973), p. 8.

3. See Szuppe, "La participation des femmes de la famille royale."

4. Charles Grey, ed. and trans., *A Narrative of Italian Travels in Persia in the Fifteenth and Sixteenth Centuries* (New York: Burt Franklin, 1873), pp. 59, 223, 173.

5. See *'Alam-ara-yi Shah Isma'il,* ed. A. Montazer-Sahib (Tehran, 1349/1970), pp. 80–81. For more on Tajlu Khanum, see Szuppe, "La participation des femmes de la famille royale," pp. 71–72.

6. Szuppe, "La participation des femmes de la famille royale," p. 65; also Anthony Jenkinson, *Early Voyages and Travels to Russia and Persia,* ed. E. Delmar Morgan and C. H. Coote (London: Haklyut Society, 1886), pp. 447–48.

7. Grey, "The Travels of a Merchant in Persia," in *A Narrative of Italian Travels in Persia in the Fifteenth and Sixteenth Centuries,* p. 173.

8. "Most Noble Vincento d'Alessandri," in ibid., p. 223.

9. Michele Membre, *Relazione di Persia* (Naples, 1967), trans. Alexander H. Morton:

Mission to the Lord Sophy of Persia (1539–1542) (London: School of Oriental and African Studies, 1993), p. 25.

10. Shohreh Gholsorkhi, "Pari Khan Khanum: A Masterful Safavid Princess," *Iranian Studies* 28 (1995): 143–56. There is a disagreement in the Persian sources as to whether she was the daughter of Shah Isma'il and therefore the sister of Shah Tahmasb or his daughter. See E. G. Browne, *A Literary History of Persia,* 4 vols. (Cambridge: University Press, 1969), 4:101–2. This confusion is due to the fact that Shah Isma'il also had a daughter called Pari Khan Khanum. For both Pari Khan Khanums, see Szuppe, "La participation des femmes de la famille royale," pp. 72–76, 79–89.

11. For more on Khayir al-Nisa Bigum, see Szuppe, "La participation des femmes de la famille royale," pp. 90–100.

12. Many examples illustrating this fact appear in Wiebke Walther, *Women in Islam* (Montclair, N.J.: Abner Schram, 1981).

13. This illustration is from one of the earliest surviving copies of Nizami's text. I am deeply indebted to Dr. Massumeh Farhad of the Freer Gallery of Art, Washington, D.C., for first guiding me toward this painting and for helping me with analysis of it.

14. The original of this miniature is in the Fogg Art Museum, Harvard University; colored reproductions can be seen in Basil Gray, *Persian Painting* (Cleveland: World Publishing Company, 1961), p. 137; and Stuart Cary Welch, *Persian Painting: Five Royal Safavid Manuscripts of the Sixteenth Century* (New York: George Braziller, 1976), p. 63. Sam Mirza was a younger son of Shah Isma'il, born in 1517. He was a prominent patron of the arts throughout his life until his imprisonment by his brother Shah Tahmasb in 1561.

15. Basil Gray disagrees with Cary Welch's attribution and considers the miniature to be the work of an unknown artist. I am indebted to Professor Welch for his help and guidance on this painting and its artist, Sultan Muhammad.

16. For more on Sultan Muhammad, see Stuart Cary Welch, "Chap. I: Sultan-Muhammad," in *The Houghton Shahnama,* ed. Martin Bernard Dickson and Stuart Cary Welch, 2 vols. (Cambridge, Mass: Harvard University Press, 1981), 1:51–86. Although it is anticipating the argument of the present essay, it should be noted that it was this Sufi spirit that was suppressed as a result of Majlisi's influence.

17. Sir John Chardin, *Travels in Persia* (1724, rpt. New York: AMS Press, 1988), pp. 215, 76, 193.

18. Muhammad Hashim Asif (Rustam al-Hukama), *Rustam al-Tavarikh,* ed. Muhammad Mushiri (Tehran, 1969), pp. 106–8.

19. A lithographic edition of *Bihar al-Anwar* was published by Haj Muhammad Hasan Amin al-Zarb (1834–98), the major entrepreneur of the period, at his own expense in twenty-two volumes and distributed freely among the public. A new edition was published recently in Iran in more than one hundred volumes. Karl-Heinz Pampus did a doctoral dissertation on Majlisi and his *Bihar,* published as *Die Theologische Enzyklopädie Bihar al-Anwar des Muhammad Baqir al-Majlisi (1037–1110 a.h. = 1627–1699 A.D.): Ein Beitrag zur Literaturgeschichte der Ši'a in der Safawidenzeit* (Bonn, 1977).

20. Browne, *A Literary History,* 4:359–60.

21. For a detailed account of Majlisi's life and works, see the introduction to Muhammad Baqir Majlisi, *Bihar al-Anwar,* vol. 13, translated into Persian by 'Ali Davani as *Mahdi Maw'ud* (Tehran: Dar al-Kutub-i Islami, 1971), pp. 1–180.

22. Vladimir Minorsky, ed. and trans., *Tadhkirat al-muluk: A Manual of Safavid Administration (circa 1137/1725),* E. J. W. Gibb Memorial Series, n.s. 16 (London: Luzac, 1943),

commentary, p. 110; also *The Encyclopaedia of Islam,* new ed., s.v. "Madjlisi" by Abdul-Hadi Ha'iri. Said Arjomand, however, disagrees with the above view that Majlisi was the first Mullabashi and contends that the *Tadhkirat al-muluk* is referring to another Muhammad Baqir who held the title later in Shah Sultan Husayn's reign. See Said Arjomand, "The Mujtahid of the Age and the Mulla-bashi," in *Authority and Political Culture in Shi'ism,* ed. Said Arjomand (Albany: State University of New York Press, 1988), pp. 80–97. For a short description of the office of Mullabashi, see *The Oxford Encyclopedia of the Modern Islamic World,* s.v. "Mullabashi" by Michel M. Mazzaoui.

23. Moojan Momen, *An Introduction to Shi'i Islam* (New Haven: Yale University Press, 1985), pp. 114–16 and 316–17.

24. *E.I.,* 2nd ed., s.v. "Madjlisi" by Abdul-Hadi Ha'iri.

25. The number of Indians in Isfahan during this period has been estimated by Chardin and others at 10,000. See Stephen Dale, *Indian Merchants and Eurasian Trade, 1600–1750* (Cambridge: Cambridge University Press, 1994), p. 67. No doubt such a large community had its own houses of worship (with Hindu idols, etc.). Apparently Shah 'Abbas was against the Indians' settling in Persia. His successor Shah Safi allowed them to stay (ibid., p. 70).

26. For similarities in the views of Majlisi and the Ayatulla Khomeini on women, see Adele K. Ferdows and Amir H. Ferdows, "Women in Shi'i Fiqh: Images through the Hadith," in *Women and Revolution in Iran,* ed. Guitty Nashat (Boulder: Westview Press, 1983), pp. 55–68.

27. Muhammad Baqir Majlisi, *Hilyat al-Muttaqin* (The Ornament of the Pious; Tehran: Markaz-i Pakhsh va Chap-i Kitab-i Salehi, n.d.).

28. *Encyclopaedia Iranica,* s.v. "Adab" by Ch. Pellat; and "Akhlaq" by G. M. Wickens.

29. Nasir al-Din Tusi, *The Nasirean Ethics,* trans. G. M. Wickens (London: George Allen and Unwin, 1964), pp. 154–84.

30. Majlisi, *Hilyat,* pp. 68–102 (hereafter cited in the text).

31. Potiphar's wife came to be known as Zulaykha, although no name is mentioned for her in the Qur'an. For a discussion of the Surah Yusuf as it appears in Islamic tradition and literature to portray female sexuality and guile, see Gayane Karen Merguerian and Afsaneh Najmabadi, "Zulaykha and Yusuf: Whose 'Best Story'?" *International Journal of Middle Eastern Studies* 29 (1997): 485–508.

32. Mahmud Katira'i, ed., *'Aqa'id al-Nisa* (Tehran: Kitabkhana Tahuri, 1349/1970). An English translation of this work has appeared: J. Atkinson, *Kulsum Nani: Customs and Manners of the Women of Persia and Their Domestic Superstitions* (London, 1832); and a French one: J. Thonnelier, *Kitabi Kulsum Naneh, ou le livre des dames de la Perse* (Paris, 1881).

33. For a detailed discussion of this work, see Kathryn Babayan, "The 'Aqa'id al-Nisa: A Glimpse at Safavid Women in Local Isfahani Culture," in *Women in the Medieval Islamic World: Power, Patronage and Piety,* ed. Gavin R. G. Hambly (New York: St. Martin's Press, 1998), pp. 349–81.

34. Ibid., p. 358.

35. Ibid.

36. This research was submitted for an M.A. in history: see Shireen Mahdavi, "Women, the 'Ulama and the State in Iran: A Study in Shi'i Ideology" (M.A. thesis, University of Utah, 1982), appendices B and C.

37. Majlisi, *Hilyat,* p. 70; Tusi, *The Nasirean Ethics,* p. 162

38. Ibid., p. 164.

39. Mahdavi, "Women, the 'Ulama and the State in Iran."

5

Anti-Ottoman Concerns and Caucasian Interests

Diplomatic Relations between Iran and Russia, 1587–1639

Rudi Matthee

INTRODUCTION

Few questions preoccupied early modern European diplomacy as intensely and persistently as what was known at the time as the Turkish threat. Sultan Mehmed II's capture of Constantinople in 1453 prompted the first organized Western reaction to the Ottoman march into the Balkans, but it was only with the second Ottoman siege of Vienna in 1683 that the tide definitively turned in favor of the coalition of European powers that had been formed to fend off the advance of the Turks. The intervening two centuries witnessed an unending series of efforts to deliver Christian Europe from the Ottoman fury—efforts that halted and ultimately succeeded in repelling the sultan's armies. Leadership in this endeavor varied, switching back and forth between a papacy keen on rekindling the Crusades; Venice, the maritime republic that forever hesitated between Christian solidarity and its own commercial interests; and Poland-Lithuania, the state that in the late seventeenth century would play an important role in the coalition that helped put a definitive halt to the Ottoman thrust into central Europe.

Much has been written on this episode in history; an extensive literature examines the struggle between the Sublime Porte and Europe's leading powers from the moment in 1453 that Pope Nicholas V called Christianity to a Crusade against the Turks until the protracted Ottoman retreat from central Europe that commenced in the late 1600s. Quite a few studies address questions pertaining to Europe's efforts to forge an anti-Ottoman alliance, focusing on the complexity of intra-European relations and its effect on these efforts or on relations between individual Western countries and the imperial court at Istanbul.[1] The existing scholarship even encompasses Romanov Russia, which, being separated from Ottoman territory by a permeable steppe frontier, was at times approached as a partner in the endeavor and participated in the Holy Alliance with the Polish-Lithuanian commonwealth and the Austro-Hungarian Empire that came into being in 1684.[2]

Attention has also been paid to European initiatives toward Iran, a country that, though remote, was potentially attractive for the West as a force that might close the *cordon sanitaire* around the Ottoman Empire by attacking the Turks from the rear.[3] In fact, it has been recognized that the very antecedents of Europe's anti-Ottoman policy involve Iran, for as early as the thirteenth century various European powers had approached the Il-Khanids, the Mongol rulers who at that time ruled on the Iranian plateau, in the hope of gaining their assistance in recapturing the holy Christian sites of Palestine from the Mamluks. In the centuries that followed, the Ottomans took over from the Mamluks as the main adversary of the Christian powers, and the Aq-quyunlus and later the Safavids replaced the Il-Khanids as potential allies of the West. Yet the stakes remained the same.

The missing link in this search for alliances remains the relationship between Iran and the Russian state, originally called Muscovy after the city that formed the nucleus of its expanding power. It is easy to see why few Western or Iranian scholars have paid much attention to this connection. Safavid chroniclers pay little heed to Iran's relationship with the world beyond the realm of Islam; and Russia, a land located in a remote northern clime and populated by people who enjoyed a rather low reputation among Iranians, shares in their aloofness. Much of the material relevant to the relationship is found in Russian archives, and the mostly Russian scholarship on the issue remains little known among non-Russian students of Iran. The massive collection of primary documents assembled and published by N. I. Veselovskii and the studies of P. P. Bushev—which draw heavily on Veselovskii's source material—in particular contain a wealth of information on Russo-Iranian political and economic relations in the Safavid period and are indispensable for anyone who wishes to gain a comprehensive picture of the diplomatic and commercial interface between these two states.[4]

The present essay draws mostly on this Russian scholarship—in addition to alternative sources such as sporadic references in the Persian chronicles, the odd merchant report, and contemporaneous observations by foreign travelers—to outline the development of Russo-Iranian contacts around the common Ottoman threat. Its particular focus is the period from the accession of Shah 'Abbas I—which marked a return to stability in Iranian domestic politics and, by extension, its relations with the outside world—to 1639, the year when Shah 'Abbas's successor, Shah Safi I, made peace with Istanbul and ceased being an active partner in the multilateral quest to encircle and isolate the Ottoman Empire. My focus here is on the nature of these contacts and on the reasons why, as far as the Safavids are concerned, they never rose above the level of rhetorical, almost ritual expressions of intent. An overview of the antecedents of the relationship precedes the actual discussion.

ANTECEDENTS

Coin hoards from Russia and as far away as Scandinavia provide evidence that commercial links between Russia and Iran go back to pre-Islamic times. The main route between the two had always been the fluvial Volga route and the Caspian Sea basin, where merchants would either follow the western littoral or (at least until the thirteenth century) avoid bandit-infested Daghistan by crossing the sea itself between the northern ports and Darband, traditionally the point of entry into Iran.[5] Over time, the interaction between the two lands followed a certain rhythm according to stability and prosperity or political unrest and economic crisis in either the north or the south, all of which was predicated on the existence or absence of viable political and commercial centers at either end and a modicum of safety en route. Thus the heyday of the Khazar state in the eighth and ninth centuries saw a certain degree of commercial activity between Rus' and the Middle East. The same is true for the emergence of the Kievan Empire in the tenth century and the rise of the Vladimir-Suzdal' state a hundred years later.[6] The Mongol invasion of Vladimir-Suzdalia and the eastern half of the Middle East in the 1300s destroyed much of this trading link, though the subsequent consolidation of Il-Khanid rule in Iran and that of the Golden Horde in northeastern Rus' created a relatively stable environment conducive to a resumption of trading activities.

It was only with the decline of the Golden Horde and the rise of Muscovy as an independent and expansionist city-state as of the early fourteenth century that a lasting revival of trade between Russia and Iran was made possible. By the early 1500s Moscow's influence reached far enough south into the Don basin to lead to direct contacts with the Ottoman state, which by that time had extended its control to the northern shores of the Black Sea, reducing the Crimean Tatars to vassalage in 1475. Commercial relations along the River Don as far as the Sea of Azov dominated the contacts between Moscow and the ean Tatars. Until 1521, when the Crimean Tatars attacked Moscow, these contacts were based on the mutual benefit flowing from the assistance given by the khanate in Russia's struggle against the remnants of the Golden Horde as well as from the free passage granted by the Tatars to Russian caravans in exchange for the payment of protection costs.[7] The Crimean Tatars operated in a mediating role as well. Thus, in the first diplomatic contacts between Moscow and the Sublime Porte in 1492, Mengli-Giray Khan (the ruler of the Crimean Tatars and at that point a vassal of the Ottomans) seems to have acted as representative and go-between for Tsar Ivan III.[8]

Contacts between Russia and the various post–Il-Khanid principalities that ruled over parts of Iran were sporadic at this time and appear to have concerned mostly commercial matters. Russian envoys visited Timurid Herat in 1464–65, while in the latter year an envoy called Hasan Beg appeared in Moscow as the representative of Farrukh Yasar, the ruler of Shamakhi and Baku. Tsar Ivan III in turn dispatched an envoy by the name of Papin to Shamakhi. Yet these contacts were incidental, and their true import was most likely the exchange of trade commodities.[9] Two obstacles stood in the way of closer and more sustained diplomatic relations: the vast stretch of unpacified territory subject to a punishing climate separating the lands under Moscow's jurisdiction from the world of Islam; and the fact that, in the aftermath of the turmoil caused by Timur's campaigns at the turn of the fifteenth century, conditions in Iran long remained little conducive to sustained political and commercial contact with the outside world. Both circumstances were to change in the course of the sixteenth century. Iran, coalescing around a clearly defined political center, at this time entered a new period of relative stability. Russia, meanwhile, extended her dominion southward by incorporating the Muslim khanates of Kazan and Astrakhan.

In Iran the foundations were laid for a viable and enduring center of authority with the rise of Shah Isma'il as a warrior-king keen to extend his realm beyond Tabriz, where he had proclaimed his sovereignty in 1501. Within a short period Shah Isma'il managed to conquer large parts of western and central Iran, building a reputation as an intrepid leader whose fame reached far beyond the borders of his realm. Upon the shah's death in 1524, the throne passed to his son Tahmasb. Shah Tahmasb I (r. 1524–76) first had to contend with a serious tribal challenge to his authority that almost overwhelmed him. Emerging victorious from this power struggle, he ended up reigning for over half a century and during that period succeeded in consolidating and strengthening the legitimacy of the dynasty and its territorial claims.

Russia, meanwhile, was in the process of broadening her power and influence as well. Muscovy had long been part of a triangular relationship with Kazan and the Crimean Tatars that was aimed at a common enemy, the Golden

Horde. This alliance did not, however, prevent each of these parties fr boring its own expansionist dreams. Vulnerable because negative, the c broke up as soon as the Golden Horde ceased to be a common threat by submitting to Mengli-Giray, the ruler of the Crimean Tatars.[10] In 1521 he attacked Moscow, forcing the Russians to reassess their strategic interests and to seek assistance from the khanate of Astrakhan, situated north of the Caspian Sea at the mouth of the Volga. Muscovy's annexation of the city-states of Kazan and Astrakhan provided a stepping-stone for a further southward thrust.

The first diplomatic contact between Safavid Iran and the rulers of Muscovy appears to have taken place in 1521, when an Iranian envoy visited Tsar Vasilii III (r. 1505–33) on behalf of Shah Isma'il. Unfortunately, nothing more is known about this encounter, and no more envoys seem to have been exchanged during the reign of Shah Isma'il.[11] It is quite conceivable, however, that part of this envoy's mandate was to probe Moscow's willingness to join ranks against the Ottomans. After all, following his defeat against the Ottomans on the battlefield of Chaldiran, Shah Isma'il had approached Western rulers with similar intentions.[12] Information about Shah Tahmasb's contract with Russia is equally scanty. In 1552 he sent an emissary named Sayyid Husayn to Moscow with the intent of establishing diplomatic relations with the Russians.[13] Other envoys traveled back and forth between Iran and Russia in this period as well, though on the Iranian side most of these represented the semi-autonomous regions of Shirvan and Gilan rather than the central Safavid state. Commercial relations are likely to have been central to such contacts. In 1544, for instance, Alqas Mirza, the brother of Shah Tahmasb and the *beglerbeg* (governor) of Shirvan, petitioned Tsar Ivan IV for a renewal of the privileges of Armenian merchants with respect to their trading activities in Russia.[14] The ruler of Shamakhi in 1554 sent representatives to Moscow to request a revival of the old Armenian trade.[15] The envoy who visited Moscow in 1562 probably represented Shirvan as well.[16] And the emissary who entered Moscow in late 1563 had been dispatched by the *beglerbeg* of Shamakhi.[17]

In the aftermath of Muscovy's annexation of Kazan and Astrakhan, the Caucasus and by extension Iran became more accessible for merchants and diplomats coming from the north. The results are seen in the various expeditions undertaken shortly thereafter by the English Muscovy Company, an enterprise established with the purpose of opening up a trade route to Iran and India via Russia that undertook a series of commercial expeditions to the Safavid state between 1550 and 1580.[18] Yet commercial and diplomatic traffic continued to face huge obstacles. Primitive circumstances, a lack of safety, and the forbidding climate of the south Russian steppes often made the route impracticable, as a result of which the exchange of wares remained limited. Rus' offered leather, fur, and metal wares, while Iran furnished precious cloth and silk. Caravans, usually equipped by Armenians, were forced to travel in great number and accompanied by armed convoy and even then were exposed to attacks by bandits.[19]

THE BEGINNING OF ANTI-OTTOMAN ALLIANCES

As stated earlier, Russo-Iranian diplomatic contacts in the Safavid period built on long-standing efforts by the Christian powers of Europe, including the papacy, to enlist Iran in their struggle against the Ottomans. In fact, these efforts go back as far as the Crusades and the quest of the Christian states participating in them to find eastern allies ready to join in the battle against the forces of Islam. The same quest had motivated the contacts between European courts and the Il-Khanid rulers of Iran, which lasted until the latter converted to Islam. The phenomenal rise of Timur Gurgan at the turn of the fifteenth century had given rise to similar expectations, though by that time the targeted enemy was no longer the Mamluk state but the upstart Ottomans, whose defeat of the Crusaders at Nicopolis in 1396 raised the specter of an unchecked Muslim advance into south-central Europe. Timur's rout of the Turks at Ankara in 1402 brought temporary relief, rekindling hopes among European rulers of joint action against the Ottomans.[20]

The fall of Constantinople in 1453, though it dealt a severe blow to Christian morale, also revived the Crusader spirit, prompting the pope to call for a combined reconquest of the capital of Eastern Christianity and the liberation of the Holy Sepulcher in Jerusalem.[21] This led to a series of contacts between Europe and the Aq-quyunlu ruler Uzun Hasan (r. 1453–78), the only remaining eastern ruler of consequence to be approached after the fall of the Christian enclave of Trebizond (Trabzon) in 1461.[22] Several missions went back and forth between Tabriz, the Aq-quyunlu capital, on the one hand, and Venice and to a lesser extent Rome, on the other. When Uzun Hasan requested weapons, it briefly looked as if these contacts might bear fruit in spite of the complications involved in transporting armaments by sea. Yet Venetian opportunism quickly doomed the enterprise. Though the Venetians knew themselves threatened by the Ottoman march into central Europe, they also realized that Istanbul held the key to the lucrative Levant trade. The Serenissima therefore reacted halfheartedly to the initiatives and in 1479 eventually bowed to a Turkish peace proposal.[23]

A new round in relations between Europe and Iran was launched with the establishment of Safavid power in 1501. Shah Isma'il's fame as a ruler able and willing to take on the Turks soon grew to mythical proportions among Europeans, who, desperate for relief from the Turkish scourge, were eager to believe the inflated stories of a superhuman warrior coming out of the East. Isma'il was thus quickly incorporated into the new crusading project that was launched by Pope Leo X in 1517.[24] In fact, at that point Safavid interests paralleled those of the Christian West, for Shah Isma'il, bruised by his defeat by the Ottomans at Chaldiran in 1514, was keen to find allies as well. Missions were again exchanged (mostly with Rome, which had begun to overshadow the declining Venetian republic), but little was achieved. Nor were the diplomatic exchanges between Shah Tahmasb and the Emperor Charles V any more fruitful. The Ottomans, after all, were not Iran's only concern; the Safavids also had to include in their strategic considerations their eastern neighbors, the Uzbegs, who maintained diplomatic contacts with the Ottomans that were partly directed against the Safavid state. In 1530 Tahmasb, mindful of the dangers of having to fight on two fronts at once, made peace with the sultan before waging war against the Uzbegs. This naturally diminished the chances of an alliance between Iran and the European powers.[25]

Moscow had been part of the western efforts to form a coalition against Istanbul since 1497, when it had formed an anti-Ottoman alliance with Moldova, Hungary, and Poland.[26] Further contacts between Russia and states such as France, the Habsburg Empire, and Spain took place during the reign of the Habsburg emperor Charles V.[27] These did not immediately generate communications between the tsar and the shah over the same issue. Russia had her own agenda, and the Ottomans were hardly at the top of it. Thus, when Muscovy dispatched envoys to Uzun Hasan, it was not with the intent of finding common ground against the Ottomans so much as to seek assistance against the Golden Horde.[28] Shah Isma'il engaged in diplomatic traffic with western European states and (as seen earlier) also approached Russia. Though receptive to European overtures, especially after his defeat at Chaldiran, the Safavid ruler was prevented from pursuing too close a bond by the strategic dilemma that the Safavids would face until the mid-seventeenth century: a need to balance Ottoman and Uzbeg threats. More serious contacts, including contacts with Russia, took place in the reign of Shah Tahmasb, when the Ottomans repeatedly invaded Azerbayjan and Shirvan. The Ottoman attempt to take both provinces was no doubt the direct reason for the shah to send envoys to Moscow. But Shah Tahmasb, too, proved reluctant to antagonize the Ottomans by openly allying himself with a third party, especially after concluding the Peace of Amasya with Istanbul in 1555.

The role played by the Golden Horde in Russia's strategic considerations suggests how misleading it would be to regard the triangular relationship of Europe, Russia, and Iran as it emerged after 1550 as a simple configuration aimed at a common enemy. To be sure, the expansionist policy of especially the

Russians in the Black Sea zone would eventually lead to a clash between the two, but not until the late seventeenth century.[29] Until that time, they occasionally encroached upon each other's spheres of influence, such as happened in the 1560s, when Sultan Selim II launched a campaign against the eastern Caucasus and Astrakhan, blocking the transit route to Iran by occupying the western littoral of the Caspian between Baku and Darband.[30]

Yet the ambivalent position of Moscow in the international geopolitical balance of power renders its relationship with Istanbul a good deal more complex than a simple antagonism pointing to Russia's inevitable incorporation into an alliance with western Europe that would also include Iran. First and foremost, Europe's desire to include Russia in such a coalition was at variance with that country's reputation as a primitive and barbarian realm—a reputation that earned it the nickname of "Alter-Turca" in western Europe.[31] Second, the Russians considered the Ottomans far less threatening than the Poles or, for that matter, the Crimean Tatars, who as late as 1571 marched on Moscow and torched the city. Indeed, Moscow saw the Ottomans as potential allies in its struggle against those two enemies, and the Russians naturally were reluctant to give up good or at least working relations with Istanbul in exchange for vague promises from either western Europe or Iran. During the entire subsequent episode, Russia, while increasingly willing to entertain anti-Ottoman proposals, left the door open for initiatives from the sultan and never ceased to exchange embassies with the Sublime Porte.[32]

The aggression of the Crimean Tatars and heavy losses in its wars against Poland and Sweden in the early 1570s must have motivated Moscow to keep its options with Istanbul open. Yet the simultaneous Ottoman thrust toward the Caspian Sea and beyond it, toward Central Asia, probably made the Russians realize the fragility of relations with the Porte. When the Ottomans launched a direct attack in 1569 against Astrakhan, by then a rising commercial emporium serving international trade, Tsar Ivan IV understandably turned to Iran, a country that had long felt threatened by Turkish expansionism. The first mission he sent to Qazvin was clearly designed to underscore the importance Russia attached to opening relations, for it carried a number of German-made cannons, varyingly reported as 30 and 100, 500 arquebuses, and 4,000 muskets, all items that were in great demand in the Safavid realm.[33]

Shah Tahmasb, bound by the Treaty of Amasya and reluctant to antagonize the Ottomans, did not take advantage of this and other opportunities to join an anti-Turkish alliance. He thus declined a Venetian proposal to that effect in 1571, and until the end of his reign Iran and the Ottoman Empire would coexist in peace. It was under his successor, Shah Khudabandah, whose accession in 1576 was shortly followed by an outbreak of yet another round in the Safavid-Ottoman wars, that Iran's policy underwent a change. Following a Russian decision in 1586 not to enter into joint military action with the Ottomans against Iran, Khudabandah—buffeted by the loss of Azerbayjan, including Tabriz, and large tracts of Shirvan stretching as far as the Caspian Sea—sent the first official and full-fledged Safavid diplomatic mission to Moscow. Its leader, Hadi Beg, is said to have suggested an anti-Ottoman alliance, promising the Russians sovereignty over Baku and Darband, even if the shah himself would recapture these cities from the Ottomans.[34]

That promise reflects the fact that in this period relations between Iran and Russia were increasingly influenced by developments in the Caucasus. Russia's offensive against Astrakhan in the mid-sixteenth century was soon followed by a further penetration of the lands between the Black and Caspian seas. In an attempt to extend her power farther into the Caucasus, Russia entered a mountainous region inhabited by a bewildering variety of mostly tribal peoples who often engaged in plundering raids against each other's territory. Further complicating the instability caused by regional conflict was the geopolitical status of the Caucasus as a frontier region where the territorial claims of adjoining powers—Safavids, Ottomans, and eventually the Russians as well—collided. Safavid claims to Georgia went back to 1521, when a Qizilbash regiment entered the eastern region of Kakhet'i and plundered the towns of Zagam and Giram, forcing King Levan (Lavand Khan) to submit to the authority of Shah Isma'il.[35] Shah Tahmasb's expedition against Georgia in 1540 caused a great deal of destruction and formed the prelude to further campaigns and a more lasting Safavid presence in the region. The Ottoman defeat of a combined Georgian army a few years later enabled Istanbul to extend its influence over Imeret'i, the western half of Georgia.

As for the Russians, they were initially drawn into the area in part because various (especially Christian) groups living there approached them, seeking protection against aggressive neighbors and expansionist outsiders. The Daghistanis in 1567 sent an envoy to Moscow to request help against the Kabardians and the Crimean Tatars.[36] It was a Kabardian request for protection against the Ottomans and their vassals, the Crimean Tatars, that led to the building of a Russian fortress on the confluence of the Terek and Sunzha rivers, the first of what would become a string of strongholds on this segment of Russia's southern frontier. And it was the building of that fortress that gave the Ottomans the excuse to invade the area and attack Astrakhan in 1569, thus prompting the local rulers to draw even closer to the Russians as potential protectors against hostile neighbors and encroaching outside forces.[37]

For the time being, however, the Russians were in no position to give their full attention to the south, preoccupied as they were with a protracted struggle with Poland and Sweden over domination of the Baltic region. Only the (temporary) conclusion of the Livonian War in 1583 and a succession crisis in the khanate of the Crimean Tatars enabled Tsar Feodor, who in 1584 succeeded Ivan IV, to turn his attention southward again. Ever since the outbreak of a new Ottoman-Safavid war in 1578, large parts of the Caucasus had fallen to the Ottomans. In 1583–84 Osman Pasha's armies had taken control of Shirvan in addition to Daghistan and Georgia; and in 1588–89 their domination would extend to Ganja in Qarabagh and Nakhjavan in Armenia. In the process the Ottomans had destroyed the fort that the Russians had constructed at the mouth of the Terek River. The Russians reacted to these developments by establishing diplomatic and commercial relations with Kakhet'i, the richest part of Georgia (which had not fallen under direct Ottoman domination and which managed to balance both outside powers), and by building new fortifications in the Caucasus.[38] Moscow was now ready to resume relations with the Safavid state as well as with the khanates of Central Asia.[39] This reorientation coincided with the coming to power of Shah 'Abbas I in Iran.

RELATIONS UNDER SHAH 'ABBAS I

The Russian reaction to Shah Khudabandah's dispatch of the Hadi Beg mission was swift. Iran's promise with regard to Baku and Darband, which in any case was of little weight since it had only been transmitted orally, did not elicit the enthusiastic Russian response and commitment to assistance that the Iranians may have hoped for. Yet Moscow did reciprocate, for Hadi Beg returned to Iran accompanied by a Russian envoy named Grigorii Borisovich Vasil'chikov. We know precious little about this mission; but since it concerned a so-called light delegation, intelligence gathering and, perhaps, official or "royal" trade are likely to have been its main task. Vasil'chikov no doubt also was to probe the chance of continuing friendly relations with Iran, in addition to requesting more details about the promises with regard to Darband and Baku.[40]

Regardless of Tsar Feodor's motives for dispatching Vasil'chikov to Iran, circumstances had changed since the accession of Shah 'Abbas. His extensive military campaigning brought the new Safavid ruler face to face with a series of adversaries and the constant risk of having to fight simultaneously on two fronts against his most formidable external enemies, the Ottomans and the Uzbegs. He therefore naturally searched for ways to be relieved on either front and in the end resolved to conclude a temporary peace with his western neighbors in order to have the time and opportunity to take on the Uzbegs as well as to engage in pressing domestic reforms. This must have been the nature of his dealings with the Ottoman embassy that stayed in Iran while Vasil'chikov was awaiting the shah's return from Khurasan. Seeking an accommodation with the Ottomans was also the aim of the mission that Shah 'Abbas sent to Istanbul later in 1589.[41] This priority of concerns explains why the shah was not in a particular rush to meet Hadi Beg and Vasil'chikov and only received them after his return from Khurasan in April 1589.[42]

The missions that Shah 'Abbas dispatched to Moscow and Istanbul in 1589 (Budaq Beg and Hadi Beg went north, while Mihdi-quli Khan, the governor of Ardabil, headed west) further reflect the difference in the importance that 'Abbas attached to relations with Russia and the Ottoman Empire, respectively. Whereas Budaq Beg and Hadi Beg set out for Moscow accompanied by a mere thirty-six men (including a separate contingent from Gilan) and without a mandate, the mission going to Istanbul consisted of one thousand persons.[43] Of course, this discrepancy illustrates the inherently greater weight and significance that Safavid rulers tended to accord to the Ottoman state, both as a neighboring empire and a Muslim realm and as Iran's most formidable adversary. Yet it also suggests that the shah, unwilling to jeopardize a pending agreement with the Ottomans, had no obvious plans to join the Russians in an alliance. The letter presented in Moscow on behalf of Shah 'Abbas expressed a generic desire for cordial and firm relations; and Hadi Beg and Budaq Beg spoke of a military alliance only in the vaguest of terms, thus dispelling any illusions about concrete plans in that direction. The reiteration of the previously made commitment with regard to the cession of Baku and Darband, also stated in the letter, suggests an attempt to create a rift between the Russians and the Ottomans (who were, after all, still in possession of those two cities) while appearing amenable to the Russians.[44] The same design is reflected in the apparent approval given to the construction of a number of Russian fortresses south of the Terek and Koisu rivers.[45] The only other result of the mission—the expression of a Russian desire to improve economic relations—must have pleased above all the separate delegation from Gilan, whose main task it was to complain about the poor treatment of Iranian merchants in Astrakhan.[46]

Shah 'Abbas continued his policy of disinformation with the so-called Kay mission, which set out for Moscow in 1591.[47] Through this mission he reiterated his previously made proposal to form a military alliance, in spite of the fact that he had just made peace with the Ottomans. In reality, the shah did not intend to jeopardize the peace, which, though humiliating, gave the Safavid army a free hand against the Uzbegs. Nor were the Russians deceived by this policy, having known about a pending Ottoman-Safavid accord since 1589. The tsar was clearly not interested in peaceful relations between the Safavids and the Ottomans, fearing that the Ottomans might be tempted to use Cossack incursions into the Azov region as an excuse to threaten Russia with an attack by their proxies, the Crimean Tatars.[48] In a show of their dissatisfaction with the direction of Shah 'Abbas's policy, the Russians returned the presents brought by the Iranian envoy. Simultaneously, Moscow prodded

Istanbul to keep the Cossacks in check. Moreover, its relations with Poland having taken center stage, Moscow even gauged the sultan's interest in forming a joint anti-Polish alliance. That strategy would remain an abiding factor in Russia's foreign policy, even if it failed against the Ottoman condition that it give up Kazan and Astrakhan in return.[49]

The Russians reacted with the same reluctance to the next Iranian mission, led by Hajji Khusraw. Shah 'Abbas, buffeted by losses against the Uzbegs, had dispatched the Hajji Khusraw mission to Moscow in 1592, even before the return of the Kay mission. Awaiting the results of talks with the Habsburg ruler, Rudolph II, with regard to the formation of an anti-Ottoman coalition, the Russian tsar was not in a rush to receive Hajji Khusraw.[50] It was Hajji Khusraw's task to communicate Shah 'Abbas's conquest of Gilan to the Russians, but commercial motives seem to have prevailed. He was charged with buying weaponry in Russia; as a result of the talks he conducted, the Russians granted toll freedom to the goods that were imported into their country under the shah's auspices. Once again 'Abbas did not await the return of the envoy before he sent yet another mission to Russia, this one led by Hajji Iskandar, the first Safavid state merchant to travel north.[51] Neither Hajji Khusraw nor Hajji Iskandar achieved much in the way of closer political relations; obviously, little common ground for this existed. For the time being, Iran and Russia would concentrate on maintaining and strengthening their commercial relations.

At this point, Iran's preoccupation with Russia's expansionism in the Caucasus region moved into the foreground as a complicating factor and an additional obstacle to closer relations between the two states. This development had its origins in the turbulent state of the Caucasus, where especially the fiery tribes inhabiting Daghistan frequently launched incursions into the territory of surrounding peoples. Matters were further complicated by the fact that, with the Russian penetration and the Ottoman expedition against Astrakhan in 1569 and their subsequent occupation of Azerbayjan and parts of Georgia a decade later, the area had become fiercely contested by Ottomans, Safavids, and Russians. As noted earlier, a number of local khanates in the Caucasus turned to Moscow to seek protection against the Ottomans, the Crimean Tatars, and the Daghistani tribes. Over time, the Russians more and more sided with the rulers of Kakhet'i, acting as the overlords of this Georgian kingdom. In 1587, as King Alexander of Kakhet'i and his sons decided to seek protection against the Qumuqs of Daghistan by declaring themselves vassals of the Russian tsar, the Russians announced that they would build a fortress on the River Terek for Georgia's safety. In the next five years Russian armies went to war several times, routing the Kabardians and briefly occupying Tarkhu, the residence of the *shamkhal,* the Qumuq ruler. In the process the Russians built new fortresses on the Sunzha and Koisu rivers.[52]

As long as Shah 'Abbas was preoccupied with his wars against the Ottomans and the Uzbegs and engaged in his internal administrative and military reforms, he was forced to acquiesce to Russia's activities in and on behalf of Kakhet'i and in particular the ongoing building of Russian fortresses on the Caucasian frontier. After 1590, however, as he made peace with the Ottomans and his domestic power and authority became more firmly established, Russia's southern forays became one of Shah 'Abbas's direct preoccupations. Iran's subsequent diplomatic missions to Moscow reflect this. A Russian expedition against Daghistan in 1593 prompted Shah 'Abbas to dispatch Hadi Beg to Moscow once again, charging him with finding ways to prevent the Russians from encroaching further on the Caucasus.[53] Mindful of the possibility that Iran might need Russian support in a future conflict with the Ottomans, however, the Safavid ruler decided to move cautiously in his resistance to Russian claims on Daghistan and other parts of the Caucasus that were still tied to Iran in a tributary relationship.[54]

As it was, 'Abbas did not have immediate plans to resume war with the Ottomans. For the time being, his time and energy were absorbed by his struggle against his domestic enemies, the Qizilbash tribes, and his continuing confrontation with the Uzbegs. The Russians, meanwhile, having been rebuffed by the Ottomans, were seeking a rapprochement with Iran. An embassy led by Andrei Dmitrievich Zvenigorodskii arrived in Iran in 1594 with the task of exhorting the Safavids to move against the Ottomans (as well as the Uzbegs). The timing was auspicious, for at the same time Shah 'Abbas was about to conclude an anti-Ottoman alliance with Simon I, the ruler of Kartli (the Georgian principality adjacent to Kakhet'i), and Alexander II, the ruler of Kakhet'i.[55] Zvenigorodskii and his men were well received in Qazvin; and during the Nawruz festivities of 1595, when the shah celebrated his recent victories against the Uzbegs, they were paraded in full view of the Ottoman and Bukharan merchants present in town to show Iran's rivals that she had important allies.[56] During the audience granted on the occasion of the New Year, the shah brought up the issue of the *shamkhal,* asking the Russians not to wage war on this vassal of the Iranians but to turn their armed forces against the Ottomans who were still occupying Shirvan. As a way of encouraging the Russians to assist him in ousting the Ottomans from that region, the shah reiterated his promise of Darband and Baku should the Russians wrest those towns from the Ottomans.[57] This seems to have been little more than rhetoric, however; and though well treated at the Safavid court, Zvenigorodskii returned without any commitment on the part of the Safavid ruler.

Things deteriorated from there. The next Russian mission, which was sent to Iran in 1595 to explore the shah's position on the Ottoman question and Russia's expansionism, was rather coolly received at the Safavid court. Vasilii

Portrait of a Russian ambassador, reign of Shah 'Abbas I. This envoy has been identified as Andrei Dmitrievich Zvenigorodskii by Adel T. Adamova ("Persian Portraits of the Russian Ambassadors," in Sheila R. Canby, ed., *Safavid Art and Architecture* [London: British Museum Press, 2002], pp. 49–53.) Topkapi Palace Museum, Istanbul. *Muraqqa'* H. 2155, fol. 19b.

Vasil'evich Tiufiakin, who headed south in 1597 in the company of Imam Quli Beg, a commercial agent whom the shah had previously sent to Russia, was the next envoy to try to convince Iran's ruler of the need to join the Russians in their struggle against the Ottomans.[58] His mission met a tragic end, for Tiufiakin himself died before reaching Iran; his successor, Emel'ianov, succumbed to the plague in Gilan; and a third leader, Dubrovskii, perished in Iran as well.[59] The rather uncivil manner in which Shah 'Abbas treated the surviving members of the mission bespeaks the general Iranian contempt for Russians—people they thought boorish and primitive—but no doubt also reflects the Safavid ruler's lack of interest in Russia as an ally by that time.[60]

Shah 'Abbas responded to the hapless Tiufiakin mission by sending the Pir Quli Beg delegation to Moscow in 1599. Pir Quli Beg did not command a full-fledged diplomatic mission. Trade, so often the raison d'être of official relations between early modern courts, seems to have been its most important rationale, judging by the fact that he was accompanied by a number of merchants who carried precious cloth with them.[61] Though its members appear to have misbehaved rather badly while in Russia, they were nevertheless treated quite cordially by that country's authorities.[62] Bushev plausibly sees the indulgence of the Russians and the tolerance with which they met the many demands of the Iranians as a sign that Moscow was keen on forging an anti-Ottoman coalition with Shah 'Abbas.[63]

By this time a clear asymmetry had developed in the energy with which the two states pursued their contacts. How much the Iranians and Russians differed in the importance they attached to the formation of an anti-Ottoman coalition becomes abundantly clear from the way in which the regent Boris Godunov responded to the rather insignificant Pir Quli Beg mission following his accession as tsar in 1600. The head of the mission that headed south in that year to explain Russia's behavior and designs in the Caucasus and to suggest the formation of a military mission with Iran, Prince Alexander Zhirov-Zasiekin, is called *veliko-posol'* (great envoy) in the Russian sources. Apparently still hopeful that Iran might provide real military assistance, the tsar instructed Zhirov-Zasiekin to act cautiously with regard to Russian claims on the Caucasus.[64] Shah 'Abbas, meanwhile, having concluded his Uzbeg campaigns, was little inclined to consider the Russian proposal, which was in part intended against the Uzbegs, whom the Russians considered a growing military threat. According to the Safavid court chronicler Mulla Jalal Munajjim, the Russian envoy implored the shah to grant him the favor of the *pa-bus* (the foot kiss) but was even denied the *zamin-bus* (the ground kiss).[65] The shah's renewed plans for a confrontation with the Ottomans did not translate into a changed position vis-à-vis the Russians; they merely prompted him to intensify his strategy of trying to convince Moscow that an alliance was still among the possibilities.

In 1603, shortly before the outbreak of the new Safavid-Ottoman conflict, Shah 'Abbas dispatched a new mission, headed by Lachin Beg, to Moscow. Its mandate did not include a joint military strategy but merely a discussion of Russian military action in the Caucasus with the aim of indirectly weakening the Ottomans.[66]

At this point Shah 'Abbas had other reasons to distance himself from Moscow, despite the outbreak of yet another round in the war with the Ottomans. For one thing, Russia now seemed less keen on cultivating closer relations with Iran, perhaps because Russian leaders now envisioned a wider European coalition against the Ottomans.[67] Rather more important was the fact that Russia by that time had fallen victim to a period of widespread internal chaos, manifested in unstable leadership and loss of control over outlying areas in revolt. This so-called Time of Troubles (1598–1613) severely diminished the country's status as a credible military partner—and a potential threat—for Iran. To be sure, the Russians did not cease to interfere in Caucasian affairs in this period. In 1604–5, for instance, they attacked Daghistan in an attempt to avenge their earlier defeats by the Qumuqs, though they justified their campaign as a defense of Kakhet'i (which had suffered an invasion by the Daghistanis the year before). The Russians did little to resist Shah 'Abbas's own expansionism in this period, however; and even when the shah attempted to strengthen his hold on Kakhet'i, their reaction was rather muted. In the same years in which the Russians took on Daghistan, the Safavid armies recaptured Azerbayjan and Armenia from the Ottomans. Shah 'Abbas next engineered the death of King Alexander of Kakhet'i through Alexander's son Constantin, a renegade living in Iran as a hostage. This was ostensibly a way of punishing the Georgians for their suspected pro-Ottoman leanings and for having established diplomatic relations with Tsar Boris Godunov; but in reality the shah's aim was to put his own protégé on the Georgian throne.[68]

The shah's subsequent expeditions into Transcaucasia led to the eviction of the Ottomans from Kartli, parts of Kakhet'i, and Shirvan. In the process the shah took the cities of Ganja, Baku, Darband, and eventually Shamakhi, ordering Zu'l Fiqar Khan, the newly appointed ruler of Shirvan, to build defensive fortresses on the border between Tabarsaran and Daghistan.[69] All the while the Safavid ruler merely sought guarantees that the Russians would not form a threat to his northern borders.[70] As it was, Iran's annexation of these cities and regions elicited but a faint Russian response. Moscow did dispatch an embassy to Isfahan to convey its displeasure with the course of events as well as to affirm that the Russians considered the *shamkhal* their vassal. The tsar's reaction to these conquests never reached Iran, however, since the mission's leader, Ivan Petrovich Romodanovskii, perished en route.[71] Instead of continuing to seek Russian partnership, the Safavid ruler now turned to western

Europe, which at the same time began to show an active interest in Iran as a potential ally in its anti-Ottoman strategy. In 1603–4 Shah 'Abbas sent six to seven missions to various European courts, requesting military assistance and implying that, in exchange, he would be willing to entertain a diversion of Iran's silk trade from the Levant route to the maritime route around the Cape of Good Hope.[72]

As a result, the period between 1604 and 1613 witnessed relatively little interaction between Isfahan and Moscow. It did not help that, as a result of the unsettled state of Russia, the connecting route was frequently made impassible by bandits and rebels—so much so in fact that the road north of the Caspian Sea became temporarily blocked at this time.[73] Even the Peace of Sitva Torok between the Habsburg Empire and the Ottomans in 1606 was unable to alter this situation, though it raised fears in Iran about a new Ottoman offensive, causing the shah to launch a new search for potential allies. Following the rapprochement between the Austrians and the Ottomans, Shah 'Abbas sent several missions to Moscow, in part to gauge Russia's interest in assisting in his struggle against the Ottomans, in part to gain information on the troubled state of the country after the death of Boris Godunov. Sayyid 'Azim headed north in 1606, just after the shah had taken Ganja following a long and arduous siege. The inclusion in his mandate of a suggestion to form a military union against the Ottomans may be explained by the length and difficulty of that siege, which must have convinced the shah that it would not be easy to fully oust his enemies from Shirvan and Daghistan. As Bushev surmises, the shah may also have been prompted momentarily to seek Russian assistance by his knowledge of the ongoing peace talks between the Austrians and the Ottomans—talks that would lead to the Peace of Sitva Torok in late 1606.[74]

Sayyid 'Azim's mission did not achieve its goal, however. Neither did that of Mujib Beg, who set out for Russia the following year (carrying with him the news that the shah had taken Shamakhi on June 25, 1607) and would only return to Iran in 1613.[75] Something similar happened to yet another Safavid envoy, Amir 'Ali Beg, who was dispatched in 1608 to gather intelligence about political conditions in Russia as well as to resume ties with Moscow. Owing to the turmoil in Russia, it was only in 1613 that he was able to hand his letters to the newly acceded tsar, Mikhail Romanov. The Cossack occupation of Astrakhan forced Amir 'Ali Beg's mission to travel via Khiva and Khurasan on the way back to Iran, where the delegates arrived six years after their departure.[76] In early 1611, finally, Shah 'Abbas commissioned the Carmelite friar John Thaddeus to journey to the tsar of Russia, the king of Poland, and the pope and to propose the diversion of Iran's silk and carpet trade via the northern route. The mission never even made it to Russia; for upon arrival in Astrakhan, its members were taken prisoner by the Cossacks who held the town. After much effort, the Iranians managed to secure their release three years later. Shah 'Abbas never sent Thaddeus back to Moscow, possibly because he had made peace with the Ottomans shortly after the envoy's first departure in 1611.[77]

It was only the return of order and stability in Russia, symbolized by the accession of the Romanov dynasty in 1613, that allowed a resumption of diplomatic and commercial traffic between the two countries. By that time Shah 'Abbas had concluded a peace treaty with the Ottomans (November 20, 1612) that stipulated Iran's neutrality in Ottoman dealings with Russia.[78] The first Russian mission to make its way to Iran following the Time of Troubles was that of Mikhail Tikhanov. Sent to Isfahan in 1614 to inform the shah of the enthronement of Tsar Mikhail Romanov, Tikhanov was also charged with the task of finding a solution for the problem of the Cossacks who continued to occupy Astrakhan and trying to reestablish diplomatic and commercial relations with the Safavid state. In receiving Tikhanov, Shah 'Abbas displayed little of his usual diplomatic charm. As if to show his contempt for the impoverished Russian state, he welcomed the tsar's envoy, whose meager presents reflected Russia's financial plight and were accordingly deemed unworthy of a Safavid ruler, in a most undiplomatic manner—and, adding insult to injury, in the company of an envoy representing the very same Cossacks whose aggression had been the main reason for the Russian mission.[79] In the negotiations that followed, Shah 'Abbas applied his habitual strategy: while demanding that Moscow safeguard Iran's northern border against Ottoman aggression, he made vague promises about financial and military assistance. With Astrakhan still occupied, Tikhanov (like Amir 'Ali Beg before him) was forced to follow the eastern littoral of the Caspian Sea on his return to Russia.[80]

The Tikhanov mission was followed by embassies headed by Shahmatov in 1615–16 and Leont'ev in 1616–17, respectively. Their request for financial assistance and the circumspection with which they raised the issue of Georgia and the savage campaign that Shah 'Abbas had conducted there can only be interpreted as a reflection of Russia's continued weakness.[81] It is therefore not surprising that the various Safavid missions that headed north between 1614 and 1617 exhibited little spontaneity or energy. One of those was that of Hajji Murtaza, who went north at the same time that Tikhanov set out for Iran. Hajji Murtaza's mission was typical of diplomatic exchange at the time in being concerned with trade as much as with politics. In fact, the commercial task of this personal merchant of Shah 'Abbas—who brought a quantity of silk with him and was to inquire about buying gerfalcons, sable tigers, and squirrels for the shah—is likely to have overshadowed his political mandate. This mandate centered on Isfahan's concern about the fate of Iranian subjects living in Russia, the tsar's request for military and financial aid, and, most importantly, the question of sovereignty over the Caucasus and (more specifically) the territory of the *shamkhal.* His standing as an embassy merchant did not, however, prevent Hajji Murtaza from promising the Russians not just Safavid monetary aid but also military assistance. He may have acted on his own initiative in making such statements, though it seems more likely that he operated under instructions from the shah—who, after all, had a long record of making promises to Russia's rulers that were designed to buy goodwill and time and to safeguard his northern borders rather than as pledges to be honored in fact.[82]

Shah 'Abbas's response to the Tikhanov mission and the first official Safavid diplomatic initiative toward Russia following the Time of Troubles was a delegation led by Bulat Beg, who accompanied Tikhanov on his way back to Moscow in late 1614. Dispatched to congratulate the new tsar on his accession, Bulat Beg's mission also represented a return to the themes that Shah 'Abbas had pursued before the interruption in relations with Russia. The letter that Bulat Beg submitted to the tsar spoke of Iranian assistance to Russia; and in his talks he relayed the shah's wish to strengthen the Irano-Russian border by a rebuilding of Russian strongholds on the Sunzha and Koisu rivers and a ceding to Russia of Shamakhi. Yet neither in the letters nor in his negotiations was mention made of the specific promises extended by Hajji Murtaza.[83]

Shah 'Abbas's subsequent diplomatic initiatives continued in the same vein. A second mission, led by Muhammad Qasim (1616–17), and the third mission, again led by Bulat Beg (1617–18), were meant as a response to the Leont'ev mission, aimed at obtaining further guarantees with respect to the borders in the Caucasus following Iran's bloody quelling of a revolt in Kakhet'i in 1616.[84] The potential usefulness of Russia as a military coalition partner and Russian territory as a conduit for trade diminished even further when Iran's armies defeated the Ottomans in 1618 and the shah concluded the peace of Sarab with the sultan later that year. Moreover, Shah 'Abbas, in a reorientation of his foreign policy, at this very same time turned his attention to his southern shores, where a new outside force had made its appearance. Though the English had come to Iran to engage in trade, Shah 'Abbas saw in the armed ships of the English East India Company a useful instrument to further his political agenda. In 1622 he persuaded them to assist him in the ouster of the Portuguese from the isle of Hurmuz. Needless to say, the Russians did not play any role in this project.

How far Russia's stock had fallen at this juncture is illustrated by the rather rude manner in which a Russian delegation led by Mikhail Petrovich Bariatinskii and Ivan Ivanovich Chicherin was treated at the Safavid court in 1618–20. When Bariatinskii died on the way to Qazvin, Chicherin (the second in command) became the head of the delegation.[85] The Italian traveler Pietro della Valle, witnessing the collective audience that Shah 'Abbas granted to a number of foreign envoys including the Russians, noted that only the shah and the Indian ambassador entered the *maydan* of Qazvin on horseback, while the Muscovite envoy and his retinue were made to dismount and enter on foot.[86] Della Valle also observed how Chicherin was snubbed in his request for a loan for his master and forced to return empty-handed.[87]

'Abbas's resumption of war preparations against the Ottomans shortly thereafter had the effect of changing his Russia policy once again. This redirection explains the generous attention the Iranians accorded to the V. G. Korob'in mission, which visited Isfahan in 1622–23. Just as in the case of the Zvenigorodskii mission almost three decades earlier, the Iranians seem to have been especially keen to demonstrate to the Ottomans that they had close ties with the Russians.[88] Yet this time around Shah 'Abbas may have underestimated the complexity of the Russian interests, which (as seen earlier) went well beyond a desire to join forces with Iran in an anti-Ottoman coalition. In the absence of concrete objectives, the Korob'in mission illustrates how radically Moscow's position had changed. Russia's traditional anti-Polish orientation now prevailed, and the significant third party here was the Ottoman Empire rather than the Safavid state. It is true that in 1618 the Russians had concluded the Treaty of Deulino with Poland-Lithuania. Yet this agreement did little to change their long-term strategy, which continued to be strongly anti-Warsaw. Thus, while Moscow officially remained neutral in the Thirty-Year War that broke out in the same year, in reality it leaned toward participating on the side of the Ottomans against Poland-Lithuania, which had joined the Austrians in their fight against Istanbul. Such considerations formed the backdrop for the intensive contacts that the Russians had maintained with the Ottomans ever since 1613.[89] These circumstances also explain why the mandate that Korob'in brought with him to Iran did not include an anti-Ottoman proposal.[90]

This Russian reorientation seems to have continued during the last few years of Shah 'Abbas's reign, for nothing points to a revival of Irano-Russian diplomatic traffic in this period despite the resumption of the Safavid-Ottoman wars and Shah 'Abbas's seizure of Baghdad in 1623. Two Russian embassies are known to have visited Iran in 1624 and 1626, but both seem to have concerned mostly trade matters.[91]

AFTER SHAH 'ABBAS

The death of Shah 'Abbas in 1629 and the enthronement of his grandson Shah Safi marked the beginning of considerable change in the relationship between the Safavid and Romanov states. Shah 'Abbas's successors paid much less attention to bilateral relations; the continuous interaction that had characterized his reign began to level off, to the point where a delegation led by an obscure

Iranian envoy may have been the extent of Shah Safi's interest in sending representatives to Russia. This diminished frequency may have been due in part to a change in commercial relations between the two countries. From the sources one gets the impression that the Safavid state's involvement in trade relations diminished with the death of Shah 'Abbas I, giving private initiative the upper hand in trade relations. This is clearly true for the trade in silk. Shah 'Abbas had turned the export of his country's silk into a royal monopoly in 1619. Shah Safi canceled this monopoly upon his accession, and the role of commerce as a rationale for sending missions north may have decreased. The frequency of official traffic between the two states leveled off accordingly.[92]

The Russians in this period also showed themselves less keen on continuing cordial relations with Iran. Aggressive behavior on the part of the Crimean Tatars and the perennial enmity of the Poles, made worse by a Polish-Swedish alliance, led them to seek closer ties with the Ottomans. As early as 1627 an Ottoman envoy visited Moscow with a proposal to form an alliance against the Crimean Tatars, who (supported by the Zaporozhian Cossacks) at that point presented a threat to both the Turks and the Russians. Beyond that there was the ever-present threat from Poland-Lithuania as a mutual concern. Istanbul, for instance, seems to have seen King Sigismund III as the instigator of unrest in the Crimea. Russia's enmity was further sharpened when Poland-Lithuania concluded the Treaty of Altmark with Sweden in 1629. All this prompted the Russians to seek support in what appeared to be an imminent war with Poland-Lithuania. This policy automatically led to closer ties with the Ottomans, the other foe of the Poles and a state that might be willing to provide military support. The Ottomans, in turn, were interested in Russian assistance against the Zaporozhian Cossacks.[93]

As a result, the number of Russian emissaries sent to Iran in the 1630s remained limited to just a few; and it was only in 1636–37, seven years into Shah Safi's reign, that a Russian envoy offered the tsar's congratulations on the shah's accession.[94] Relations sharply deteriorated in the 1640s as the Iranians threatened to invade Daghistan and began to meddle in that region's internal affairs, as a result of which its rulers once again turned to Russia for protection. Conflict also arose over a series of caravan robberies in the Caucasus, the detention in Iran of a number of Russian merchants, and the construction of Russian garrison towns on the Iranian side of the river Terek. This conflict briefly turned violent when in 1652 Khusraw Khan (*beglerbeg* of Shirvan) torched one of those garrison towns, after which it would take a full decade and the exchange of a number of missions for the outstanding issues to be resolved.[95] By then Moscow was again keen to seek Iran's assistance against the Ottomans; but since the Safavids had definitively made peace with the Ottomans in 1639, their new overtures failed to resonate in Isfahan. Until the end of the Safavid era, Iran would conduct a foreign policy designed not to provoke the Ottomans into breaking the Peace of Zuhab.[96] The imbalance is suggested by the number of embassies traveling back and forth during the reign of Shah Sulayman. While three major Russian ambassadors and eleven envoys visited Iran between 1670 and 1692, the Iranians reciprocated with just two delegations. The second, led by Muhammad Husayn Khan Beg, was mainly designed to congratulate Tsar Peter I on his accession. The Iranians also notified the Russians that they were not willing to engage in an anti-Ottoman coalition, thus formally rejecting a proposal that Shah Khudabandah had made more than a hundred years earlier.[97]

NOTES

A different and slightly shorter version of this article was published in Dutch in the Dutch journal of Middle Eastern Studies *Sharqiyyat* 5 (1993): 1–22. I would like to thank Victor Ostapchuk for his valuable comments on the penultimate draft of this paper.

1. See, in chronological order, C. D. Rouillard, *The Turk in French History, Thought and Literature (1520–1660)* (Paris, 1940); Sydney Nettleton Fisher, *The Foreign Relations of Turkey 1481–1512* (Urbana, Ill., 1948); Dorothy M. Vaughan, *Europe and the Turk: A Pattern of Alliances 1350–1700* (Liverpool, 1954); Massimo Petrocchi, *La politica della Santa Sede di fronte al'invasione ottomana (1444–1718)* (Naples, 1955); K. M. Setton, "Pope Leo and the Turkish Peril," *Proceedings of the American Philosophical Society* (1969): 367–427; Carl Göllner, *Turcica III Bd., Die Türkenfrage in der öffentlichen Meinung im 16. Jahrhundert* (Bucharest, 1978); and Ekkehard Eickhoff, *Venedig, Wien und die Osmanen: Umbruch in Südosteuropa 1645–1700*, 2nd ed. (Stuttgart, 1988).

2. A selection of the available literature on this aspect of the "Turkish Question" in Western languages other than Russian includes H. Uebersberg, *Österreich und Russland seit dem Ende des 15. Jahrhundert* (Vienna/Leipzig, 1906); idem, *Russlands Orientpolitik in den letzten zwei Jahrhunderten*, 2 vols. (Stuttgart, 1913); R. Neck, "Diplomatische Beziehungen zum vorderen Orient unter Karl V," *Mitteilungen des österreichischen Staatsarchiv* 5 (1952): 63–86; W. E. D. Allen, *Problems of Turkish Power in the Sixteenth Century* (London, 1963); B. H. Sumner, *Peter the Great and the Ottoman Empire* (Oxford, 1949); Georg von Rauch, "Moskau und die europäischen Mächte des 17. Jahrhundert," *Historische Zeitschrift* 178 (1954): 25ff.; Günther Stökl, "Russland und Europa vor Peter dem Grossen," *Historische Zeitschrift* 184 (1957): 531–54; and Philip Longworth, "Russian-Venetian Relations in the Reign of Tsar Aleksey Mikhailovich," *Slavonic and East European Review* 64 (1986): 380–400.

3. Studies on this topic include C. Piot, "Relations diplomatiques de Charles V avec la Perse et la Turquie," *Messages des Sciences Historiques de Belge* (1843): 44–70; V. Minorsky, "The Middle East in Western Politics in the 13th, 14th, and 15th Centuries," *Journal of the Royal Central Asian Society* 27 (1940): 427–61; Hans Robert Roemer, "Die Safawiden: Ein orientalischer Bundesgenosse des Abendlandes im Türkenkampf," *Saeculum* 4 (1953): 27–44; Barbara von Palombini, *Bündniswerben abendländischer Mächte um Persien 1453–1600* (Wiesbaden, 1968); Niels Steensgaard, *The Asian Trade Revolution of the Seventeenth Century: The East India Companies and the Decline of the Caravan Trade* (Chicago,

1974); Jean Aubin, "Per viam portugalensem: Autour d'un projet diplomatique de Maximilien II," *Mare Luso-Indicum* 4 (1980): 45–88; Jean-Louis Bacqué-Grammont, *Les Ottomans, les Safavides et leurs voisins: Contributions à l'histoire des relations internationales dans l'Orient islamique de 1514 à 1524* (Istanbul, 1987); and Rudi Matthee, "Iran's Ottoman Diplomacy during the Reign of Shāh Sulaymān I (1077–1105/1666–1694)," in *Iran and Iranian Studies: Essays in Honor of Iraj Afshar,* ed. Kambiz Eslami (Princeton, 1998), pp. 148–77.

4. See N. I. Veselovskii, *Pamiatniki diplomaticheskikh i torgovykh snoshenii moskovskoi Rusi s Persiei,* 3 vols., in *Trudy Vostochnogo Otedeleniia Imperatorskogo Russkogo Archeologicheskogo Obshchestva* (St. Petersburg, 1890–98). See especially P. P. Bushev, *Istoriia posol'stv i diplomaticheskikh otnoshenii russkogo i iranskogo gosudarstv v 1586–1612 gg.* (Moscow, 1976); and idem, *Istoriia posol'stv i diplomaticheskikh otnoshenii russkogo i iranskogo gosudarstv v 1613–1621 gg.* (Moscow, 1987). Modern Persian studies that include sections on relations between Iran and Russia in the Safavid period are Sayyid Muhammad 'Ali Jamalzadah, "Rus va Iran," *Kavah* 3:28 (7 Day 1287 H.Q./May 25, 1918): 1–6; idem, "Tarikh-i ravabit-i Rus va Iran," supplement to *Kavah* 5:1 (January 22, 1920): a, b, j; Najaf Quli Hussam Mu'izzi, *Tarikh-i ravabit-i siyasi-yi Iran ba dunya* (Tehran, 1326 Sh./1947), pp. 333ff.; Nasrullah Falsafi, *Zindigani-yi Shah 'Abbas-i avval,* 4th ed., 5 vols. in 3, paginated as 1 (Tehran, 1369 Sh./1990); 'Abd al-Husayn Nava'i, *Ravabit-i siyasi-yi Iran va Urupa dar 'asr-i Safavi* (Tehran, 1372 Sh./1993), pp. 183–260; and 'Ali Akbar Vilayati, *Tarikh-i ravabit-i khariji-yi Iran dar 'ahd-i Shah 'Abbas-i avval-i Safavi* (Tehran, 1374 Sh./1995), pp. 195–212.

5. Hans Wilhelm Haussig, *Die Geschichte Zentralasiens und der Seidenstrasse in islamischer Zeit* (Darmstadt, 1988), pp. 25, 170.

6. See Wilhelm Heyd, *Geschichte des Levantehandels im Mittelalter,* 2 vols. (Stuttgart, 1879), 1:53–54, 69ff.; H. A. Manandian, *The Ancient Trade and Cities of Armenia in Relation to the Ancient World Trade,* trans. from the Russian (Lisbon, 1965), p. 135; and Bushev, *Istoriia posol'stv, 1586–1612,* p. 32.

7. Janet Martin, "Muscovite Relations with the Khanates of Kazan and the Crimea (1460s to 1512)," *Canadian-American Slavic Studies* 17 (1983): 442–43.

8. Fisher, *Foreign Relations of Turkey,* pp. 34–35; and Robert M. Croskey, *Muscovite Diplomatic Practice in the Reign of Ivan III* (New York and London, 1987), p. 129.

9. Bushev, *Istoriia posol'stv, 1586–1612,* pp. 34–35. Papin was accompanied by Afanasii Nikitin, the famous Russian merchant who later was to visit India and was the first Russian to write an account of India.

10. In a seminal article, Leslie Collins has refuted the long-held and oft-repeated notion that the Great Horde was destroyed and utterly vanished in 1502. See Leslie Collins, "On the Alleged 'Destruction' of the Great Horde in 1502," *Byzantinische Forschungen* 16 (1991): 361–99.

11. Bushev, *Istoriia posol'stv, 1586–1612,* p. 36. This in contrast to Falsafi, *Zindigani,* p. 1827, who claims that the earliest diplomatic contacts between Russia and Iran in the Safavid period only occurred in the reign of Shah Tahmasb I.

12. See Arnulf Hartmann, O.S.A., "William of St. Augustine and His Time," *Augustiniana* 20, nos. 3–4 (1970): 182.

13. Bushev, *Istoriia posol'stv, 1586–1612,* p. 39.

14. Ibid., p. 40.

15. V. A. Baiburtian, *Armianskaia koloniia Novoi Dzhul'fy v XVII veke: Rol' Novoi Dzhul'fy v irano-evropeiskikh politicheskikh i ekonomicheskikh sviazakh* (Erevan, 1969), p. 86.

16. Bushev, *Istoriia posol'stv, 1586–1612,* p. 42; and Jenkinson's report in E. Delmar Morgan and C. H. Coote, eds., *Early Voyages and Travels to Russia and Persia,* 2 vols. (London, 1886), 1:125–26.

17. Bushev, *Istoriia posol'stv, 1586–1612,* p. 42.

18. See Morgan and Coote, *Early Voyages;* and T. S. Willan, *The Early History of the Russian Company 1553–1603* (Manchester, 1956, repr. 1968), for the various expeditions of the Muscovy Company to Iran.

19. Bushev, *Istoriia posol'stv, 1586–1612,* pp. 61–62.

20. See Adam Knobler, "The Rise of Tīmūr and Western Diplomatic Response, 1390–1405," *Journal of the Royal Asiatic Society,* 3rd ser., 5 (1995): 341–49.

21. Von Palombini, *Bündniswerben,* p. 9.

22. For the diplomatic traffic between Rome and the court of Uzun Hasan, see Angelo Michele Piemontese, "La représentation d'Uzun Hasan sur scene à Rome (2 mars 1473)," *Turcica* 21, no. 3 (1991): 191–203; and idem, "The Nuncios of Pope Sixtus IV (1471–84) in Iran," in *Iran and Iranian Studies,* ed. Eslami, pp. 90–108.

23. Von Palombini, *Bündniswerben,* pp. 16–31.

24. For this, see Jean Aubin, "La politique orientale de Selim Ier," in *Itinéraires d'Orient: Hommages à Claude Cahen,* ed. Raoul Curiel and Rika Gyselen (Bures-sur-Yvette, 1994), pp. 207ff.; and Palmira Brummett, "The Myth of Shah Ismail Safavi: Political Rhetoric and 'Divine' Kingship," in *Medieval Christian Perceptions of Islam: A Book of Essays,* ed. John Victor Tolan (New York and London, 1996), pp. 331–59.

25. Von Palombini, *Bündniswerben,* p. 68.

26. Fisher, *Foreign Relations of Turkey,* p. 55.

27. Ana Maria Schop Soler, *Die spanisch-russischen Beziehungen im 18. Jahrhundert* (Wiesbaden, 1970), pp. 21–22.

28. See Michel M. Mazzaoui, *The Origins of the Ṣafawids: Šhīʿism, Ṣūfism, and the Ġulāt* (Wiesbaden, 1972), p. 11.

29. The notion that a confrontation between Russia and the Ottoman was the inevitable outcome of a rivalry that goes back to the sixteenth century has recently been refuted as anachronistic by Victor Ostapchuk. He argues that prior to the Chyhyryn/Chrehrin campaign of 1678 very little fundamental antagonism can be detected and that an image to the contrary is an anachronistic projection originating in the bad blood that has existed between the two states since the reign of Peter the Great. The Ottomans, in this revisionist portrayal, showed little zeal for expansionism into the steppes beyond the northern shores of the Black Sea. They rather conducted a defensive policy designed to perpetuate the status quo by establishing a mutually beneficial relationship with the Crimean Tatars, the main force of the steppes, whom they used as a buffer against Poland-Lithuania and Muscovy. See Victor Ostapchuk, "The Ottoman Black Sea Frontier and the Relations of the Porte with the Polish-Lithuanian Commonwealth and Muscovy, 1622–1628" (Ph.D. dissertation, Harvard University, 1989); and idem, "The Human Landscape of the Ottoman Black Sea in the Face of the Cossack Naval Raids," *Oriente Moderno* n.s. 20 (2001): 23–95, esp. 30–36.

30. This expedition is discussed in Alexandre Benningsen, "L'Expédition turque contre Astrakhan en 1569," *Cahiers du Monde Russe et Soviétique* 8 (1967): 427–46.

31. Von Rauch, "Moskau und die europäische Mächte," p. 27.

32. For the diplomatic exchange between Russia and the Ottoman Empire, see Hans Uebersberger, *Russlands Orientpolitik* (Stuttgart, 1913–), 1:pt. 1.

33. Bushev, *Istoriia posol'stv, 1586–1612,* p. 44. The figure of 30 cannons is reported by the

Polish envoy Andrzej Taranowski, who in 1559 traveled to Istanbul and from there to Astrakhan, where he witnessed the Ottoman expedition, siege of the city, and retreat. Taranowski does not mention 500 arquebuses but instead, and rather implausibly, claims that 500 expert arquebusiers accompanied the mission to Iran. See Maria Szuppe, "Les Polonais dans l'espace ottoman au XVIe siècle: Deux relations de voyage (E. Otwinowski, 1557, et A. Taranowski, 1569)," in *Europa e Islam tra i secoli XIV e XVI/Europe and Islam between 14th and 16th Centuries,* ed. Michele Bernardini et al. (Naples, 2002), pp. 643–84 (671).

34. Bushev, *Istoriia posol'stv, 1586–1612,* pp. 63–64.

35. Hasan Bayg Rumlu, *Ahsan al-tavarikh,* ed. 'Abbas Husayn Nava'i (Tehran, 1357), p. 225.

36. B. B. Piotrovskii, ed., *Istoriia narodov severnogo Kavakaza s drevneishikh vremen do kontsa XVIII v.* (Moscow, 1988), ch. 13, "Nachalo prisoedinenniia severokavkazskikh narodov k Rossii v XVI–XVII vv.," p. 340.

37. Ibid., ch. 12, "Severniy Kavkaz v mezhdunarodnoi obstanovke XVI–XVII vv.," p. 317; and ch. 13, "Nachalo prisoedinenniia," p. 330.

38. Carl Max Kortepeter, *Ottoman Imperialism during the Reformation: Europe and the Caucasus* (New York, 1972), pp. 90–92; and Alexandre Benningsen, "La poussée vers les mers chaudes et la barrière du Caucase: La rivalité Ottoman-Moscovite dans la seconde moitié du XVIe siècle," *Journal of Turkish Studies* 10 (1986): 31.

39. For the beginning of Russian contacts with the khanates of Bukhara, see M. Iu. Iuldasev, *K istorii torgovykh i posol'skikh zviazei srednei Azii s Rossiei v XVI–XVII vv.* (Tashkent, 1964), pp. 47ff.

40. Falsafi, *Zindigani,* p. 1833. The Russians distinguished between three types of mission: "heavy" (*velikie*), "light" (*legkie*), and those performed by messengers (*gontsi*). See Iuldashev, *K istorii torgovykh i posol'skikh zviazei,* pp. 23–24.

41. Joseph Hammer von Purgstall, *Geschichte des osmanischen Reiche,* 10 vols. (Pest, 1963), 4:181.

42. Bushev, *Istoriia posol'stv, 1586–1612,* p. 72. Falsafi, *Zindigani,* pp. 1832–33, erroneously states that the shah received these envoys in Jumadi I, 996 H.Q./April 1588.

43. Hammer von Purgstall, *Geschichte,* p. 181; Bushev, *Istoriia posol'stv, 1586–1612,* p. 121; and Muhammad Amin Riyahi, ed., *Sifaratnamahha-yi Iran: Guzarishha-yi musafirat va ma'muriyat-i safiran-i 'Usmani dar Iran* (Tehran, 1368 Sh./1989), pp. 38–39.

44. The letter appears in Falsafi, *Zindigani,* p. 1835; and is discussed in Bushev, *Istoriia posol'stv, 1586–1612,* p. 131.

45. Bushev, *Istoriia posol'stv, 1586–1612,* pp. 118–19.

46. Ibid., pp. 136ff., 149ff. It is hardly surprising that Russia's interest in diplomatic relations with Gilan was minimal compared to the weight accorded to entertaining ties to Iran proper. Diplomatic and commercial initiatives on the part of Gilan were doomed anyhow, as Shah 'Abbas incorporated the region into his realm in the mid-1590s.

47. Kaia, the name under which this mission appears in Veselovskii, *Pamiatniki,* 1:160ff., is likely to refer to the rank rather than the name of its main envoy. See W. E. D. Allen, ed., and Anthony Manog, trans., *Russian Embassies to the Georgian Kings (1589–1605),* 2 vols. (Cambridge, 1970), 2:534.

48. Bushev, *Istoriia posol'stv, 1586–1612,* pp. 165–66. Russia had to operate carefully, however, in light of the same threat. The Russians were also reluctant in their relations with Iran because they wished to await the results of simultaneous talks with various European powers as well as the end of the war with Sweden. See ibid., p. 177.

49. Uebersberger, *Russlands Orientpolitik,* p. 13.

50. Bushev, *Istoriia posol'stv, 1586–1612,* pp. 177–81. It seems that in Moscow Hajji Khusraw conducted talks with the Habsburg envoy Nikolai Varkac, who was staying in Moscow to discuss a grand European coalition against the Ottomans. Varkac apparently proposed that Iran be included in this coalition as well. See ibid., pp. 191–92, 201.

51. Ibid., p. 202.

52. See M.-F. Brosset, ed. and trans., *Histoire moderne de la Géorgie, depuis l'antiquité jusqu'au XIXe siècle,* 2 vols. (St. Petersburg, 1857), 2:336–37.

53. Bushev, *Istoriia posol'stv, 1586–1612,* pp. 217–27.

54. Ibid., pp. 228–29.

55. M. Svanidze, "Une ambassadrice géorgienne (sur l'histoire du traité de paix turco-persan de 1612)," *Revue des Etudes Géorgiennes* 4 (1988): 110.

56. Audrey Burton, *The Bukharans: A Dynastic, Diplomatic and Commercial History 1550–1702* (London, 1997), pp. 79–80. This must be the Russian ambassador mentioned by Iskandar Munshi as having visited Iran in 1003/1594–95. See Iskandar Beg Turkaman, *Tarikh-i 'alam-ara-yi 'Abbasi,* 2nd ed., 2 vols. paginated as 1 (Tehran, 1350/1971), p. 504.

57. Bushev, *Istoriia posol'stv, 1586–1612,* p. 258.

58. Imam Quli Beg is one the few Safavid envoys to Russia mentioned by name in the Safavid chronicles. See Iskandar Beg Turkaman, *Tarikh-i 'alam-ara-yi 'Abbasi,* p. 507.

59. The story of the Tiufiakin mission may be found in Bushev, *Istoriia posol'stv, 1586–1612,* pp. 294–320.

60. On the Safavid perception of the Russians, see Rudi Matthee, "Between Aloofness and Fascination: Safavid Views of the West," *Iranian Studies* 30 (1998): 233–35; and idem, "Suspicion, Fear and Admiration: Pre-Nineteenth-Century Iranian Views of the English and the Russians," in *Iran and the Surrounding World: Interactions in Culture and Cultural Politics,* ed. Nikki R. Keddie and Rudi Matthee (Seattle, 2002), pp. 121–45.

61. Augustin Courbe, ed., "Relation d'un voyage de Perse faict es années 1598–99 par un gentilhomme de la suite du Seigneur Scierley Ambassadeur du roy d'Angleterre," in *Relations véritables et curieuses de l'isle de Madagascar et du Brésil* (Paris, 1651), pp. 151–52. Originally, the Pir Quli Beg delegation was not part of the mission led by Sir Anthony Sherley and Husayn 'Ali Beg that set out for Russia from Iran in 1599. The two groups did, however, travel together from the time they met in Astrakhan.

62. Pir Quli Beg was severely punished by Shah 'Abbas upon his return to Iran. His tongue was cut out, and his eyes were gouged. See Maria Szuppe, "Un marchand du roi de Pologne en Perse, 1601–1602," *Moyen Orient et Océan Indien* 3 (1986): 98; and Mulla Jalal al-Din Munajjim, *Tarikh-i 'Abbasi ya ruznamah-i Mulla Jalal* (Tehran, 1366 Sh./1987), p. 212.

63. Bushev, *Istoriia posol'stv, 1586–1612,* p. 357.

64. Ibid., pp. 362ff. Zhirov-Zasiekin apparently carried a letter from the Habsburg monarch Rudolph II, perhaps in response to a proposal made by Bayat Husayn Beg in Prague. Nothing is known about its contents, however. Since the surviving Russian archives remain silent about the stretch of the journey beyond Astrakhan, relatively little is known about the mission's activities and results. Bushev suggests that the mission never even reached Iran, speculating that it may have been recalled once it became clear to the Russians that Shah 'Abbas did not intend to sign a treaty. Yet Maria Szuppe, based on documentation provided by an Armenian merchant residing in Safavid territory at the time, has demonstrated that Zhirov-Zasiekin mission did stay in Iran in 1601. See Szuppe, "Un marchand," pp. 90–91.

65. Munajjim, *Tarikh-i 'Abbasi,* p. 212.

66. Bushev, *Istoriia posol'stv, 1586–1612,* p. 383.

67. Ibid., p. 387.

68. David Marshall Lang, *The Last Years of the Georgian Monarchy 1658–1832* (New York, 1957), p. 12. Antonio de Gouvea, a Portuguese friar who was in Iran at the time, explained the murder as part of a conflict involving the shah's desire to retake Shirvan from the Ottomans. Since Alexander showed little inclination to move against the Ottomans, the shah had him and his other son (Gurgin) eliminated and replaced by Constantin, who was then ordered to conquer Shirvan. See Antonio de Gouvea, *Relation des grandes guerres et victoires obtenues par le roy de Perse Cha Abbas contre les empereurs de Turquie Mahomet et Achmet son fils,* trans. A. de Meneses (Rouen, 1646), pp. 254–59. Bushev, *Istoriia posol'stv, 1586–1612,* p. 408, based on Georgian historians, is a little more circumspect in speaking out on the reasons why the shah had King Alexander and Grigorii/Gurgin killed.

69. See Muhammad Mufid Mustawfi, *Mukhtasar-i mufid,* ed. Seyfeddin Najmabadi, 2 vols. (Wiesbaden, 1991), 1:184–85.

70. Bushev, *Istoriia posol'stv, 1586–1612,* pp. 382–83.

71. Ibid., p. 420.

72. See Steensgaard, *Asian Trade Revolution,* pp. 237–44.

73. Bushev, *Istoriia posol'stv, 1586–1612,* p. 432–33; and idem, "Iranskii kuptsina Kazim Bek v Rossii, 1706–1709 gg.," *Iran: Sbornik statei* (Moscow, 1973), p. 168.

74. Bushev, *Istoriia posol'stv, 1586–1612,* p. 429.

75. Ibid., pp. 429–32.

76. Bushev, *Istoriia posol'stv, 1613–1621,* pp. 13ff.

77. [H. Chick, ed.,] *A Chronicle of the Carmelites in Persia and the Papal Mission of the XVIIth and XVIIIth Centuries,* 2 vols. (London, 1939), 1:194–97.

78. Svanidze, "Une ambassadrice," p. 122.

79. Bushev, *Istoriia posol'stv, 1613–1621,* pp. 49ff.

80. Ibid., p. 62.

81. Ibid., pp. 44–45, 53. Shahmatov protested against the Iranian invasion and occupation of Georgia; but his remonstration was categorically rejected, and he was sent back home without a letter for the tsar. See ibid., pp. 129–30.

82. Ibid., pp. 109–19.

83. Ibid., pp. 89–96.

84. In response to a Russian request for the huge sum of 400,000 rubles (ca. 40,000 tumans), Shah 'Abbas eventually included a sum of 7,260 rubles in the presents carried by Bulat Beg, who accompanied Leont'ev on his return voyage. See ibid., pp. 154ff.

85. Ibid., pp. 198–99.

86. Pietro della Valle, *Viaggi di Pietro della Valle il pellegrino,* ed. G. Gancia, 2 vols. (Brighton, 1843), 1:832.

87. Ibid., 2:41. This is no doubt the embassy referred to by Iskandar Beg Turkaman, *Tarikh-i 'alam-ara-yi 'Abbasi,* p. 940, which he says was received by the shah in Qazvin. Iskandar Munshi, however, does not mention anything about the fate of the mission and only talks about its handing over of gifts and letters.

88. P. P. Bushev, "Posol'stvo V. G. Korob'ina i A. Kushinova v Iran v 1621–1624 gg.," in *Iran: Ekonomika, istoriia, istoriografiia, literatura (Sbornik statei)* (Moscow, 1976), pp. 135, 142.

89. See Uebersberger, *Russlands Orientpolitik,* 1:19.

90. Bushev, "Posol'stvo V. G. Korob'ina i A. Kushinova," p. 124.

91. H. Dunlop, ed., *Bronnen tot de geschiedenis der Oostindische Compagnie in Perzië 1611–1638* (The Hague, 1930), pp. 60, 191. The 1624 embassy also seems to have been sent to seek the release of the Georgian queen Ketivan (called Didemal in the Persian sources), who, with her grandson Alexander, had been held as a hostage by Shah 'Abbas since 1615. See "De la gloriosa muerte que la Sereníssima reyna Gativanda Dedopoli padeció en Xirás, metrópoli de la Persia, por mandato de Xá Abbás, rey de ella: Año 1624 a dos de septiembre," in Carlos Alonso, O.S.A., *Misioneros Agustinos en Georgia (siglo XVII)* (Valladolid, 1978), p. 133.

92. For more information on this, see Rudolph P. Matthee, *The Politics of Trade in Safavid Iran: Silk for Silver, 1600–1730* (Cambridge, 1999), pp. 139–42.

93. B. N. Floria, "Russko-osmanskie otnosheniia i diplomaticheskaia podgotovka smolenskoi voiny," *Sovietskoe Slavianovedenie* (1990): 17–27. Poland at this point also actively tried to form an anti-Ottoman coalition, seeking to include Iran in it. The arrival of a Polish envoy in Isfahan in 1637 must be seen in this light. It was his task to conduct negotiations with the Safavid court about a silk contract, but his mandate also included the Ottoman question. In the same year a Safavid embassy visited Poland. See Dunlop, *Bronnen,* p. 614; and Vaughan, *Europe and the Turk,* p. 214.

94. Iskandar Beg Turkaman and Valah Isfahani, *Zayl-i tarikh-i 'alam-ara-yi 'Abbasi,* ed. Suhayli Khansari (Tehran, 1317 Sh./1938), p. 188. For the various embassies, see Dunlop, *Bronnen,* pp. 505, 528, 566.

95. E. Zevakin, "Konflikt Rossii s Persiei v seredine XVII stoletiia," *Azerbaidzhian v nachale XVIII veka* 8, no. 4 (1929): 24–31.

96. For Iran's Ottoman policy in the second half of the seventeenth century, see Matthee, "Iran's Ottoman Diplomacy."

97. P. P. Bushev, "Puteshestvie iranskogo posol'stva Mokhammeda Khosein Khan-Beka v Moskvu v 1690–1692 gg.," *Strany i Narody Vostoka* 18 (1976): 135.

6

The Central Asian Hajj-Pilgrimage in the Time of the Early Modern Empires

R. D. McChesney

The hajj-pilgrimage (the four or five days of ritual ceremonies at Mecca from the ninth to the twelfth or thirteenth of the month of Dhū'l-Ḥijjah that every able Muslim is obliged to perform at least once in his or her lifetime) has recently been the subject of a number of substantial historical studies.[1] Several of these (the books of Suraiya Faroqhi and Michael Pearson and the articles by Sanjay Subrahmanyam, Naim Farooqi, and Hélène Carrère d'Encausse) focus on the later Muslim imperial era (in particular the tenth H./sixteenth C.E. and eleventh H./seventeenth C.E. centuries) from the perspective of two of the great imperial formations, the Ottoman in western Islamdom and the Mughal in the east. No work has as yet been devoted to the subject of the hajj-pilgrimage from Central Asia, the lands of Mawarannahr, Khwarazm, and Khurasan, and parts north and east, although three of these studies do attempt to characterize in a general way the phenomenon of the Central Asian pilgrimage. The purpose of the present study is to address some of the interpretations of pilgrimage relating to Central Asia put forward in these works and to suggest some of the subjects that need more detailed study in any comprehensive work on hajj-pilgrimage from the populated regions of Central Asia in the tenth/sixteenth and eleventh/seventeenth centuries.

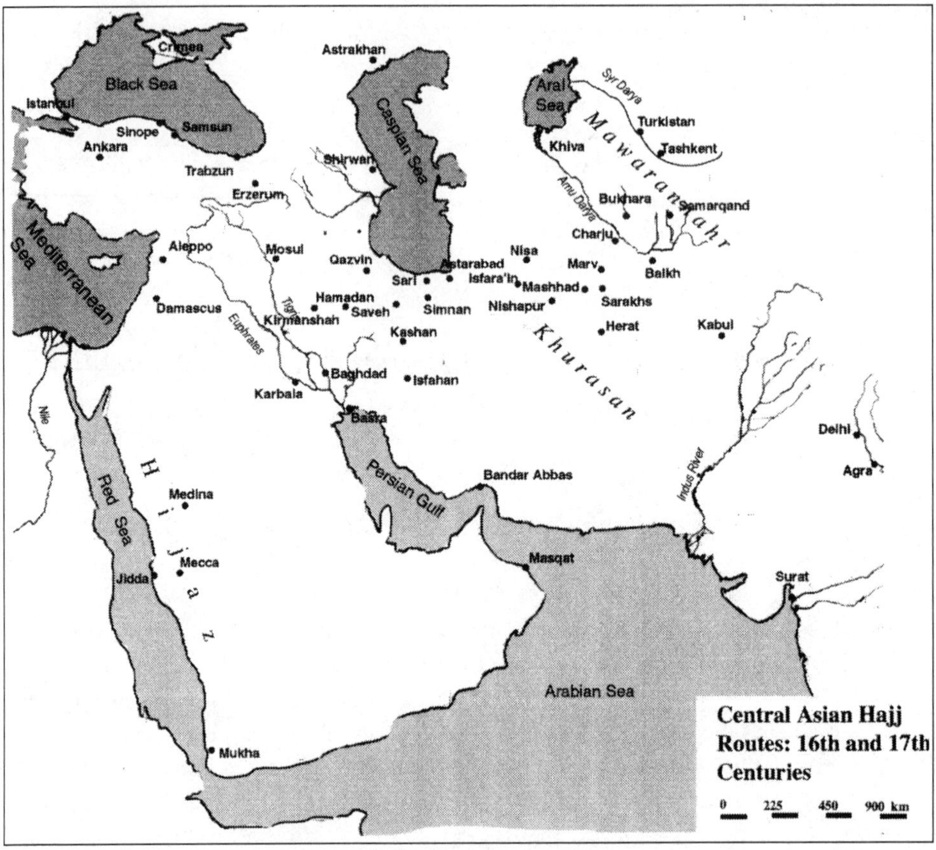

THE ISSUE OF HAJJ ROUTE SELECTION FROM CENTRAL ASIA TO THE HIJAZ

For prospective pilgrims from the major urban centers of Central Asia (Samarqand, Bukhara, Balkh, Tashkent, Urganj) there were three major routes by which one reached the Hijaz. These were the northern route around the Caspian to Anatolia then south through Syria, the southern route to India and the port of Surat and then by sea to Mukha or Jiddah, and the central route through Iran and then either by sea or by land to Mecca. Each route had innumerable alternate subroutes and had its own geographical, political, meteorological, and cultural features that could either attract or repel the prospective pilgrim depending on the time of year, the prevailing degree of security for the traveler, and the costs associated with the route. It is difficult, if not impossible, for the early twenty-first century observer to conceive of the factors that went into any individual's decision as to which route to take; the best we can do today is extrapolate from the evidence on the routes actually taken as to which were most attractive and at which times.

Unlike the case in the Ottoman and Mughal states, there is very little evidence that the political leadership of the Central Asian khanates organized a pilgrimage caravan, at least on a regular basis. We know there were at least occasional pilgrimage caravans organized in conjunction with the pilgrimage of a major political or religious figure (see below), but the office of "commander of the *ḥajj*" (*amīr al-ḥajj* in the Arab lands and *mīr-i ḥajj* in India) does not appear in the available lists of offices for the governmental structures of the neo-Chinggisid states of Mawarannahr and Khwarazm (Khiva).[2] There is thus no apparent reason to assume the existence of a regular pilgrimage caravan with a predetermined route. Nonetheless, it is reasonable to assume for any given year that information would have been available to guide the prospective pilgrim in choosing one route over another. From an early twenty-first century perspective, distance, time, cost, and safety might seem to have been critical factors in any decision as to which route to follow; yet without a good deal more information about individual choices, motives, and objectives, such considerations must remain purely speculative. Here I consider the known routes, what historians have said about them, the problems that inhered in them, and what evidence we have of how these routes were used. Through most of this period, all three major routes remained options for the prospective pilgrim. Yet the evidence seems to show a great preference for only one of them.

A complicating factor for the modern observer is the "hecto-historical" approach familiar from the works of most historians of the period and to some degree followed here. The fallacy of conceptualizing decision-making and action within the vast chronological parameters of a century is all too evident when reading what has been written about the hajj. The two centuries that have been rather casually grouped here included 206 occurrences of the hajj-pilgrimage, not to mention six to eight generations of Muslims who would be born, grow up, and confront the questions of whether to perform the hajj at all and if so which route to take. Although modern historians have found it fairly easy to characterize certain kinds of behavior during this long stretch of time, usually based on one obvious and prominent factor—the political situation—a closer look at actual experience is a useful corrective.

When considering route selection over such a long span of time, climatic and weather conditions also need to be considered, although it is far more difficult to know what weight to give them than to describe them. The time of the pilgrimage is fixed by the lunar calendar, which does not keep pace with the seasons. This meant that over the course of the sixteenth and seventeenth centuries, the time of the hajj cycled six times through the seasons. There were six clusters of years, therefore, when the time for the pilgrimage trek coincided with the depths of winter; and it seems reasonable to assume that during those years the northern route might have been decidedly less attractive, all other conditions being equal. The seasonal rhythms of wind and weather are perhaps more apparent as a factor on the southern route (as we will see); but certainly winter weather on the northern route as well as summer heat on the eastern desert part of it probably would have been as much a factor in route choice as the pattern of the monsoon winds of the Arabian Sea on the southern. Yet we do not really know what part the factor of climate played. Is it an anachronism to assume that weather conditions on the route were a consideration at all in route selection or that the length of time required for the journey was a factor in fixing the time of departure from home? I have not yet found written evidence that pilgrims thought about the length of time required to complete the journey to the Haramayn. Yet since individuals knew when the hajj rituals had to be performed, time and distance must have been, in some way at least, factors in planning for the hajj. Some pilgrims may have left Central Asia with the object of performing the hajj of that particular year. Others may have set out only with the intention of fulfilling the hajj, whether that year, the next, or the year after.

THE NORTHERN OR ASTRAKHAN ROUTE

We begin with the northern route. Both Carrère d'Encausse and Faroqhi believe this was the preferred route for Central Asian pilgrims. Carrère d'Encausse, reflecting the more or less conventional wisdom of the time in which she was writing, saw the advent of the Safavid state in Iran in 1501 as foreclosing the possibility of Central Asian pilgrims' following the most direct route to the Hijaz across Iran and forcing them instead to make a long detour to the north, around the northern shore of the Caspian Sea.

> Il suffit de regarder une carte pour constater que les routes traditionelles de pèlerinage passaient par l'Iran et que le triomphe séfévide était, à cet égard, particulièrement pénible pour l'Asie Centrale. En effet, empêchés de passer par l'Iran, les pèlerins turkestanais devaient faire un détour considérable par le nord . . . pour atteindre Astrakhan, par terre ou par mer, et continuer ensuite par des voies diversement compliquées.[3]

Thus a political factor, the emergence of the Safavid state in Iran, becomes the decisive element leading the prospective pilgrim to choose the northern route. This route would have taken the pilgrim, starting the journey in Bukhara, down the Amu Darya to Khiva, then west of the Aral Sea, around the northern end of the Caspian through Astrakhan, west to the Crimea, and by ship across the Black Sea to Anatolia (Istanbul, Sinope, or Samsun). Although a more direct route south from Astrakhan through the Caucasus existed, there is not much evidence that it was particularly attractive, perhaps because of a general lack of security on the roads.[4] Once in Anatolia the pilgrim had a choice of two major routes—either Trabzon-Erzerum-Mosul-Baghdad then overland to the Hijaz or to Basra and thence by ship to Jiddah; or Sinope-Ankara-Aleppo, thence to the great assembly point at Damascus, from whence the pilgrimage caravan took thirty days or so to reach Mecca. The whole journey, starting in Samarqand or Bukhara, could last from six months to a year.

Like Carrère d'Encausse, Faroqhi accepts as given the argument that the establishment of the Safavid state meant that pilgrims from Central Asia were barred from the central, presumably more direct route, and she concludes from evidence available to her that they therefore chose the northern route: "Central Asian pilgrims generally travelled from Bukhara and Samarkand through the steppe to the Caspian Sea. After a stopover in Astrakhan they continued their journey through present-day southern Russia until they arrived at one of the Ottoman ports of the northern Black Sea coast. . . ."[5]

A third scholar, Toru Horikawa, also found Ottoman documents showing that passage through Iran was so difficult that pilgrims were compelled to go via the northern route. But he does not generalize from this evidence that this situation prevailed throughout the sixteenth and seventeenth centuries, as both Carrère d'Encausse and Faroqhi do.[6]

It is of interest to note that all of the evidence that these three scholars cite dates from a single fifteen-year period; and most of the documents date to 975/1568, when at least two political factors may have been momentarily influential in the choice of route. In the north, the attention of Ottoman policy-makers was focused on the effort to retake Astrakhan from the Russians in this period. The hajj-pilgrimage was a major issue for the Ottoman state, and appeals for military assistance on the grounds of the need to protect pilgrims were a calculated if ultimately futile effort to persuade Sunni rulers to the east to support the Ottoman campaign to retake Astrakhan.[7] In addition, and perhaps more influential for the pilgrim setting out from Mawarannahr, was the campaign into Khurasan of the Jānī-Begid prince 'Abd Allāh, son of the reigning khan, Iskandar, in the summer of 1567.[8] July 1567 fell at the very beginning of the Hijri year 975; and the uncertainty of travel in Khurasan because of military movements may partly explain the applications for travel permits dating to the middle and second half of 975/early 1568.[9]

The Pilgrimage Record for the Astrakhan Route

We have the identities of a number of pilgrims who traveled the northern route, the earliest during the time of the Abu'l-Khayrid/Shibanid 'Ubayd Allāh at Bukhara (1512–40). A contemporary, Zayn al-Dīn Wāṣifī, describes at least two instances of Bukharans making the hajj via the northern route. One was a Sayyid Shams al-Dīn Muḥammad, who left Bukhara—taking a route through Tashkent and Turkistan (perhaps because of perils on the Khwarazmian route)—but nearly perished in the summer desert heat along the way.[10] Another was a Mawlānā Ṣubhī, who in 933/1526–27 left for the Holy Cities, also by way of Tashkent. His is one of the rare instances of traveling via the Caucasus, through Shirvan, at a time when it was still independent of Safavid control.[11]

As noted above, Ottoman records provide evidence of two Central Asian pilgrims taking this route in 975–76 (July 1567–June 1569), one a Bukharan named Shaykh Zangī, a descendant of the Turkestani shaykh Aḥmad Yasavī; and the other, a figure called "Shaykh Khwārazmī" who began his journey in Samarqand but died en route.[12] A decade later another shaykh, 'Abd al-Qahhār al-'Ulwī, received Ottoman travel documents; and six years after him a shaykh claiming descent from the caliph 'Umar b. al-Khaṭṭāb rounds out the list of Central Asian pilgrims traveling the northern route, at least as far as the records cited by the Ottomanists show.[13] From these few instances, all grouped within a fairly limited period, Faroqhi concluded that pilgrims from Bukhara and Samarqand "generally travelled" the northern route.

Few as the sixteenth-century examples are, the seventeenth century produces even fewer, suggesting that the northern route grew relatively less attractive over the years. It is difficult to say why so little evidence exists of pilgrim traffic on this route in the seventeenth century. Weather and banditry were more or less constant factors. The hostility between Khiva and Bukhara that marked the late sixteenth and the late seventeenth centuries may have contributed to a diminishing of travel from Bukhara and Samarqand. Perhaps the Russian presence in Astrakhan and the expansion of its influence around the northern shore of the Caspian bore on the relative unattractiveness of the route. Commercial documents from seventeenth-century Astrakhan do reveal the names of a few Bukharan and Khivan "ḥajjīs" in Astrakhan.[14] These documents provide no clue, however, as to how or when these men had acquired the title.

Suffice it to say here that there is only one record (so far discovered) from a Central Asian source that describes individuals taking the northern route for the pilgrimage in the seventeenth century. Indeed, the reference to the pilgrimage suggests that the northern route was selected for reasons other than simply the hajj itself. The pilgrim was a man later to be known as Manṣūr Ḥajjī *dādkhwāh* (chamberlain). He was the son of a magistrate, Amīr Qāżi Shāhum; and at the age of twenty-two, probably sometime in the second decade of the seventeenth century, he and his brother 'Abd al-Raḥīm, who also later became a magistrate, made the pilgrimage via the Caspian Sea, Astrakhan, the Black

Sea, Istanbul, and Damascus.[15] Our source tells us that the Tarkhān family to which Manṣūr belonged had come from Astrakhan in the middle of the sixteenth century. One can perhaps too easily imagine a youthful desire on the brothers' part to seek out their origins in Astrakhan and see something of the world while undertaking the obligation of a hajj-pilgrimage. The hajj as a life experience is underscored by his biographer, who says that Manṣūr "in that land [identified vaguely as 'Egypt and Syria' but probably Damascus] found particular pleasure in the company of [the Christian] Shaykh Ḥabīb Allāh Shīrāzī and was strongly attracted by [his] Christian benedictions."[16] It is reasonable to assume in this case that the northern route was chosen for personal reasons—to see where the family's origins were, to visit Istanbul, and to sample some of the ecumenical attractions of the West.

THE SOUTHERN ROUTE THROUGH INDIA AND BY SEA TO ARABIA

While Ottomanists have focused on the northern route, historians of India have emphasized the importance of the southern maritime route. For the pilgrims leaving Mawarannahr, the normal route would have taken them through the Hindu Kush Mountains to Kabul and then east through the Afghan tribal regions to the Punjab. From there the prospective pilgrims would travel through the Punjab southeastward to Delhi and Agra, then south to Surat on the Bay of Cambay. The pilgrims sailed thence to Mukha (or, if the winds were favorable, to Jiddah) and trekked overland to Mecca. Although the land route via Qandahar, Quetta, and the Indus Valley to its mouth at Daybul (Dabhol) near present-day Karachi and then by ship to the Hijaz appears shorter, it seems to have been far less frequented than the road from Delhi and Agra to Surat.

M. N. Pearson has provided the best and most recent study of the southern route, although his focus is exclusively on pilgrims whose journeys originated within India. But his conclusions and hypotheses also apply to Central Asian pilgrims who chose the southern route. Although Pearson's approach is Indocentric, he too, like Carrère d'Encausse and Faroqhi, has a clear view of the obstacle posed by the Safavid state in Iran to pilgrims from Mughal India contemplating the overland rather than maritime route.

> If the Ottomans at least sometimes tried to help Indian pilgrims, Ṣafavid Persia was an obstacle. This was partly for reasons of geopolitical hostility between Persia and Mughal India, for there was more or less constant tension between the two in the northwest of India and Afghanistan, then part of India, focussed on the strategic fortress of Qandahar. But religious cum doctrinal differences were also important, for the Ṣafavids were strict and proselytizing *shia* Muslims while the Mughals were, to varying degrees,

> committed *sunnis.* A sign of this was the way in which in 1544 Shah Tahmasp forced the exiled ruler Humayun to convert to *shia* Islam before he would try to help him regain his throne. Subsequently, the Ṣafavids frequently impeded the passage of Indian pilgrims.[17]

This section of Pearson's work does not reflect his main interest, and perhaps it is unfair to examine it too closely. But since it is a good example of the "barrier of heterodoxy" school of historiography,[18] it is worth taking a moment to examine the internal logic and the evidence on which he relies. Pearson's work covers the period 1500–1700; and from this paragraph he seems to be saying that there was no period during these two hundred years when Sunni pilgrims were permitted to transit Safavid Persia in order to reach Mecca. His argument is not that there were economic or weather-related reasons for choosing the sea route but rather that Sunni pilgrims were consistently refused passage for purely sectarian reasons, a conclusion that Carrère d'Encausse, Faroqhi, and Farooqi all arrive at as well.[19]

The only evidence Pearson cites for this rather sweeping conclusion is contained in the synopsis of a letter from the neo-Chinggisid (Tuqāy-Timurid) khan at Bukhara, Imām Qulī Khān (r. 1609–41), to the Timurid/Mughal ruler at Agra, Jahangir (r. 1605–27).[20] In the undated letter (probably written ca. 1625) Imām Qulī speaks of "the friendship between Jahangir's father, Akbar, and the late 16th century khan at Bukhara, the Abu'l-Khayrid-Shibanid 'Abd Allah b. Iskandar, that led to the latter's victories in Khurasan and to opening the pilgrimage route."

But the letter itself is only an announcement of Imām Qulī's intent to campaign in Khurasan and his proposal that Jahangir join him in an alliance against Shah 'Abbās. It also indicates that Imām Qulī is aware of Jahangir's problems at the time with his ambitious son Prince Khurram, later Shah Jahan; and in the elusive diplomatic language of the time the Bukharan leader may have been warning Jahangir against any involvement that would imperil Imām Qulī's plans. The letter gives a most distorted view of history when it refers to Akbar's friendship with 'Abd Allāh Khān and asserts that this friendship helped 'Abd Allāh in his decade-long series of campaigns between 1587 and 1598 that brought most of Khurasan under Bukharan control or indeed that those campaigns had any overall effect on the pilgrimage route across Iran. The fact that pilgrimage is mentioned at all seems to be far more a rhetorical rather than a substantive issue.

If taken at face value, this letter—rather than indicating that the Safavids were impeding Sunni pilgrims—would seem to support the notion that pilgrimage through Iran for Sunnis, whether starting their journey in South or Central Asia, had been opened thanks to the efforts of Akbar and 'Abd Allāh some three decades earlier. It certainly does not support Pearson's generalization that Shīʿī authorities in Iran impeded Sunni pilgrimage traffic for sectarian reasons. But Pearson was primarily concerned with pilgrimage via the sea route, and his coverage of the hajj-pilgrimage from India is thoroughly researched and convincingly presented.

Maritime Obstacles to the Pilgrimage

The sea route held special dangers and posed unique logistical problems for the prospective pilgrim. Piracy was one concern in the sixteenth and seventeenth centuries. The maritime records of the Indian Ocean suggest that piracy was as common at sea as banditry on land. But with the arrival of the Portuguese, piracy was raised to a fine art and a sectarian component was added to justify it. For a time, at the very beginning of the sixteenth century, this presented a serious and constant menace to seagoing pilgrims. When the Portuguese first established themselves, according to Pearson, "they were keen both to oppose Islam and to monopolize the spice trade."[21] They viewed it as their Christian duty to intercept pilgrim ships and kill pilgrims. In one of the more egregious cases, Vasco da Gama captured a large ship owned by the Mamluk ruler Qanṣūḥ al-Ghawrī that was on its way from Calicut on the Malabar Coast of India with a rich cargo of spices and an untold number of pilgrims. Sparing only the pilot and twenty children who were seen as fit for conversion to Christianity, the Portuguese reportedly killed or left to drown the rest of those on board.[22]

The Portuguese crusade against Islam was soon mitigated by their greater desire to maximize profit from sea trade; so ships with passes issued at Portuguese ports were in theory spared from piracy, at least from Portuguese piracy. But there were always renegades who refused to acknowledge the theoretical protection provided by a *cartaze*. As Subrahmanyam has shown, the western Indian Ocean remained a risky place for Muslim ships as late as the middle of the seventeenth century.[23] The system of passes did not provide perfect security for pilgrims; nor was it completely effective in bringing commercial shipping under Portuguese protection, but it was effective enough to compel even the most powerful land-based politicians to accede to it, through the sixteenth century at least. The Mughal ruler Akbar (r. 1556–1605), at the height of his power, was forced to pay for passes for members of his family and entourage to make the pilgrimage by sea, which was deeply irritating not to say humiliating for him. His correspondence with his Central Asian and Iranian contemporaries in which he repeatedly vows that he will rid India of the Franks reflects his frustration.[24]

In the seventeenth century, the Dutch and English joined their Christian brethren in preying on ships (including pilgrim ships) that refused to accept their protection. At least one Central Asian pilgrim, the Bukharan poet Mullā Muḥammad Jān, who had gone to India in an unsuccessful search for work, set sail for Mecca sometime not long before 1690 and perished when his ship was reportedly attacked by "Franks" and all aboard were killed.[25]

Besides piracy, the monsoon cycle of the Arabian Sea, the regular shift of winds from northeast to southwest, and the stormy seasons that linked those shifts were a major factor in the southern route. The sailing technology of the time did not permit sailing closer than about 90 degrees to the direction of the wind. Thus there were clearly defined sailing seasons from east to west and west to east. As repeatedly noted by contemporaries, ships sailing for the Red Sea generally had to leave Surat in March and reach the Red Sea toward the end of April and no later than the end of May.[26] When the ship landed at Mukha in Yemen, another thirty to forty-five days of overland travel were required to reach Mecca.[27] This set of circumstances combined with the ever-changing seasonal time of the hajj meant that any hajj that occurred earlier than about mid-June would be impossible to make by sea with that season's northeast monsoon.

But here we must grapple again with how people thought about time, distance, and travel schedules. Although the authorities could plan for the great pilgrim caravan overland from Damascus to depart the Syrian capital thirty to forty-five days before the time of the hajj, planning an approach to Mecca by sea (whether the Red Sea or the Arabian Sea) would have been a far less precise affair. Still, we do not know whether pilgrims setting off from Bukhara or Samarqand had in mind a timetable for their arrival in the holy cities. It would surely have been disappointing and considerably more expensive to arrive late, say on or after the tenth of the month of Dhū'l-Ḥijjah, when one could no longer fulfill the hajj requirement for that year and would have to spend another year in the Hijaz in order to do so. But we have no way of knowing whether individuals setting off from Central Asia in any given year during these two centuries were particularly concerned about whether they would perform the hajj that year or the next.

In the late 1580s the sultan of Golconda, Muḥammad Qulī (Quṭb Shāh), began to send a ship to the Hijaz annually. The ship was to carry textiles from the Coromandel coast for the Middle East market, carry alms in the name of the sultan to the Holy Cities, and provide direct passage for pilgrims to Mecca and for Arabs coming to India. On its return trip it would carry gold and silver directly to Golconda through its principal port, Masulipatnam, and would carry returning pilgrims as well as Arab merchants and immigrants to Golconda. The fact that this ship was subject to the dictates of the monsoon seasons meant that its schedule could not be correlated with the time of the hajj. Depending on the year, pilgrims could wait nearly a year for the hajj to occur and then an equally long time to return home. Therefore, the issue of whether the monsoon would be favorable or not for making the hajj may have been of far less importance in an individual's route choice than other factors that we can only guess at now, such as personal plans for stops and visits along the way, business duties, and the route recommended in that particular year by people whose judgment the pilgrim could rely on.

If the monsoon cycle affected Central Asian pilgrims at all, then there would have been alternating cycles of desirable and undesirable years for the sea routes, depending on how many months the pilgrims were willing to cool their heels at Mecca or en route. Of course, the longer one was prepared to wait, the less significant the issue of the monsoon cycle became.

There is also the factor of the return from the hajj by sea. If returns by sea to India tended to be limited to September and October, then the most desirable years to have made the hajj over the sea routes (to go and come in the same year) would have been those years when the hajj occurred between mid-June and mid-August (allowing thirty to forty-five days to make the overland journey between Mecca and Mukha). In the sixteenth and seventeenth centuries these years are 1496–1502, 1528–35, 1561–67, 1595–1601, 1627–33, 1660–66, and 1693–98. Until some correlation can be made between these years and the records of known and dated pilgrimages over the sea routes, however, it is highly speculative to say that Central Asian pilgrims were concerned about the time spent on the hajj journey and that this was a factor in whether they chose the southern route.

In any event there is sufficient counter-evidence of sailings *against* the monsoons, suggesting that there could always be overriding factors. For instance, an Iranian embassy sailing from Bandar 'Abbās to southeast Asia in 1685 set sail on June 25 (25 Rajab 1096), the worst time of year to be at sea. But the embassy had been delayed six months at Bandar 'Abbās and was willing to take the risk.[28] The ship was soon pummeled by storms and nearly driven aground, and it took two weeks to cover the miles from Bandar 'Abbās to Masqat.[29] At Masqat the ship picked up a pilgrim, an Iranian resident of India, who had completed the pilgrimage and was on his way back to India. After three days in port at Masqat, the ship sailed again and for twenty days (until mid-July) enjoyed calm seas. But another severe storm hit; and the *ḥajjī,* sleeping on deck, was washed overboard and drowned.[30]

Besides piracy, the weather, and the problems (if there were any) of coordinating the time of the hajj with the monsoon winds, inlanders from Central Asia had to transit the always dangerous routes through Afghan territory to reach the Punjab. Despite generally firm Mughal control at Kabul, officials had as difficult a time then as now controlling the roads eastward through the tribal territories. Moreover, there was no guarantee of security even in the areas more closely subject to Mughal control. There was always the possibility of local trouble. The Mahdawī movement in the late sixteenth century was one such unsettling factor.[31] Sometime in the 1570s there was an exchange of embassies between Bukhara and Agra. Akbar's letter of response to 'Abd Allāh Khān survives and sheds some light on conditions for pilgrims attempting the southern route at this time. The letter informs the Bukharan khan that, with the conquest of Gujarat and the subjugation of the Mahdawī Afghans, the obstacles to the hajj had been removed, "so that the people of Turan, Khurasan, and 'Iraq [presumably 'Irāq-i 'Ajam] may come to India in order to proceed on pilgrimage by the sea route."[32] About a decade later, in September 1586, Akbar sent another letter to 'Abd Allāh, now reigning khan, in which he rebuffed the latter's overtures concerning an alliance against the Safavids (embroiled at the time in a succession struggle) and expressed his hope that he could eliminate the infidels (the Portuguese) from the sea routes where they continued to plague pilgrims.[33] Whether this was to encourage the Bukharan ruler to continue to direct pilgrims toward Agra or was simply a conventional rhetorical gesture it is difficult to say.

This was a complicated period in Agran-Bukharan relations, for the khan had just ousted the Timurid ruler of Badakhshan, who fled to Akbar's protection in India. Moreover, Akbar appeared reconciled at this point to Safavid control of Qandahar and was opposed to any Bukharan attempt to exploit the current internecine struggle in Iran (the second civil war that lasted from 1577 to 1590 and pitted various Qizilbash factions against each other for control of the throne) for its own benefit. 'Abd Allāh Khān ignored Akbar's advice regarding the Safavids; he seized Herat and much of Khurasan from the Safavids and held them for the next decade. The "friendship" that Imām Qulī would cite in his letter to Akbar's son and successor was quite notional. The Sunni Shibanids and the Sunni Mughals had few foreign policy interests in common during the last quarter of the sixteenth century.

The Pilgrimage Record for the Southern Route

The scanty information on Central Asian pilgrims reflects the relative undesirability of the southern route. As in the case of the northern route via Astrakhan, contemporary sources produce very few names of people who traveled to Mecca via India and the sea route. Of those who traveled that way, most seem to have gone to India for work, for residence, or on official assignment and only then decided to make the pilgrimage, rather than choosing India as the pilgrimage route before leaving Central Asia.

The earliest record of a Central Asian making the pilgrimage via India is in this mode. Sometime before 1566 a grandson of Khwājah 'Ubayd Allāh Aḥrār,

'Abd al-Ḥaqq (having already settled in India), made the pilgrimage, afterward returning to India.[34] In 1587 the Nayman amir Naẓar Bī, who had been governor of Balkh until 1582, accompanied the Bukharan embassy to Agra that informed Akbar of the capture of Badakhshan.[35] Naẓar Bī was with the embassy not as an official member but because he had been exiled after some dispute with the khan and was ultimately bound for Mecca along with three of his sons, Qanbar, Shādī, and Bāqī.[36]

In the early seventeenth century there is information about Mawlānā Ḥasan Qubādyānī's intended hajj. Qubādyānī was one of the leading scholars at Balkh (Maḥmūd b. Amīr Walī calls him *a'lam al-'ulamā'*—"most learned of the learned"). He had held concurrent professorships in Balkh at the 'Abd Allāh Khān Madrasah and the Nazr Muḥammad Khān Madrasah and sometime not long before 1633 left Balkh with Mecca as his destination. He reached Agra, where he reportedly (according to the Central Asian source) made a great impression on Shah Jahan. He never did make the hajj, however, and fell mortally ill in Delhi in 1043/1633. His remains were brought back to Balkh and buried on the 9th of Rabī' al-Thānī 1044/October 2, 1634.[37]

Between 1683 and 1696 five prospective pilgrims attempted the southern route. The first of these, a native Samarqandi named Muḥammad Ṣalāh, spent a number of years studying in Balkh and then traveled to India, where he donned "mendicant's garb" (*libās-i tajrīd*) and made the hajj in 1093/1682. Afterward he returned to Central Asia overland ("through 'Irāq," i.e., through Safavid domains) and eventually wound up back in India, where his anthologist heard he was killed in Lahore in 1100/1689–90.[38]

About this same time, Mullā Muḥammad Jān "Musta'idd-i Bukhārī," disappointed in his search for a job in the Mughal administration, also set sail for Mecca from India but (as noted above) perished at sea when his ship was attacked by "Frankish" pirates.[39]

Another Samarqandi, Mullā Baqā "Tamāshā," a cloth merchant (*bazzāzī*), was in Bukhara in 1684 on business when the Khwarazmian khan Anūshāh briefly occupied Samarqand. Instead of returning home, Mullā Baqā decided to undertake the pilgrimage and headed for India. According to reports, however, he was unable to fulfill his goal because of a lack of resources and when last heard from was wandering from *takiyah* to *takiyah* in India as a mendicant.[40]

A third Samarqandi, a professor at the Shībānī Khān Madrasah, set off for India to undertake the hajj circa 1689 but was persuaded by the Mughal padshah, Awrangzib, to postpone his plans long enough to serve as the ruler's agent in reviving the endowment of the Gūr-i Amīr, the Timurid mausoleum in Samarqand.[41]

The last case I have found of Central Asian pilgrimage in the seventeenth century via India was that of Imām Qulī Qushbegī, father of the author of the *Tārīkh-i Qipchāq Khānī,* Khwājum Qulī Balkhi "Qipchāq Khān." Imām Qulī left Bukhara in 1107/1695. Some of the difficulties of his journey are suggested in his son's description of the preparations: "The writer's father, only by dint of great effort, obtained permission from Subḥan Qulī Khān [his patron and khan at Bukhara at this time] to make the pilgrimage. He stayed in Balkh for nearly six months [making preparations for the rigors of Hindustan] and then on the first of Muḥarram 1107 [August 12, 1695] he left the homeland [*waṭan-i ma'ūf*] for the Haramayn."[42]

Thus far, this is the available record for use of the southern route by prospective Central Asian pilgrims. The individual cases show a certain common pattern: the associated interest, often involving possible economic opportunity, of a visit to Hindustan. There is little to suggest that the route was more convenient or offered better security than the other main routes.

THE CENTRAL ROUTE

The last and most important pilgrimage route was the one that was most direct and least subject, by comparison, to the insecurities posed by banditry and weather on the northern and southern routes. Despite what modern-day historians have written, the route through Safavid Iran consistently proved through the sixteenth and seventeenth centuries the route most favored by Sunni pilgrims from Central Asia.

Beginning in Bukhara, the pilgrims would head southwest for the Amu Darya (Oxus) crossing at Charju then continue through the desert to Marv. From there the route would take them to Sarakhs, Mashhad, Nishapur, and Isfara'in. Depending on time of year and road conditions, the pilgrims might angle north toward Astarabad and then west along the Caspian coast, where there were numerous sacred sites and other tourist attractions,[43] before turning south at Sari and joining the more direct route from Isfara'in just west of Simnan.

At Simnan, there was another choice: either the cross-desert route angling to the southwest to Kashan or the route west through Saveh, Hamadan, and Kirmanshah to Baghdad, where the pilgrims could link up with the feeder caravan that brought pilgrims from Baghdad to the great assembly point at Damascus.

Pilgrims choosing the Kashan road would make their way to Isfahan and from there could continue westward across the Zagros Mountains to Dizful and thence to Basra. In 'Irāq-i 'Arab, the route branched again; depending on travel conditions, pilgrims might take a ship from Basra to Mukha or Jiddah or choose one of several overland routes.

The Advantages and Disadvantages of the Central Route

The obvious advantages of the central route for the Central Asian pilgrim were that it was the most direct, offered the most predictable weather conditions, and could avoid the always dreaded sea. Less obvious advantages included the high degree of personal and property security provided during this period on the roads under Safavid jurisdiction and the numerous points of interest to the pilgrim en route to the Hijaz.

Much has been made, with little evidence, of the seeming obstacle that the Shīʿī state in Iran would pose to Sunni pilgrims during these two centuries. Both Faroqhi and Carrère d'Encausse assume from the very limited evidence of Ottoman *laissez-passers* issued mainly around 1568 that for the entire two centuries Central Asian pilgrims preferred the northern route. Faroqhi, citing a single rather curious case, concludes that Central Asian pilgrims were simply unable to cross Safavid territory because of "constant conflict":

> The Timurid principalities of Central Asia in the sixteenth century were governed by Sunni rulers, many of them in constant conflict with the Safawid shahs of Iran. Due to frequent wars between the Iranian ruler and the khan of the Uzbeks, Sunni pilgrims could not travel to Mecca by the direct route, and all politically feasible detours were enormously long and difficult. Certain pilgrims reached Mecca by way of Istanbul and returned to their Central Asian homelands by way of Delhi. Apparently one of these pilgrims was asked by the Ottoman authorities to deliver an official missive from Sultan Ahmed I (reigned 1603–17) at the court of the Mughal ruler Djihangir (reigned 1605–27). However Akbar's son [Djihangir] refused to recognize the credentials of this improvised ambassador.[44]

First, a small point: there were no Timurid principalities left in Central Asia at the time Faroqhi is writing about, unless one includes the small and isolated holdouts in Badakhshan. At the beginning of the century the Chinggisid dispensation had been revived by a Jochid lineage, the Shibanids. There is no denying that the Shibanids waged war against the emerging Safavid polity—they waged war against their Sunni brethren as well, including the Qazaqs, the Timurids, and their own cousin clans at various times. But just how armed conflict between Safavids and Shibanids in the sixteenth century or Safavids and Tuqāy-Timurids in the seventeenth might have affected pilgrimage routes is not addressed. Nor does she provide any evidence for the sweeping statement that "Sunni pilgrims could not travel to Mecca by the direct route."

Furthermore, the conclusion that "[c]ertain pilgrims reached Mecca by way of Istanbul and returned to their Central Asian homelands by way of Delhi" is drawn from a single example. Had Faroqhi not generalized from this that they had to do so because the direct route was not open, there would be no reason to raise a question about the quality of her evidence. Of course, over a 200-year period, some pilgrims reached Mecca by way of Istanbul and returned via Delhi. In fact, they reached Mecca and returned home—or on occasion did not, as the case may have been—by every conceivable route.

Faroqhi chooses a poor example to prove her argument, a single case from Riazul Islam's *Calendar of Documents,* which refers to an individual who turned up in Istanbul claiming to be of Mawarannahrid origin and styling himself an "uncle" of Imām Qulī Khān, the Bukharan ruler from 1612 to 1641. The Ottoman letter dated 1035/1625 names the bearer Ay Muḥammad Khān. A Mughal source (*Tuzuk-i Jahāngīrī*) called him "'Āqūm ḥājjī" and thought him an impostor.[45] As the Mughals were well aware, Imām Qulī had only two known uncles, both deceased at the time.

In any event, there is nothing in the evidence of this incident to show that the man had actually come to Istanbul from Mawarannahr or had not come through Iran if he did so. Nor is there any evidence here that he had come to Anatolia with the intent of making the hajj. In fact it appears much more likely that once having deceived the Ottomans about his background and convincing them to fund his journey to India, he took the opportunity to perform the hajj en route. His case hardly backs the assertion that "[c]ertain pilgrims reached Mecca by way of Istanbul." This is not to say that they did not. Manṣūr Tarkhān, the son of Qażī Shāhum mentioned above, is one such case. But the evidence of Aqum Ḥajjī (aka Ay Muḥammad) certainly does not support the conclusion. Compounding the felony, as it were, Faroqhi treats the matter as demonstrated and goes on to generalize that pilgrims from Bukhara and Samarqand therefore only used the northern route, as noted above.

Pearson, too, attributes to the Safavid authorities a kind of blanket hostility to Sunnis that made pilgrimage through Iran impossible. He likewise cites but one example, the highly problematic one of the Ottoman admiral Sīdī 'Alī Reis, who was shipwrecked on the coast of Gujarat in 1553 and then made his way overland back to Ottoman territory, reaching Baghdad in the spring of 1557.[46] "Indeed, *sunni* visitors in general appear to have been subjected to slights and insults in Persia. For example, the *sunni* Turkish traveller, Sidi Ali Reis, was three times challenged on sectarian grounds."[47]

Actually, the admiral was more than "challenged." He was arrested, stripped, and detained at Mashhad when he arrived there on the 1st of Muḥarram 964/November 4, 1556; but his arrest probably had far more to do with his being a high Ottoman military officer than with any sectarian concern. Certainly his Sunni Mughal hosts had hardly been more cooperative during his effort to transit India. It is very difficult to extrapolate from the rather singular case of Sīdī ʿAlī Reis that Sunni travelers were routinely "subjected to slights" when passing through Iran.

Besides the sectarian issue, modern historians have not unreasonably assumed that warfare also disrupted, if it did not shut down, the pilgrimage routes. The kind of warfare that the available materials describe, however, is hardly the total war of the twentieth century. Borders were not sealed with mines and barbed wire and guardposts. According to contemporary descriptions, armies tended to concentrate in siege positions in and around towns. Business travelers and pilgrims might well have noticed no difference between the usual problems of bandits in the countryside and the movements of more organized war-bands except when towns were in the grip of a siege. Yet Farooqi speaks of the conflicts between the Safavids and their enemies as "virtually" blocking the roads, implying that this state of affairs held good for the entire sixteenth and seventeenth centuries.

Even if one were to accept the problematic notion that sixteenth- and seventeenth-century warfare disrupted travel between regions at war with each other, the actual periods of such warfare were fairly limited. At most, for example, there were approximately forty-five years between 1500 and 1700 when the Safavids and their neighbors to the northeast, the neo-Chinggisids and their Uzbek supporters, engaged in acknowledged and official warfare.[48] Therefore the great bulk of the period was one of nominal peace. Moreover, there is a fair amount of evidence that during some of these periods of war the authorities on both sides were making at least token efforts to ensure that pilgrims crossing Iran from Central Asia were protected and supported despite the state of hostilities between the two sides.

In 1004/1595, at the height of the conflict between the Shibanid/Uzbek and Safavid/Qizilbash forces in Khurasan, Mīr Qulbābā Kukaltāsh, the Uzbek governor at Herat since its conquest in 1588, sent gifts and an embassy to Shah ʿAbbās, saying that people from Mawarannahr had been unable to make the pilgrimage because of the fighting. Fearing for their lives, they had been unwilling to set foot in Iran, which lies across the road to the Hijaz (*sadd-i rāh-i Ḥijāz*). He requested that permission be granted to those of "the Uzbek tribe" (*ṭāʾifah-i uzbekīyah*) and "the people of Mawarannahr" who wished to make the pilgrimage so that they could do so without fear. Qulbābā's envoys were welcomed in Qazvin, and the shah sent Islām Beg Shāmlū, a centurion (*yūz bāshī*), back to Herat with a decree (*manshūr*) that permitted *ḥajjī*s from the "Uzbeks of Mawarannahr" to transit Iran.[49] Apparently as part of his response to Qulbābā Kukaltāsh's letter, Shah ʿAbbās also sent a letter to ʿAbd Allāh assuring the khan that he would do all he could to provide assistance to pilgrims and merchants coming from Turan.[50]

One could argue that these letters are simply diplomatic posturing for domestic consumption, and they may indeed have served that end. We do not yet have actual examples of individual pilgrims who took advantage of this solicitude on the part of the politicians. In the famous exchange of correspondence between Shah ʿAbbās and ʿAbd al-Muʾmin as they faced each other in Khurasan in the 1590s, there are two other letters that bear on the issue of Central Asian pilgrims through Iran. In one ʿAbd al-Muʾmin calls on the shah to return to the policy of the (very idealized) time of Sultan Ḥusayn Mīrzā (Bayqarā) and Ūzūn Ḥasan and secure the roads for wayfarers and pilgrims. "Now the best policy for us is that those heading for Mecca and businessmen [*tujjār*] should feel secure against attack." He repeats the formula—*tujjār wa ʿāzīmān* [or *ṭālibān*] *-i rāh-i makkah-i muʿaẓẓamah*—three times in this letter. The linkage of businessmen with pilgrims (sometimes adding terms for unspecific travelers: *mutaraddidīn, musāfirīn*) is common,[51] and it may simply be a rhetorical expression for "everyone," especially those who are assumed defenseless and in need of protection.

In a second letter ʿAbd al-Muʾmin wrote to ʿAbbās: "At this time there is nothing between us and the Urganji sultans [the Yadgarid Shibanids of Khwarazm] that contravenes friendship. Between them and us is amity and concord. They are writing us now about the problems of the Turkmen of Astarabad and Girayli and that they have eliminated problems of travel for wayfarers, businessmen, and pilgrims on the hajj."[52] Here the reference is not to the northern route but rather to one of the alternate routes through Iran, the route to the Caspian coast through Nisa along the southern edge of what is now Turkmenistan. Implicit in his letter is the message that it was now incumbent on the shah to take care of things on his side to ensure safe passage for travelers.

Some twenty-five years later the theme of Safavid safeguarding of Central Asian pilgrims is raised again with the visit to Isfahan of a member of the Jūybārī family of Bukhara, a wealthy and politically well-connected family of shrinekeepers. The versions of his visit suggest the difficulties in attempting to separate the political rhetoric from the facts on the ground. In late Shaʿbān 1030/early July 1621 Khwājah ʿAbd al-Raḥīm, the son of Khwājah Saʿd Jūybārī, arrived in Isfahan from Bukhara en route to Mecca.[53] He was received with deference and cordiality: Shah ʿAbbās reportedly paid a visit to the khwājah's quarters as a signal of his respect. As was often the fate of travelers, illness forced a delay in the Bukharan shaykh's journey; and he was still at the Safavid capital in early 1031 (end of 1621). About that time, according to the hardly impartial contemporary Safavid chronicler Iskandar Beg, he petitioned the shah, asking "forgiveness" for "Uzbek misdeeds."[54] This may have been a reference to the heightened level of march raiding in Khurasan that occurred during the ataliqate of Uraz bi Ming in Maymanah.[55] Maḥmūd b. Amīr Walī characterizes the military activity at the time as a fight against "troublemakers" in Panjdah, Maruchaq, and Murghab.[56] Not surprisingly, Maḥmūd makes no mention of any petition of repentance. Quite the contrary: he alleges that the Jūybārī khwājah was actually prevented from completing the hajj by the shah.[57] It is difficult to credit either Iskandar Beg or Maḥmūd here, given the contexts within which each was writing. In any event, the khwājah missed the hajj that year (whether because of his illness or on account of other circumstances), and he returned to Bukhara.

Perhaps while 'Abd al-Raḥīm was still in Isfahan or not long after his departure, Shah 'Abbās sent a letter to the khwājah's older brother, Tāj al-Dīn Ḥasan,[58] in which he reiterated his concern for the welfare of all people, as he had assured Khwājah 'Abd al-Raḥīm during his visit. "Thanks to this understanding, pilgrims to Mecca and Medina and traders and travelers have been coming and going in perfect security." Whether pilgrims enjoyed perfect security in Safavid Iran or not, these and other examples at least provide a counterweight to the received notion that there was a deliberate policy of impeding pilgrims,[59] even when there were open hostilities between the Sunni and Shī'ī states of West Asia.

In the following summer (1622), probably as part of his diplomacy to prevent the Tuqāy-Timurids from interfering with the planned Safavid campaign to retake Qandahar from the Mughals, Shah 'Abbās sent a letter to 'Abd al-Raḥīm in which he expressed a desire for peace with the ruler of Balkh, Nazr Muḥammad. With peace, he wrote, pilgrims, businessmen, and travelers would be able to move about in safety. He asked the khwājah to continue to correspond with him and expressed hope that they would see each other again.[60]

The Central Asian ruling caste seems to have been equally adept at posturing as guardians of the pilgrimage route. In 1563 or so, Pir Muḥammad, the Shibanid appanage-holder at Balkh at the time, led an unsuccessful campaign to take Mashhad.[61] The justification for it, like its predecessors under 'Ubayd Allāh and Shībānī Khān, was to open the pilgrimage route. But as Martin Dickson was perhaps the first to note, this must be seen as mere propaganda, apparently effective, because it is repeatedly used, but not to be mistaken for an accurate account of the existing situation.[62] The Shibanids, like the Safavids, were interested in expansion of their territory, the chief means to economic growth. Ensuring the kind of security over the pilgrimage route that their propaganda proclaimed would have meant the complete subjugation of the Safavid state. But, like the Safavid rulers, they were not unskilled at making a virtue of necessity. Perhaps the oft-expressed wish for an Ottoman-Mughal-Shibanid alliance was more than just a pious one, frequently expressed for its propaganda value. There is little to suggest that such an alliance would have led either to the downfall of the Safavid state or to any drastic change in pilgrimage routes.

The reality for Central Asian pilgrims was that the route through Safavid Iran was no more hazardous than the route via India or Astrakhan. But the professed Shiʿism of the Safavid state gave the powers in Agra, Bukhara, and Istanbul a propaganda weapon not available for the other routes (except in the case of the Portuguese and other Frankish infidels on the sea route). Despite the explicit and implied charges of Safavid obstructionism found in the diplomatic correspondence, I have yet to discover a single instance of a Sunni pilgrim or pilgrim caravan being blocked, if we discount the case of Khwājah ʿAbd al-Raḥīm Jūybārī. Yet the propaganda continued through the sixteenth and seventeenth century, presumably because it was effective at home.

In 1568 ʿAbd Allāh, son of the newly enthroned khan at Bukhara, Iskandar b. Jānī Beg, led a force into Khurasan. Despite some early success, it was withdrawn suddenly because of political problems at home.[63] He too justified the campaign in terms of (among other things) providing freedom of passage for pilgrims heading for Mecca. As mentioned earlier, this particular campaign may have encouraged some pilgrims to choose the northern route; or at least we have circumstantial evidence that some Central Asia pilgrims did choose the northern route about the time when the campaigning began or shortly thereafter.

The propaganda continued to reverberate down through the years; and in 1687 Subhān Qulī, the khan at Bukhara, sent a letter to Awrangzib in which he "expresses gratitude that now, being free from domestic worries, he can turn his entire attention to the task of shattering Shiʿite power in order to ensure complete freedom of access to the holy Kaʿba." This was merely a formulaic wish, not to be taken too seriously, as underscored by the khan's wholly incredible boast that, having "liberated" Bala Murghab (one of the towns in the Iranian/Mawarannahrid marches that continually changed hands), he had "stopped the people of ʿIraq and Khurasan from cursing the first three caliphs."[64]

The Pilgrimage Record for the Central Route in the Sixteenth and Seventeenth Centuries

Writings that describe pilgrimage across Iran by and large record only the activities of a privileged class of people with the means to travel, like ʿAbd al-Raḥīm Jūybārī, for example. For the laborers, artisans, or servants whose work was all that stood between their family and starvation, travel expenses and lost earnings probably rendered a hajj-pilgrimage inconceivable. Yet as time passed, those same individuals might perhaps raise children whose labor would eventually free them to travel. Locating such a subaltern group is difficult. For the time being we may assume that those who made the pilgrimage were by definition the privileged. The wealthy and privileged took their servants with them, however, presumably thereby affording them the opportunity to perform the hajj. Behind the names that appear in the texts we have to imagine other nameless but no less real participants in the adventure.

For it was an adventure. The journey through Iran was never seen as mere transit but as an opportunity to visit and pay one's respects at shrines all along the way. In the sixteenth and seventeenth centuries shrine visits were what tourism is in our time—a reason for travel and perhaps a way to learn about another society. The attraction of shrines was ecumenical. The shrine of the Eighth Imam, Imam Riza, for example—viewed today as a particularly Twelver Shīʿī shrine center—was equally appealing to and served as a destination for Sunni visitors in earlier times. For a Central Asian prospective hajji, the shrine at Mashhad was an obligatory stop.[65]

The earliest instance I have found for an individual from Central Asia transiting Safavid Iran on pilgrimage is Mīrzā Ṣabrī, a famous *rubāb* and *ʿūd* player from Bukhara who typifies this interest. He traveled to the Hijaz via Isfahan; and it is recorded that, like many Sunni pilgrims, he was eager to visit shrines. In his case, it was the tombs of ʿAlī and Ḥusayn; and he is reported to have spent some time at the *maqām-i Ḥusaynī* in Karbala before continuing on to the Haramayn. After fulfilling his hajj obligations, he returned to Bukhara. No precise date is given for his pilgrimage, but it must have been before 1566–67 (when the source that records it, the *Mudhakkir al-aḥbāb,* was written).[66]

Another early pilgrim who probably traveled via Iran, although the account does not specifically say so, was a high-ranking Uzbek amir, Shujāʿ al-Dīn Dūst Nī (alternately Dūst Muḥammad Jānī), son of one of the principal supporters of Muḥammad Shībānī Khān, Jān Wafā Bī. Nizārī, author of the *Mudhakkir al-aḥbāb,* tells us that Dūst Nī made the pilgrimage in 973/1565–66.[67]

Most of the individuals who made the pilgrimage through Iran and whose names have been recorded traveled with the pilgrimages of four of the seventeenth-century Tuqāy-Timurid khans, Walī Muḥammad in 1611–12, Imām Qulī in 1642, Nazr Muḥammad in 1651, and ʿAbd al-ʿAzīz in 1681–82.

After being ousted from his throne by his nephews Imām Qulī and Nazr Muḥammad, Walī Muḥammad went to Isfahan, intending by all accounts to make the hajj; there he was persuaded by Shah ʿAbbās to return to Mawarannahr and retake his throne. He took the advice and some Qizilbash troops but was killed in the attempt to regain the khanate.

Imām Qulī also abdicated under some duress but apparently not because of rivals for the khanate. He suffered some form of ocular degeneration and surrendered the throne because he could no longer see. Like his uncle before him and his brother and nephew afterward, he was attended by a large party on the trip to the Holy Cities. He announced in a letter to the governor of Marv that he was accompanied by 200 people, presumably so that sufficient provision could be made for the group.[68] Among them were some of his closest political supporters—Nadr Bī Arlāt *diwānbegā,* Raḥīm Beg *parwānajā,* Bayram Khwājah *yasāwul-ī ṣuḥbat,* and Khwājum Qulī Qalmaq.[69] The khan spent some time in Marv and then moved on to Mashhad, where he performed *ziyārat* rites at the tomb of the Eighth Imam. According to *Khulāṣat al-siyar,* on a Wednesday in Ẕū'l-Qa'dah 1051/February 1642, Shah Ṣafī dispatched a Dulgadir (Dhū'l-Qadr) amir, Khāndān Qulī Beg, with 1,000 tumans in cash and 500 tumans worth of supplies for Imām Qulī. Although Khāndān Qulī Beg is not styled a *mihmāndār* or chief of protocol, he clearly was assigned as an official escort, a functionary depicted in some detail in the case of 'Abd al-'Azīz Khān forty years later.

Either at Mashhad or shortly after leaving the city, Imām Qulī received news of the death of Shah Ṣafī and sent his congratulations to the new shah, 'Abbās II.[70] 'Abbās replied with a letter of welcome, expressing his pleasure at the khan's performing *ziyārat* at the shrine of the Imam Riza. 'Abbās himself then traveled to Qazvin to welcome the former khan. Imām Qulī was feted at Qazvin and invited to spend the rest of the (Turki) year there; but he declined the invitation and continued on to Mecca, where he obviously arrived in time to perform the hajj of 1052/1643. He lived only a short time longer, dying in 1053/1644, and was buried (according to *Silsilat al-salāṭīn*) at the "*ṣuffah* of Khwājah Muḥammad Pārsā behind the *qubbah* of Hazrat-i 'Abbās and Imam Ḥasan."[71]

Besides the officials mentioned by Muḥammad Maḥsūm, Imām Qulī was also accompanied on the pilgrimage by several other named individuals and countless unnamed ones. Muḥammad Badī' Samarqandī mentions two poets: one was Ḥajjī Muḥammad "Ṣābir," who left the Hijaz after performing the pilgrimage with Imām Qulī and sailed to India, where he spent twenty years before returning to Samarqand.[72] The other was Ākhūnd Ḥajjī "Bahrām." Ḥajjī Mīr Muḥammad Sālim also names Khwājah Mīrak, a *dīwān,* and Ibrāḥīm Khwājah, a *naqīb.*[73]

In 1061/1651 Nazr Muḥammad abdicated the khanate under pressure from his son 'Abd al-'Azīz and his son's amirid supporters and set out to perform the hajj. He never reached his goal. At Simnan he was struck by illness and died. At first his body was reportedly interred next to a *chahārbāgh* belonging to Jamshīd Khān, governor of Erivan in the late 1670s.[74] Subsequently, his remains were disinterred and reburied in Medina at the Baqī' Cemetery, probably near his brother's. Among the named individuals accompanying the former khan were two brothers, Allāh Yār Khwājah and Nūr Allāh Khwājah, sons of Shah Muḥammad Khwājah b. Muḥammad Yār Khwājah, members of a Sayyid Aṭā'iyyah (Yasavī) lineage. The brothers returned from Simnan with the khan's personal effects.[75]

Between 1651 and 1681 Muḥammad Badī' Samarqandī reports on one other pilgrim, of Central Asian origin but at this stage more a citizen of the Persianate ecumene—Shah Shawkat, whom he met and became friends with while on an embassy sent by 'Abd al-'Azīz to Shah Sulaymān in Isfahan in 1090/1679.[76]

The last of the Mawarannahrid khans to abdicate and make a farewell pilgrimage via Iran was 'Abd al-'Azīz Khān, who left Bukhara in the autumn of 1681. As I treat his pilgrimage in more detail elsewhere, I only note here that he too was accompanied by a large party; the names of nine of them were recorded and have survived thanks to Muḥammad Badī' Samarqandī. The khan's party spent nine months in Iran, at no small expense to Shah Sulaymān's treasury. The party visited dozens of shrines, Sunni and Shī'ī, as well as some associated with mythological and literary figures.

CONCLUSION

We thus have more than enough evidence to lay to rest the notion that the Safavids made it impossible for Sunni pilgrims from Central Asia and India to cross their territory. No doubt there were moments when—because of war or weather or the economy or banditry—the route looked less desirable to the prospective pilgrim from points east than at other times. As historical evidence to the contrary, there is little more than the routine and formulaic propaganda of the Sunni politicians to suggest that the Safavids ever adopted actual measures to turn pilgrims back.

A question that cannot be answered but might prove more fruitful to pursue in the long run is whether the Safavid government sponsored facilities for the annual hajj across its territory. The assignment of *mihmāndārs* to escort very important pilgrims safely and smoothly across the country shows that at the level of intergovernmental relations the will and the means existed to support at least individual parties of pilgrims in transit. Whether similar support for less well-placed pilgrims at ordinary times existed remains to be documented.

Although the Safavid sources emphasize the sums of money spent on the notables from Mawarannahr, there were certainly potential economic benefits from encouraging transiting pilgrims. Active competition for the pilgrim traffic seems to have occurred elsewhere, and we might assume Safavid officials would have been equally interested in exploiting it. On at least one occasion shaykhs along the Gulf and lower Mesopotamian routes petitioned the Safavid court to send pilgrim caravans through their territory, presumably for the money to be made from the hire of guides, escorts, transport, food, and other services, though the arguments were couched in terms of the care to be accorded the pilgrims and the dangers lurking elsewhere.[77] One assumes that Mawarannahrid pilgrims passing through Iran would have been expected to bring the same kinds of benefits that Shīʿī Iranian pilgrims would bring to "ʿArabistan."

The main obstacle to a detailed and persuasive study of the pilgrimage routes through Iran has been the foregrounding of sectarian difference as if it were in itself a sufficient explanation. Sectarianism has become a catchall rationale for human and institutional behavior that seems not to demand high standards of proof. This is certainly not to say that on occasion, or even routinely, individuals or institutions did not arbitrarily (and violently) discriminate on sectarian grounds. I imagine such discrimination was as common in the sixteenth and seventeenth centuries as it was in the late twentieth century. I would only argue that it serves as a very unsatisfactory way to explain two centuries of mutual relations and personal encounters related to both hajj and *ziyārat*-pilgrimage. Those who postulate sectarianism as a sufficient explanation for these encounters must willfully ignore an extensive body of incompatible evidence. Perhaps it would be more useful to examine the phenomenon of the pilgrimage in a comparative context, looking for evidence in the Safavid case of institutions and responses to the needs of "pilgrims, businessmen, and travelers" that appear more readily in the historiography of other regions, where the sectarian issue has not come to dominate the discourse.

NOTES

1. Suraiya Faroqhi, *Herrscher über Mekka: Die Geschichte der Pilgerfahrt* (Munich: Artemis, 1990); and idem, *Pilgrims and Sultans: The Hajj under the Ottomans 1517–1683* (London and New York: I. B. Tauris, 1994), a revised version of the preceding; Ian Richard Netton, ed., *Golden Roads: Migration, Pilgrimage and Travel in Medieval and Modern Islam* (London: Curzon Press, 1993); F. E. Peters, *The Hajj: Muslim Pilgrimage to Mecca and the Holy Places* (Princeton: Princeton University Press, 1994); and M. N. Pearson, *Pious Passengers: The Hajj in Earlier Times* (London: Hurst and Co., 1994; recently republished in somewhat abbreviated form as *Pilgrimage to Mecca: The Indian Experience 1500–1800* [Princeton: Markus Wiener, 1996]). Important recent articles on the subject are Sanjay Subrahmanyam, "Persians, Pilgrims, and Portuguese: The Travails of Masulipatnam Shipping in the Western Indian Ocean, 1590–1665," *Modern Asian Studies*, 22 (1988): 503–30; and Naim R. Farooqi, "Moguls, Ottomans and Pilgrims: Protecting the Routes to Mecca in the Sixteenth and Seventeenth Centuries," *International History Review* 10, no. 2 (May 1988): 198–220. A. Jan Qaisar, "From Port to Port: Life on Indian Ships in the Sixteenth and Seventeenth Centuries," in *India and the Indian Ocean 1500–1800*, ed. Ashin Das Gupta and M. N. Pearson

(Calcutta: Oxford University Press, 1987), pp. 331–49, is a summary of the sea portion of the hajj memoir *Anīs al-ḥujjāj,* written by Ṣafī b. Walī Qazvinī, who left Delhi on the 12th of Rajab 1087/September 18, 1676, to sail from Surat to Jiddah on the ship *Salamat Ras.* A somewhat earlier but nonetheless influential work from the standpoint of the hajj-pilgrimage from Central Asia (Mawarannahr, Khwarazm, and Khurasan) is Hélène Carrère d'Encausse, "Les routes commerciales de l'Asie Centrale et les tentatives de reconquête d'Astrakhan," *Cahiers du Monde Russe et Soviétique* 11 (1970): 391–422.

2. See, e.g., the mid-seventeenth-century lists of court and bureaucratic titles and officials in Maḥmūd b. Amīr Walī, *Baḥr al-asrār fī manāqib al-akhyār,* India Office Library MS no. 574, fols. 124a–26b (the Bukharan amirs); fols. 133a–58b (shaykhs and qāżīs of Mawarannahr); fols. 277b–305a (religious and military officials at Balkh), and the later (eighteenth-century) brief listing of offices and titles published by A. A. Semenov in "Bukharskii traktat o chinakh i zvaniiakh ob obiazannostiakh nositelei ikh v srednevekovoi Bukhare," *Sovetskoe Vostokovedenie* 5 (1948): 137–53.

3. Carrère d'Encausse, "Les routes commerciales," p. 405.

4. Faroqhi, *Pilgrims,* p. 140. Faroqhi has a section here entitled "Pilgrims from Central Asia" (pp. 139–42) that—perhaps because it relies exclusively on Ottoman sources and on a single case cited from Riazul Islam, *A Calendar of Documents on Indo-Persian Relations 1500–1750* (Tehran: Iranian Culture Foundation; and Karachi: Institute of Central and West Asian Studies, 1982), 2:310ff.—presents a somewhat less than comprehensive view of the Central Asian pilgrimage experience. The section also misidentifies the sixteenth- and seventeenth-century khanates of Bukhara and Khwarazm as "Timurid."

5. Faroqhi, *Pilgrims,* p. 139.

6. Toru Horikawa, "Aleppo and Central Asia in the Sixteenth Century: A Brief Note," in *Geographical Views in the Middle Eastern Cities,* ed. Akinobu Terasaka and Masanori Naito (Ryutsu Keizai University, Study Group on Middle Eastern Cities, 1990), 2:35–37.

7. See Carrère d'Encausse, "Les routes commerciales," pp. 405ff.; Faroqhi, *Pilgrims,* pp. 140, 141, 208 (notes 46, 47, 49, 51, 53, and 54); and Horikawa, "Aleppo and Central Asia," pp. 35–36, for the specific document references from Register 7 of the Mühimme Defterleri.

8. Audrey Burton, *The Bukharans: A Dynastic, Diplomatic, and Commercial History, 1550–1702* (Richmond, Surrey: Curzon, 1997), pp. 18–19.

9. See Horikawa, "Aleppo and Central Asia," pp. 35, 36; Faroqhi, *Pilgrims,* pp. 140, 208 (notes 46, 47); Carrère d'Encausse, "Les routes commerciales," p. 410 (note 1).

10. Waṣifi, *Bada'i' al-waqa'i'* (Moscow: Nauka, 161), pp. 336–42.

11. Ibid., p. 1141.

12. Faroqhi, *Pilgrims,* pp. 141, 208 (note 52); Carrère d'Encausse, "Les routes commerciales," p. 406. Faroqhi mentions only a *laissez-passer* issued to the shaykh, while Carrère d'Encausse extrapolates a pilgrimage caravan from the same document. But she does not provide a context to indicate whether this was a dedicated state-sponsored pilgrimage caravan like the one that departed Damascus every year or was simply a commercial caravan, some of whose members intended to continue on to the Holy Cities.

13. Faroqhi, *Pilgrims,* pp. 141, 208 (note 53), 209 (note 54).

14. T. D. Lavrentsova, R. V. Ovchinikov, and V. I. Shumilov, comps., *Russko-Indiiskie otnosheniia v XVII v. (Sbornik dokumentov)* (Moscow: Vostochnaia Literatura, 1958), p. 427 (column 1).

15. Maḥmūd b. Amīr Walī, *Baḥr al-asrār,* fol. 294a.

16. Ibid.: *dār ān-ḥudūd bi-ṣuḥbat-i lāzim al-bahja-i Shaykh Ḥabīb Allāh Shīrāzī bi-mayāmin-i anfās-i ʿīsāwī-asās jāḏḥibah-i qawī dar maṭāwī aḥwāl-i ū mudākhalat namūd.*

17. Pearson, *Pious Passengers,* pp. 95–96.

18. For a discussion of this perspective on early modern Middle Eastern history, see my "'Barrier of Heterodoxy'?: Rethinking the Ties between Iran and Central Asia in the 17th Century," in *Safavid Persia,* ed. Charles Melville (London: I. B. Tauris, 1996), esp. pp. 231–35.

19. Farooqi, "Moguls, Ottomans and Pilgrims," pp. 200–201. "The foundation in 1501 of the Safavid empire in Persia, and the consequent sporadic border conflicts between the Persians and the Ottomans, had virtually blocked the road, and the sectarian hostility of the Safavids towards the Sunnis had further jeopardized the free movement of pilgrims along it." He cites only Sīdī ʿAlī Reis's account as evidence for this conclusion, as does Pearson (see below).

20. The synopsis was published by Islam in *Calendar,* 2:238.

21. Pearson, *Pious Passengers,* p. 89.

22. Ibid.

23. Subrahmanyam, "Persians, Pilgrims and Portuguese," pp. 523–24.

24. Farooqi, "Moguls, Ottomans and Pilgrims," pp. 203–4.

25. Muḥammad Badīʿ Samarqandī, *Mudhakkir al-aṣḥāb,* Tashkent, IVAN MS no. 4296, fol. 194a.

26. See, e.g., Ovington: "The Ships from *Suratt* that Sail for the *Red Sea* take their departure generally about *March* and Arrive at *Mocha* towards the latter end of *April,* or before the 20th of *May* at which time . . . the Winds vary, and prevent any more Ships entering into the Sea that Year" (Pearson, *Pious Passengers,* p. 150).

27. Russell King, "The Pilgrimage to Mecca: Some Geographical and Historical Aspects," *Erdkunde* 26 (1972).

28. Anon., *The Ship of Sulaiman,* trans. John O'Kane (New York: Columbia University Press, 1972), p. 25.

29. Ibid., p. 29.

30. Ibid., p. 32.

31. On the Mahdawīs, see T. W. Arnold [B. Lawrence], "Mahdawīs," *Encyclopaedia of Islam,* New Edition 5:1230.

32. Islam, *Calendar,* 2:207.

33. Ibid., 2:210–11.

34. Khwājah Bahā' al-Dīn Bukhārī "Nithārī," *Mudhakkir al-aḥbāb* (New Delhi, 1969), p. 108.

35. The embassy is described by Abū'l-Faẓl al-ʿAllāmī, *The Akbarnama of Abu-l-Fazl* (New Delhi: Ess Ess Publications, 1987, reprint), 3:721, who mentions Naẓar Bī as a member of the party. His wording suggests that he was aware of Naẓar Bī's position with the embassy.

36. Ḥāfiẓ-i Tanīsh, *Sharaf-nāmah-i shāhī* (India Office MS, no. 574), fols. 463b–64a, makes it clear that he was not an official member of the embassy.

37. Maḥmūd b. Amīr Walī, *Baḥr,* fols. 350a–b.

38. Muḥammad Badīʿ Samarqandī, *Mudhakkir al-aṣḥāb,* Tashkent, IVAN MS no. 4270, fol. 238a–b.

39. Ibid., fol. 194a.

40. Ibid., fol. 55b.

41. Ibid., fols. 298aff.

42. Anon., *Tārīkh-i Shībānī Khān wa mu'āmalāt bā Amīr Tīmur,* Tashkent, IVAN MS no. 4468/II, identified by B. A. Akhmedov, *Istoriko-geograficheskaia literatura Srednei Azii XVI–XVII vv.: Pis'mennye pamiatniki* (Tashkent: Fan, 1985), pp. 98–99, as the *Tārīkh-i Qipchāq Khānī.*

43. Details will be published in "A Pilgrim's Progress: The 1681–2 Hajj-Pilgrimage of 'Abd al-'Azīz Khān," forthcoming.

44. Faroqhi, *Pilgrims,* p. 139.

45. Islam, *Calendar,* 2:310–11.

46. A. Vambéry, trans., *The Travels and Adventures of the Turkish Admiral Sidi Ali Reis in India, Afghanistan, Central Asia, and Persia during the Years 1553–1556* (London: Luzac and Co., 1899).

47. Pearson, *Pious Passengers,* p. 96.

48. Roughly, the periods of war are 1507–10, 1513, 1518, 1521, 1524–40 (during which there were numerous lulls), 1567, 1578, 1587–1601, 1612–13, and 1631–37. See Martin B. Dickson, "Shah Tahmasb and the Ozbeks" (dissertation, Princeton University, 1958); and Burton, *The Bukharans.*

49. Iskandar Beg Munshi, *Tārīkh-i 'ālam-ārā-yi 'Abbāsī* (Isfahan, n.d.), vol. 2.

50. Islam, *Calendar,* 2:227.

51. See for example Sultan Sulāymān's letter to the king of Portugal in October 1565, Pearson, *Pious Passengers,* 95.

52. Maḥmūd b. Hidāyat Allāh Āfūshtah-i Naṭanzī, *Nuqāwat al-āṣār fī ẕikr al-akhyār,* ed. Ehsan Eshraqi (Tehran, 1350/1971), p. 418.

53. Islam, *Calendar,* 2:233.

54. Iskandar Beg, *Tārīkh-i 'Ālam-ārā-yi 'Abbāsī,* pp. 963, 978.

55. Maḥmūd b. Amīr Walī, *Baḥr al-asrār,* 6:pt. 4, India Office Library, MS no. 575, fols. 293a–b.

56. According to Burton, *The Bukharans,* p. 158, it was in 1621 that Shah 'Ābbas sent his protégé, Rustam Muḥammad, son of the ousted Tuqāy-Timurid khan Walī Muḥammad (r. 1606–12), back in a futile attempt to recapture the khanate.

57. Maḥmūd b. Amīr Walī, *Baḥr al-asrār,* fol. 144a.

58. Islam, *Calendar,* 2:231.

59. Ibid., 2:207, 227, 233.

60. Ibid., 2:232.

61. Burton, *The Bukharans,* p. 18.

62. Dickson, "Shah Tahmasb," pp. 155ff.

63. Burton, *The Bukharans,* p. 19.

64. Islam, *Calendar,* 2:285.

65. In my forthcoming study "A Pilgrim's Progress: The 1681–2 Hajj-Pilgrimage of 'Abd al-'Azīz Khān," I give more detail on the shrines in Iran. See also my "'Barrier of Heterodoxy'" and "The Anthology of Poets: *Muẕakkir al-aṣḥāb* as a Source for the History of Seventeenth-Century Central Asia," in *Intellectual Studies on Islam: Essays Written in Honor of Martin B. Dickson,* ed. Michel M. Mazzaoui and Vera B. Moreen (Salt Lake City, 1990), pp. 57–84.

66. Bahā' al-Dīn Ḥasan Nizārī Bukharī, *Mudhakkir al-aḥbāb,* ed. Syed Muhammad Fazlullah, pp. 454–55.

67. Nithārī, *Mudhakkir al-aḥbāb,* pp. 413–14. On Jān Wafā Bī (Mīrzā), see Ẓahīr al-Dīn

Muḥammad Bābur Pādshah Ghāzī, *The Babur-nama in English,* trans. Annette Susannah Beveridge (London, 1922; 1969 rpt.), pp. 131, 133.

68. Burton, *The Bukharans,* p. 208 (note 236).

69. Ḥajjī Mīr Muḥammad Sālim, *Silsilat al-salāṭīn* (or *Tawārīkh-i badī'ā*), Oxford, Bodleian Library, MS no. 169, fol. 200a, where the date is incorrectly assigned to "Yilan Yil 1051" (Yilan is correct but the year began in 1050); and Muḥammad Ma'ṣūm b. Khwājagī Iṣfahānī, *Khulāṣat al-siyar* (Tehran, 1358/1979), p. 293. The editor of *Khulāṣat al-siyar* seems to have fallen prey to the Turki-Hijri year correspondence problem. Muḥammad Ma'ṣūm (like Iskandar Beg) organizes his work into chapters based on the Turki solar year beginning at Nawrūz. The Turki year Yilan in which Imām Qulī set out from Bukhara began on the 8th of Ẕū'l-Ḥijjah 1050/March 21, 1641, and thus fell almost entirely within 1051. But the editor carries the Hijri year of 1050 as the page heading through the chapter (because the beginning falls in 1050), easily misleading the reader (including myself at first) about the year in which the events were actually taking place. Burton, *The Bukharans,* pp. 208–11, has sorted out the numerous sources (Safavid, Mughal, and Tuqāy-Timurid) and provides a credible sequence of events beginning with the abdication on the 6th of Sha'bān 1050/ November 8, 1641.

70. Burton, *The Bukharans,* p. 210.

71. Sālim, *Silsilat al-salāṭīn,* fol. 201b.

72. Muḥammad Badī' Samarqandī, *Mudhakkir al-aṣḥāb,* fol. 314b.

73. Sālim, *Silsilat al-salāṭīn,* f. 200a.

74. This according to Muḥammad Badī', writing in the 1690s. He claims to have met Jamshīd Khān. Klaus Michael Röhrborn, *Provinzen und Zentralgewalt Persiens im 16. und 17. Jahrhundert* (Berlin, 1966), p. 36, has a Jamshīd Khān *qullar-aqāsi* as governor of Astarabad under 'Abbās II.

75. Muḥammad Badī' Samarqandī, *Mudhakkir al-aṣḥāb,* fol. 244b; also Burton, *The Bukharans,* p. 264; *Silsilat al-salāṭīn,* fol. 268b. The film *Mecca, the Forbidden City* (directed by 'Abd al-Qāsim Rizā'ī for Iranfilm, ca. 1960) has a brief segment at 18:34 of the film on the Guristan-i Baqi'.

76. Muḥammad Badī' Samarqandī, *Mudhakkir al-aṣḥāb,* fols. 139a–45a; also see my "'Barrier of Heterodoxy,'" pp. 252ff., on Shah Shawkat.

77. See, for example, Muḥammad Ibrāhīm b. Zayn al-'Ābidīn Nasīrī, *Dastūr-i shahyārān* (Tehran, 1373/1994), pp. 122–23.

7

A Seventeenth-Century Iranian Rabbi's Polemical Remarks on Jews, Christians, and Muslims

Vera B. Moreen

INTRODUCTION

From the late Middle Ages through the early modern period (fourteenth–nineteenth centuries) Iranian Jews produced a considerable body of Judeo-Persian (henceforth JP) texts—that is, texts in New Persian written in Hebrew letters. The contents of these texts are impressively varied, ranging from epic verse to folk remedies.[1] Although they are full of references to Jewish and, to a considerable extent, Muslim lore, JP texts are conspicuously devoid of legal (halakhic) and philosophical content. There are at least two explanations for this absence. First, many JP manuscripts remain uncatalogued, their contents still unknown. Second, and perhaps more importantly, legal and philosophical texts—if produced by Iranian Jews at all—were probably written in Hebrew rather than in Persian.[2] This second explanation derives from the very nature of JP texts, whose contents may be included under the general heading of "popular culture." The presence of biblical commentaries and sermons among JP manuscripts, texts that are clearly religious in content but that were aimed primarily at popularizing the teachings of the Torah, only reinforces this impression. It is therefore somewhat surprising to find at least one sophisticated philosophical treatise in the corpus of JP manuscripts. When one studies its contents, however, the author's largely didactic and popularizing agenda appears to justify his choice of the vernacular.

R. YEHUDAH AND *ḤOBOT YEHUDAH*

Ḥobot Yehudah (The Duties of Judah; henceforth *ḤY*), written by Rabbi Yehudah b. El'azar in 1686,[3] may be the only philosophical text in JP. About R. Yehudah's background we know only what he chooses to reveal about himself in this work, which is not much. R. Yehudah was a physician by profession, born in Kashan, the home of several important Jewish Iranian authors, such as 'Imrānī, Bābāī b. Luṭf, and Bābāī b. Farhād.[4] During R. Yehudah's lifetime, Kashan was a prosperous town famous in particular for its commerce in silks and the weaving of textiles and rugs, activities in which Jews also participated. It may be that R. Yehudah was the son of R. El'azar, mentioned by the chronicler Bābāī b. Luṭf in his *Kitāb-i anusī* (The Book of a Forced Convert). In any case, R. Yehudah was learned in his own right; Refu'ah b. El'azar Ha-Kohen, a fellow citizen of Kashan, who produced a condensed version of *ḤY* soon after its composition, refers to him as both *rabbi* and *dayyan* (Heb., religious judge).[5] In addition to *ḤY*, R. Yehudah wrote an astronomical treatise called *Taqvīm al-Yahudah* (The Calendar of Judah), a short treatise on the dangers of drinking wine, and a poetic rendition of the well-known legend of the seven viziers, known either as *Timsāl-nāmah* (The Book of Similitude) or as *Haft Vazīrān* (The Seven Viziers).[6]

R. Yehudah's purpose in writing *ḤY* was to expound upon the basic teachings of Judaism in order to inculcate "correct" beliefs in his coreligionists. In order to facilitate their access to eternal truths, R. Yehudah consciously turned to the vernacular, because, as he says in his introduction,

> it is well known that my contemporaries [*ahl-i zamānih*] do not pursue the sciences, especially [not] the *fundamentals of the faith*,[7] knowledge and *belief* in which convey one to *life in the world to come* and to the eternal subsistence of the soul. [Therefore I] turned to this [task], for this matter is necessary for all human beings, the exalted as well as the lowly. Not everyone is able to understand the generals and particulars written on this subject in the *holy tongue*, let alone its subtleties and details....[8]

Thus R. Yehudah's choice of JP, although he was clearly literate in Hebrew, Aramaic, and Arabic, indicates that the majority of his coreligionists were not learned, in Jewish terms—which can also be surmised from the two surviving JP chronicles, the seventeenth-century *Kitāb-i anusī* of Bābāī b. Luṭf and the eighteenth-century *Kitāb-i Sar Guzasht-i Kāshān* of Bābāī b. Farhād.[9] As in the case of his principal model, *Dalālat al-ḥā'irīn* (Guide for the Perplexed) by Moses Maimonides (d. 1204), which was written in (Judeo-)Arabic but for quite different reasons, R. Yehudah may have felt that use of the vernacular would open up his work to a broader audience.

ḤY focuses primarily on the principles of the Jewish faith as presented by Jewish thinkers (especially philosophers), chief among them Maimonides.[10] The major philosophical topics R. Yehudah addresses are: 1. the principles of the Jewish faith; 2. the existence and essence of God; 3. prophecy; 4. God's knowledge; 5. Divine Providence and free will; 6. the status of the Torah; 7. the Oral Law; 8. the resurrection of the dead; 9. Creation and the Divine Chariot (*merkabah*);[11] and 10. the essence of the soul and the intellect. On the whole, *ḤY* discusses these topics in a highly condensed fashion, which adds to the difficulty of reading this text. R. Yehudah's approach to these subjects, like that of Maimonides, on whom he relies heavily, is that of a learned rationalist, a *mutakallim* philosopher.

R. Yehudah's Persian is "richly eloquent."[12] The style of *ḤY* is somewhat repetitious due to his paraphrastic method of translating Persian phrases into Hebrew and vice-versa. Like many other Jewish Iranian authors, he introduces Persian syntax in some of his Hebrew sentences, especially in his use of the construct state. More than the language of earlier JP writers, such as the poets Shāhīn (fourteenth century) and ʿImrānī (fifteenth century) and his contemporary Bābāī b. Luṭf (seventeenth century), R. Yehudah's Persian is heavily strewn with Hebrew words (italicized in the quotations here), biblical quotations, and rabbinic references. This is not unusual, however, considering the theologico-philosophical topics of the treatise.

In *ḤY* R. Yehudah shows a fine command of numerous Jewish and non-Jewish sources. In addition to the Hebrew Bible, he quotes often from the Talmud, Zohar (and other kabbalistic works), rabbinic commentaries, and several Jewish philosophers, such as Nahmanides (d. 1270), Gersonides (d. 1344) Crescas (d. 1412?), and Albo (d. 1440). As well as including numerous references to the works of Maimonides, he singles out for praise and response the Jewish Italian Renaissance philosopher David Messer Leon (d. 1526). He quotes extensively, directly and indirectly, from these Jewish philosophers without indicating the exact source or location of his quotations, as was common in the Middle Ages. R. Yehudah enters into lively debate with his sources; the nature, extent, and especially the originality of his arguments need to be evaluated by scholars who specialize in medieval Jewish philosophy and theology.

Among his non-Jewish sources, R. Yehudah refers to the Greek philosophers Plato and Aristotle. He quotes from the works of numerous Muslim philosophers, such as al-Fārābī (d. 950), Ibn Sīnā (d. 1037), al-Ghazālī (d. 1111), Ibn Rushd (d. 1198), and Naṣīr ud-Dīn al-Ṭūsī (d. 1274). He quotes Persian belles-lettres, especially the poetry of Rūmī and Saʿdī. R. Yehudah also refers to the New Testament and the Apocrypha and quotes the Qur'ān several times.[13]

R. YEHUDAH'S POLEMICAL VIEWS ON JEWS, CHRISTIANS, AND MUSLIMS

Neither the range nor the originality of R. Yehudah's philosophical arguments is the subject of this study. Rather, I was drawn to investigate what, if anything, may be gleaned from *ḤY* about his views and perceptions of his coreligionists as well as of his non-Jewish neighbors, Muslims and Christians. In the absence of data that we may define as more appropriately "sociohistorical" and reflective of interconfessional relations in Iran in the seventeenth century, R. Yehudah's views may shed some light on how one Jewish intellectual saw the world around him. As his non-Jewish references indicate, R. Yehudah was obviously very much at home in both Muslim and Iranian milieux. It is therefore even more interesting to try to discern his views regarding the status of Jews and his Muslim neighbors.

As a seventeenth-century citizen of Iran, R. Yehudah must have witnessed the anti-Jewish persecutions described by Bābāī b. Luṭf in *Kitāb-i anusī*. Those persecutions culminated in a wave of forced conversions that lasted about seven years (1656–62), during which the Jews of many major Iranian towns and villages were *anusim* (Heb., forced converts), openly practicing Islam while secretly remaining Jews. *ḤY* was written less than twenty years after these upheavals and after the failure of the messianic Sabbatean movement (which appears to have gained adherents among Iranian Jews as well).[14] It seems likely (although R. Yehudah does not say so explicitly) that it was written in direct response to these events; for, as mentioned earlier, his stated goal was to strengthen the Jewish faith of his coreligionists. It is surely no coincidence that he undertook this project after the twin traumas of forced conversion and disappointed messianic expectations. R. Yehudah does not specifically mention these events, however. He confines himself to a guarded, circumlocutory, and rather standard explanation for undertaking his composition: namely, that his coreligionists needed to be well informed, not only from a religious but also from a rational perspective, in order to be able to answer their enemies and detractors.[15]

R. Yehudah's views about his non-Jewish neighbors are not expressed in a direct manner in one handy section of the treatise; rather they must be gleaned from several sections. While their polemical intent is not especially hidden (since the author clearly addressed his treatise to a Jewish audience), R. Yehudah's views need to be balanced with the subtext of the treatise, especially with his frequent perusal of and even direct quotations from a variety of non-Jewish sources.

The topics that best reveal (directly or indirectly) R. Yehudah's polemical views on Christianity and Islam as these relate to Judaism can be discussed under the following headings: the election of Israel; the impossibility of Jewish apostasy; the erroneous beliefs of Christians; and the erroneous beliefs of Muslims.

1. The Election of Israel

Not surprisingly, given the persecutions in his time, R. Yehudah found it necessary to stress repeatedly the concept of Israel's divine election. In section 2, chapter 7, devoted to the scriptural obligation to worship God, he declares that

> all Israel is discerning from the aspect of intelligence, for although God's beneficence [*iḥsān*] extends equally to all *mankind,* He [God] chose one people from among the nations and made them special [*makhṣūṣ*] with regard to their worship of Him; believe, therefore, that the *decrees of the Torah* are from the *Blessed One.* Since the Israelites are a chosen people, their [mode of] *worship* is different and special [in comparison with] the common one of the nations of the world.[16]

According to R. Yehudah, this chosen status manifests itself in various ways from the moment of creation of each individual Israelite, who is more pure than others due to the fact that Israelite women observe the laws of ritual purity,[17] and throughout God's continued and direct involvement with Israel in history. While the providence of other nations is under the jurisdiction of various astrological constellations, that of Israel is solely under God's guidance.[18] Thus, referring to the talmudic disputation in tractate Shabbat 156 70a–70b regarding whether Israel is under the protection of a specific constellation, R. Yehudah mentions that Scorpio rules over 'Arabistan (Khuzistan), Sagittarius over Fars; Capricorn guides the destinies of all Zoroastrians, Libra protects Armenians and Europeans (the two appear to be linked in the author's mind by virtue of their [undifferentiated] Christianity), while Taurus is in charge of all Muslims.[19] In the same vein R. Yehudah claims that "the difference between the *divine worship* which is derived from the *Torah of Moses* and the rest of the [modes of] worship of nations is that the *Holy Torah* commands that all the *worship and prayer* that we carry out is in accordance with the wish of the *Blessed One* for he rules over all the means [of worship]."[20] For this reason, the sacrificial offerings of the Israelites, presented with the greatest care and purity, were more acceptable to God than the sacrifices of other nations.[21] Similarly, true prophecy can be found only among the Israelites, because, in R. Yehudah's words, "the nations, however *proficient in wisdom,* since they are not *under the yoke of the Torah,* they cannot [truly] prophesy...."[22]

2. *The Impossibility of Jewish Apostasy*

It is very likely that the most important reason for R. Yehudah's insistence on Israel's election (quite apart from the role of this subject in medieval Jewish philosophy) is that the Jews of his time had to undergo forcible conversion to Islam. Having proved, at least to his own satisfaction, the chosen (because divinely decreed and guided) fate of Israel as well as the superiority of Moses and the Torah (see below), R. Yehudah insists forcefully that it is impossible for Jews to change their religion, for

> the *sages* said that *the Children of Israel are believers* even if they remove the *yoke of the Torah* and abandon [their] *faith* in God. They cannot belong to another faith and religion because, whether they change their religion willingly, or are forced to do so and have no escape, they still remain *Children of Israel;* whatever affects the *Children of Israel* of good and ill befalls them [apostates] also. About those who abandon their religion it is written: *Even though he sinned, he is an Israelite.*[23] [Similarly,] the prophet said: "*... when you say, 'We will be like the nations,... worshipping wood and stone.' As I live ... I will reign over you with overflowing fury*" [Ezek. 20:32–33],[24] "*... and I will bring you into the bond of the covenant*" [Ezek. 20:37], and also "*And what you have in mind shall never come to pass...*" [Ezek. 20:32]. From these verses it is clear that even if Israel should change its religion and believe in the idols of the nations, it would not be part of the assembly of nations because the latter have not been commanded whereas the Israelites, when they trespass positive and negative commandments, are sinning. That is the meaning of "*and I will bring you into the bond of the covenant*" [Ezek. 20:37]. In fact, according to R. Me'ir,[25] the Israelites are always to be regarded as *children,* even if they are strangers and are ignorant, for it is written: "*For my children are stupid...*" [Jer. 4:22], even if they reject [their] *faith,* "*They are children with no faith in them...*" [Deut. 32:21], and even if they should become idolaters, as it is written: "*depraved children...*" [Isa. 1:4].[26]

R. Yehudah goes on to state that, according to the same R. Me'ir, even if an Israelite defiantly rejects the Torah, "*profanes the Sabbaths in public and becomes an idolater,* he cannot become [part of the] assembly of nations because the Israelite *faith* is joined and is strongly attached to his rational soul [*nafs-i nāṭiqa*] in such a manner that it can never be separated from him." Moreover, R. Yehudah adds, "because their [the Israelites'] souls, through spirituality, experienced and held fast to the Divine at the time of the giving of the *holy* Torah, even if they wish to corrupt their faith through their acts and thoughts, they are unable to do so. . . ." He concludes that "from these explanations it is clear that every person, even if he were a complete sage, cannot help but agree—through these proofs and demonstrations—that the divine Torah is *true* and real, and that one cannot change one's *faith* and religion. . . ."[27]

Having absolved his coreligionists not only of apostasy but even of the possibility of apostasy, R. Yehudah also argues the superiority of Judaism by polemicizing against what he considers to be the erroneous religious beliefs of Christians and Muslims.

3. The Erroneous Beliefs of Christians

As we know, contact with Christianity in Iran in the seventeenth century meant mostly contact with Armenians and, to a much lesser extent, with Georgians and European missionaries. R. Yehudah does not distinguish between these groups and tends to lump them together under the Persian designation *armanī* (Armenian). He refers to Armenians three times; first, by declaring that they are providentially protected;[28] second, by claiming that they were biblically given the realm of Mt. Se'ir (and are thus descendants of the Edomites, a traditional Jewish view of general Christian origins);[29] and third, by referring to baptism as a symbolic event, similar to circumcision, marking a child's entrance into a particular religious covenant.[30]

R. Yehudah seems familiar with at least some basic tenets of Christianity, so that he can refer to them as erroneous (from the Jewish point of view). Thus, in the context of discussing actions impossible by their nature, he mentions the Christian belief that

> God, out of the plenitude of His mercy and righteousness toward his servants and nations, descended from heaven to earth, appeared in human form, suffered heavy persecution at the hands of the Israelites, and accepted death in order to atone for mankind's *sin* of birth, especially [for the sin of] *Adam the First,* the father of mankind, and other such heretical beliefs. [But] we see that Israelites do not accept such beliefs. They accept *expulsions, punishments, and death(s)* rather than change their faith. . . .[31]

In the epilogue to *ḤY,* written in Hebrew and tinged with messianic expectations, R. Yehudah attacks even more specifically what he views as Christian misinterpretations and misappropriations of biblical verses. He dismisses the Christian interpretation of Ps. 2:7 ("Let me tell of the decree: the Lord said to me, 'You are My son, I have fathered you this day'"), which reads the Trinity into the biblical verse, by proclaiming that this interpretation is best described by the biblical verse "all [is] futile and pursuit of wind" (Eccles. 1:14; 2:11, 2:17). He adds that all such views are built upon a "splintered reed of a staff" (II Kings 18:21), because, according to the Jewish interpretation, Ps. 2:7 is understood to be King David's prophetic retort to the future tauntings of Gog and Magog.

Nor is R. Yehudah more sympathetic toward the Christian interpretation of Isaiah 7:14 ("Look, the young woman is with child and about to give birth to a son. Let her name him Immanuel"), a verse that Jews traditionally connect with Isaiah's warning to King Ahaz. The Christian interpretation of the verse, according to R. Yehudah, is "false . . . the Christians adduce from here the view that Miriam [Mary], the wife of Joseph, was a virgin and was impregnated by the holy spirit, without a mate," which, in his view, is "conceiv[ing] evil and giv[ing] birth to fraud" (Ps. 7:15). In another place he vehemently denounces both Sufis and Christians as *ḥulūliyān* (Pers., incarnationists), the first for believing that God can manifest himself in humankind and the latter not only for believing that Jesus is the spirit of God (Ar./Pers., *rūḥ-i Allāh*),[32] but also for believing that Miriam could become pregnant without a mate. In R. Yehudah's view, such beliefs are simply *bāṭil* (Ar./Pers., vain, false).

R. Yehudah also refers to the famous verse at Ps. 22:2 ("My God, my God / Why have You abandoned me"), which, according to Jewish interpretation, was uttered by King David as a prophecy regarding both the events in the Book of Esther[33] and the present and longest period of Israel's exile. It is not

> as Christians maintain in the Injīl [New Testament] that all the verses of [this] psalm are about Jesus when he was being crucified; and they [the Christians] are grateful for this, for [they believe that] he [Jesus] suffered these punishments at the hand of the Israelites to atone for the sin of birth, and in order that these afflictions would accrue to the merit of his people to save them from their evil [ways], etc. They say that at the time of the crucifixion, as his soul was leaving his body, he called out to his father in heaven, My God. . . .

He then also quotes the verse in Arabic and in Greek and adds, "and such [is the case] with verse after verse that they [Christians] interpret [as referring to] Jesus and even change parts of the words according to their views and desire. . . ."[34]

4. The Erroneous Beliefs of Muslims ("Ishmaelites")

Not surprisingly, R. Yehudah's views about Muslims appear in equally polemical contexts. While discussing the superiority of Moses and his prophethood and the superiority of the Torah over other revelations, R. Yehudah actually displays considerable knowledge of Muslim anti-Jewish arguments.[35] In order to refute them he resorts to words of the Qur'ān itself in Arabic, thus bolstering his arguments with proofs from the rival camp, which were incumbent upon Muslims.

R. Yehudah's discussion of the superiority of Moses owes much to the views of Maimonides as expressed in *Dalālat al-ḥā'irīn*.[36] After extolling the *faḍā'il* (Ar./Pers., excellent qualities) of Moses—reminiscent of the voluble praise heaped upon Muḥammad in Muslim religious sources[37]—and while distinguishing the prophethood of Moses from all others, R. Yehudah quotes the Qur'ān (Surah 4:164), "...and Allah spake directly to Moses,"[38] thus explaining *Kalīm Allāh* (God's interlocutor), the traditional Muslim epithet bestowed on Moses. His elevated status is further acknowledged in Surah 4:153, when "the People of Scripture" asked Moses to "show us Allah plainly," even though God denied his request as far as perceiving His essence was concerned: "...thou wilt not see Me" (Surah 7:143). According to some Jewish interpretations, however, God left open the possibility that Moses would perceive even His essence in the hereafter.[39]

Replying to yet another Muslim contention—namely, that the Qur'ān supersedes the Torah—R. Yehudah's treatise includes a spirited defense of the unique "heavenly Torah," which cannot be abrogated, a reference to the Muslim charge of *naskh*.[40] R. Yehudah's reply is, in effect, a borrowing of the concept of *i'jāz al-Qur'ān* (Ar., inimitability of the Qur'ān) on behalf of the Torah, although he does not actually use this technical term. He clinches (at least in his view) the argument that the Torah cannot be abrogated by adducing the words of the Qur'ān: "...for each We have appointed a divine law and a traced out way. Had Allah willed He could have made you one community..." (Surah 5:48). Moreover, according to R. Yehudah, the permanent validity of the Torah for the Jews cannot be disputed: quoting the Qur'ān again, "How come they unto thee for judgment when they have the Torah, wherein Allah hath delivered judgment [for them]?..." (Surah 5:43). Furthermore, there can be no doubt about the accuracy of the revealed text of the Torah, because "[t]hou wilt not find for Allah's way of treatment a substitute [*tabdīlan*], nor wilt thou find for Allah's way of treatment aught of power to change [*taḥwīlan*]" (Surah 35:43). R. Yehudah responds similarly to the Muslim charge of *taḥrīf* ([scriptural] falsification) when he denies, without quoting explicitly the second half of Surah 5:45, that Jews no longer practice literally the precepts of their scripture, as exemplified in their modification of *lex talionis* (Deut. 19:21).[41]

R. Yehudah displays further acquaintance with the Qur'ān by referring to the angels Hārūt and Mārūt, whom he identifies with the angels 'Aza and 'Aza-'el of the Jewish tradition.[42] His knowledge of Shi'ism in particular, however, is not impressive. I found only one Shi'i reference, specifically to the imamate; but from that single reference it would appear that, when R. Yehudah refers to "Ishmaelites" in general, he means (naturally enough for his context) the Shi'is. Thus, in his discussion of the fundamentals of faith, R. Yehudah states that "the Ishmaelites consider monotheism [*tawḥīd*], justice [*'adl*], prophecy [*nubuwwat*], the imamate [*imāmat*], and resurrection [*ma'ād*] to be among the fundamentals of faith [*uṣūl-i dīn*]."[43]

Curiously, R. Yehudah's refers to Maḥmūd Pāsikhānī, the founder of the Nuqtawī sect in the fourteenth century.[44] He does so in the context of discussing reward and punishment and mentions that Pāsikhānī and his followers, like the Pythagoreans, believed in metempsychosis.[45] It may be that in R. Yehudah's time the memory of this sect, persecuted by Shah 'Abbās I, was not yet obliterated and that its ideas were still alive in some intellectual circles.[46]

CONCLUSION

In the treatise *ḤY,* R. Yehudah reveals no specific information about his non-Jewish neighbors. His views on Jews, Christians, and Muslims are entirely within the confines of traditional polemics. While they display the author's erudition, these views also reveal that his learning was largely derivative; in the matter of impressions about his non-Jewish neighbors they are actually stereotypical. Perhaps more interesting than R. Yehudah's commonplace (from the Jewish polemical perspective) views about Christians and Muslims are his extensive acquaintance with and use of non-Jewish sources, which bespeak a high level of acculturation. In sum, the historical value of *ḤY* is primarily that it is the effort of a learned, acculturated individual who produced what appears thus far to have been a rather solitary response to the increasing hostility directed at non-Shi'is in general and Jews in particular in his days. Thus R. Yehudah's goal was to review and reiterate, rather than reinterpret, to his fellow Jews the fundamentals of the Jewish faith, which had been dealt severe blows—internally by the lure of the Sabbatean movement and externally by forced conversions—in the second half of the seventeenth century.

NOTES

1. See my anthology *In Queen Esther's Garden: An Anthology of Judeo-Persian Literature* (New Haven: Yale University Press, 2000).

2. The nature of Hebrew texts produced in Iran during the same period is yet to be explored.

3. Originally my study of this work was based on two MSS: 8 5231 of the Jewish National and University Library, Jerusalem, and 2007 of the Klau Library, Hebrew Union College, Cincinnati. Recently, Amnon Netzer published an annotated edition of the JP text

including a Hebrew translation, introductions in both Hebrew and English, and helpful indexes. All references are therefore to A. Netzer, *Ḥobot Yehudah le-Rabbi Yehudah b. El'azar* (henceforth *ḤY*) (Jerusalem: Ben Zvi Institute, 1995). I thank Professor Netzer for sending me a copy of his book.

4. See Vera B. Moreen, *Iranian Jewry's Hour of Peril and Heroism: A Study of Bābāī Ibn Luṭf's Chronicle, 1617–1662* (New York: American Academy for Jewish Research, 1986); idem, *Iranian Jewry during the Afghan Invasion: The Kitāb-i Sar Guzasht-i Kāshān of Bābāī Ibn Farhād* (Stuttgart: Franz Steiner Verlag, 1990).

5. Netzer, *ḤY*, p. v.

6. Ibid., pp. xiii–xviii.

7. Heb., *'iqare ha-dat*, a synonym of the Ar., *uṣūl al-dīn*.

8. Netzer, *ḤY*, JP, p. 67, #19; Heb. tr., p. 274, #19.

9. See Moreen, *Iranian Jewry's Hour of Peril and Heroism;* idem, *Iranian Jewry during the Afghan Invasion.*

10. It is not clear when, and to what extent, the works of Maimonides became known in Iran. I found no evidence of copies of *Dalālat al-ḥā'irīn* in Judeo-Persian collections; but several copies of *Mishneh Torah*, his magisterial theologico-philosophical work, are found at the British Library, many of them with Judeo-Persian glosses. See Or. 10041, 10007/2, 10007/2, 10043.

11. A branch of Jewish mysticism.

12. Netzer, *ḤY*, p. xxi.

13. I am unable to determine whether R. Yehudah could have known these scriptures firsthand. In any case, he definitely had an intriguing number of appropriate quotations at his disposal.

14. Gershom S. Scholem, *Sabbatai Ṣevi: The Mystical Messiah* (Princeton: Princeton University Press, 1973), pp. 637, 640, 752–53.

15. Netzer, *ḤY*, JP, p. 70, #29; Heb. tr., p. 278, #29.

16. Ibid., JP, p. 133, #22; Heb. tr., p. 346, #22.

17. Ibid., JP, pp. 190–91, #14; Heb. tr., p. 415, #14.

18. On the rabbinic view that God alone is responsible for Israel's "troubles and redemption," see Ephraim E. Urbach, *The Sages: Their Concepts and Beliefs* (Cambridge, Mass.: Harvard University Press, 1987), pp. 153–54.

19. Netzer, *ḤY*, JP, p. 201, #49; Heb. tr., p. 428, #49. Netzer also refers to the biblical commentary (Deut. 4:19) of Abraham ibn Ezra (d. 1167) as an early medieval source promulgating the concept of nations' having guardian angels (p. 428, n. 188).

20. Ibid., JP, p. 196, #28; Heb. tr., p. 421, #28.

21. Ibid., JP, p. 237, #34; Heb. tr., p. 472, #34.

22. Ibid., JP, pp. 168–69, #21; Heb. tr., pp. 387–88, #21. R. Yehudah disqualifies Balaam's prophecy; see ibid., JP, p. 165, #11; Heb. tr., p. 384, #11.

23. *Babylonian Talmud,* Sanhedrin 44.61.

24. All English quotations of the Hebrew Bible are from *Tanakh: The Holy Scriptures* (Philadelphia: Jewish Publication Society, 1985).

25. *Babylonian Talmud,* Qiddushin, 35.72–36.71.

26. Netzer, *ḤY*, JP, pp. 222–23, #29–30; Heb. tr., pp. 455–56, #29–30.

27. Ibid., JP, pp. 223–25, #31–37; Heb. tr. pp. 456–58, #31–37.

28. See the section "1. The Election of Israel" above.

29. Ibid., *ḤY*, JP, pp. 217–18, #16, #18; Heb. tr., pp. 449–50, #16 and #18.

30. Ibid., JP, pp. 230–31, #10 (*hamchih armanī kih ʿawż-i [Heb.] millah sharbatī dar kinisht bi ṭifl mikhorānand*); Heb. tr., p. 465, #10. The context actually refers to the necessity of oral law to elucidate difficult biblical injunctions, such as Deut. 10:16, "circumcise the foreskin of your heart," interpreted by rabbinic authorities figuratively and variously, as "remove the barriers" (Rashi), "remove the barriers keeping you from the truth" (Ibn Ezra, Ramban), "remove from your hearts foolishness" (Targum), "the evil eye" (Sukkah 52a), "thoughts of sin" (Saʿadia), etc. (*The Living Torah: The Five Books of Moses and the Haftarot,* tr. Aryeh Kaplan [New York: Maznaim, 1981], p. 919).

31. Netzer, *ḤY,* JP, p. 153, #84; Heb. tr., p. 369, #84.

32. Ibid., JP, pp. 109–10, #7; Heb. tr., pp. 319–20, #7.

33. *Babylonian Talmud,* Megillah 15.60b.

34. R. Yehudah gives several additional similar examples, among them Ps. 19:2 and 19:15; see Netzer, *ḤY,* Heb. text only, pp. 541–43, #69–#71.

35. For a more detailed discussion of these issues in *ḤY,* see Vera B. Moreen, "Polemical Use of the Qur'ān in Two Judeo-Persian Texts," in *Irano-Judaica IV: Studies Relating to Jewish Contacts with Persian Culture throughout the Ages* (Jerusalem, forthcoming).

36. *The Guide of the Perplexed,* trans. Shlomo Pines, 2 vols. (Chicago: University of Chicago Press, 1974), 2:chs. 32–48.

37. A. Schimmel, *And Muḥammad is His Messenger: The Veneration of the Prophet in Islamic Piety* (Chapel Hill: University of North Carolina Press, 1985).

38. All English quotations from the Qur'ān are from *The Glorious Qur'ān,* trans. Mohammad M. Pickthall (London: George Allen and Unwin, 1984).

39. Netzer, *ḤY,* JP, p. 178, #24; Heb. tr., p. 399, #24.

40. On *naskh* and other polemical issues raised by Muslims against Judaism, see Hava Lazarus-Yafeh, *Intertwined Worlds: Medieval Islam and Bible Criticism* (Princeton: Princeton University Press, 1992), especially pp. 35–41.

41. Netzer, *ḤY,* JP, p. 232, #16; Heb. tr., pp. 466–67, #16.

42. Ibid., JP, pp. 152–53, #83; Heb. tr., pp. 368–69, #83.

43. Ibid., JP, p. 78, #56; Heb. tr., p. 286, #56.

44. See Vera B. Moreen, "The Status of Religious Minorities in Safavid Iran," *Journal of Near Eastern Studies* 40 (1981): 123.

45. Netzer, *ḤY,* JP, p. 250, #4; Heb. tr., p. 490, #4 and note 2.

46. Moreen, "Status," p. 123.

8

The Genesis of the Akhbārī Revival

Devin Stewart

In the early seventeenth century, Twelver Shi'ite jurisprudence witnessed the birth and development of a radically revisionist movement; its stated goals were to rid Shi'ite scholarship in the religious sciences of inauthentic accretions and to tie legal rulings more directly to the oral traditions of the Imams, hearkening back to an idealized early period when access to the Imams' teachings was more direct and Shi'ite thought was not contaminated by outside influences. This movement pitted the scripturalist Akhbārīs, so called because of their reliance on the oral tradition (*akhbār*) of the Imams, against the Uṣūlīs, rationalist jurists whose appellation derives from *uṣūl al-fiqh* (the science of Islamic jurisprudence and legal theory) and who approached the corpus of oral traditions more skeptically. Studies on Shi'ism have tended to view the conflict between the Akhbārīs and Uṣūlīs exclusively as one of traditionalism versus rationalism; but the Akhbārīs were extremely concerned not only with the threat of rationalism but also with the relationship between Shi'ite and Sunni jurisprudence. A crucial feature of their doctrine was an isolationist stance toward Sunni scholarship in the religious sciences, an abhorrence of assimilation to the standard modes and methods of Sunni legal thought. An understanding of this aspect of the Akhbārīs' agenda clears up a number of puzzling points concerning the genesis of the Akhbārī movement, which remains poorly understood to date.

The present essay focuses on the work of Zayn al-Dīn b. 'Alī al-'Āmilī (d. 965/1558), known as al-Shahīd al-Thānī ("the Second Martyr") in the Twelver Shi'ite legal tradition. Although he lived in Jabal 'Āmil (the Shi'ite region in what is now southern Lebanon) and never traveled to Iran, let alone settling there, his works and thought had an enormous impact on the development of the religious sciences within the Safavid Empire. His influence spread particularly through the mediation of his student and companion Ḥusayn b. ʿAbd al-Ṣamad al-Ḥārithī al-Ḥamdānī (d. 984/1576), who emigrated from Jabal ʿĀmil to Iran and served as Shaykh al-Islām of Qazvin under Shah Ṭahmāsb, and his son Bahāʾ al-Dīn Muḥammad (d. 1030/1621), who served as Shaykh al-Islām of Isfahan for many years, including the greater part of ʿShah ʿAbbās I's reign.[1] The following remarks attempt to provide a clearer picture of the place of the Akhbārī revival in the history of Twelver jurisprudence, thereby elucidating a major facet of Safavid intellectual history.

Akhbarism is arguably the most important movement in Twelver Shiʿite intellectual history during the Safavid period, given its tremendous effects on the religious sciences and related fields in the seventeenth and later centuries.[2] Like Martin Luther, who (with the famous slogan *sola scriptura*) sought to locate religious authority in the sacred text itself as opposed to the church hierarchy, the Akhbārīs argued for a system where authority was ostensibly invested in scripture itself, particularly in the oral traditions attributed to the Twelver Imams. They denied the exclusive religious authority the jurists had arrogated to themselves and rejected the claim that the jurists' speculative methods were legitimate means of discovering God's law. While the Akhbārīs espoused anti-rationalist views, they also adopted an anti-Sunni stance, arguing for an isolationist—as opposed to an assimilationist—attitude among Shiʿite scholars. They saw that, over the previous five centuries, Shiʿite jurists had largely imported their system of jurisprudence from Sunnis and that it was therefore fundamentally flawed and lacking authenticity within the Shiʿite tradition.

The only remedy for this situation was for the Shiʿites to return to the one reliable source of religious guidance, the Imams. Though direct access to the Imams was no longer possible during the Occultation, the Akhbārīs believed that their *ḥadīth*s were an adequate embodiment of the Imams' teachings, indeed the only legitimate one possible. Even the Qurʾān, the Akhbārīs argued, could only be understood in the proper manner through these reports.[3] Akhbarism had its heyday in the late seventeenth and early eighteenth centuries. By the nineteenth century it had lost its popularity and was nearly completely defunct, though its legacy remained important for Iranian and Twelver Shiʿite intellectual history.

The beginning of the Akhbārī movement in the Safavid period is marked by the completion of Muḥammad Amīn al-Astarābādī's polemical work *al-Fawāʾid al-madanīyah* (Informative Points from Medina) in the early seventeenth century. Later adherents to Akhbarism as well as opponents referred back to this famous book as a starting point, the movement's manifesto. The author's *nisbah* indicates that he was a native of Astarabad in northern Iran, but his birth date is unknown. In his youth he studied *ḥadīth*s and the biographies of *ḥadīth* transmitters in Karbala with Sayyid Muḥammad b. ʿAlī b. Abī al-Ḥasan al-ʿĀmilī (d. 1009/1600), receiving an *ijāzah* from him in 1007/1598–99.[4] He also studied under the latter's relative and companion Ḥasan b. Zayn al-Dīn al-ʿĀmilī (d. 1011/1602), the son of al-Shahīd al-Thānī, probably in Karbala as well.[5] He then traveled to Shiraz, where he studied jurisprudence for four years under the teacher Shah Taqī al-Dīn Muḥammad al-Nassābah.[6] Between approximately 1015/1606 and 1025/1616, he studied in Mecca with the Shiʿite *ḥadīth* scholar Mīrzā Muḥammad b. ʿAlī al-Astarābādī (d. 1028/1619), who seems to have exercised a strong influence on his thought and urged him to revive the method of the Akhbārīs.[7] Muḥammad Amīn wrote *al-Fawāʾid al-madanīyah,* he reports, in response to students' requests that he teach them jurisprudence. He completed the work in Rabīʿ I 1031/January–February 1622.[8] Al-Astarābādī died five years later, in 1036/1626–27.[9]

Recently, several scholars have revised the view that *al-Fawāʾid al-madanīyah* marks the beginning of the Akhbārī movement, presenting more nuanced accounts of the history of Akhbarism. In a sweeping intellectual history of Shīʾism between the ninth and the sixteenth centuries, Andrew Newman has argued that Twelver Shiʿite jurisprudence reveals a continual tension between traditionalist Akhbārī and rationalist Uṣūlī thought, so that one cannot say that the conflict began or even reemerged from a state of dormancy in the seventeenth century with the work of Muḥammad Amīn al-Astarābādī.[10] The conflict between Akhbārīs and Uṣūlīs already existed, Newman argues, in the tenth century and lasted almost continually until the sixteenth century, when it was represented by the intellectual rivalry between the prominent jurist and pro-Safavid ideologue ʿAlī b. ʿAbd al-ʿĀlī al-Karakī (d. 940/1534) on the Uṣūlī side and his opponent Ibrāhīm al-Qaṭīfī (d. after 945/1539) on the Akhbārī side. Unfortunately, Newman's account ends in the sixteenth century and does not address the issues of the relationship of *al-Fawāʾid al-madanīyah* to earlier Akhbarism.

Hossein Modarressi, while noting the persistent conflict between rationalist and traditionalist tendencies throughout Shiʿite intellectual history and admitting that an important change was introduced by al-Astarābādī's work, points to developments in the sixteenth century that facilitated or led to the revival of Akhbarism. He maintains that the roots of the Akhbārī revival predate al-Astarābādī and that two prominent sixteenth-century jurists, al-Shahīd al-Thānī (d. 965/1558) and Ḥusayn b. ʿAbd al-Ṣamad al-ʿĀmilī (d. 984/1576), were actually precursors of the movement, in effect proto-Akhbārīs:

> A suitable ground for the revival of the traditionist school had gradually been provided from the early 10th/16th century onwards. Around the middle of the same century, a tendency calling for more freedom in Shīʿī law began to gain popularity. Al-Shahīd al-Thānī wrote a treatise against following the legal judgments of the previous jurists without examining

> their bases. His pupil Ḥusayn b. ʿAbd al-Ṣamad al-ʿĀmilī, *shaykh al-islām* of the Safavid court, followed the same line and wrote a similar treatise on the same subject in which he held that *ijtihād,* i.e. the normal method of legal reasoning which is based on rational argument, is not the only way to the discovery of legal norms. In most of his other works, he criticized the legal method of Shīʿī jurists and blamed them for being imitators of the "ancients."[11]

In a note, Modarressi adds that "Ḥusayn b. ʿAbd al-Ṣamad's works were regarded as the vanguard of that dispute" (i.e., the Akhbārī–Uṣūlī conflict).[12] In an essay on the Shiʿite jurists of the sixteenth and seventeenth centuries, Rula Jurdi Abisaab also upholds this view.[13] Modarressi's remarks indicate that developments in the sixteenth century set the stage for the revival represented by al-Astarābādī's work and that the legal thought of al-Shahīd al-Thānī and Ḥusayn b. ʿAbd al-Ṣamad prefigured the Akhbārī movement.

The assessments of Newman and Modarressi both have some validity. The Akhbārī movement of the seventeenth century did not appear out of nowhere. Muḥammad Amīn al-Astarābādī indeed revived a trend in Twelver scholarship that had been important in earlier periods. He himself implies that he did so at the behest of and under the influence of his teacher in Mecca, the *ḥadīth* scholar Mīrzā Muḥammad al-Astarābādī, claiming that he intended to reestablish the methods of earlier Twelver scholars, by whom he intends such figures as Muḥammad b. Yaʿqūb al-Kulaynī (d. 329/941) and Muḥammad b. Bābawayh al-Qummī (d. 381/991). An examination of the intellectual history of the religious sciences in the sixteenth century supports Modarressi's view that developments then led to the Akhbārī revival. The impression that al-Shahīd al-Thānī and Ḥusayn b. ʿAbd al-Ṣamad were themselves proto-Akhbārīs or that their views lined up fairly squarely with those of the Akhbārīs against those of the Uṣūlīs, however, needs to be revised upon closer examination of the evidence.

The present essay suggests that the Akhbārī revival came about primarily as a critical *reaction* to developments in Shiʿite jurisprudence that took place in the sixteenth century, particularly in the work of al-Shahīd al-Thānī. Rather than standing as forerunners or pioneers of the Akhbārī movement or setting the stage for it by criticizing earlier legal scholarship and calling for freer methods in Shiʿite jurisprudence, al-Shahīd al-Thānī and his student Ḥusayn b. ʿAbd al-Ṣamad expressed ideas that were poles apart from those presented in *al-Fawāʾid al-madanīyah.* It was specifically against their works and ideas that al-Astarābādī was arguing. Rather than adopting ideas that then developed into the traditionalist Akhbārī doctrine, al-Shahīd al-Thānī and his student espoused ideas that were so far to the rationalist side of the spectrum as to provoke the traditionalist reaction embodied in the Akhbārī revival. Moreover, their ideas were seen by al-Astarābādī and others in the Akhbārī camp as so blatantly assimilationist to Sunni doctrines that they should be rejected outright.

CRITICISM OF AL-'ALLĀMAH AL-ḤILLĪ

In *al-Fawā'id al-madanīyah,* al-Astarābādī singles out al-'Allāmah al-Ḥillī (d. 726/1325), the prolific Twelver jurist of the late thirteenth and early fourteenth centuries who studied at the Ilkhanid observatory in Maragha and later served at the court of the Ilkhan Uljaytū (703–16/1304–16), as the chief author of two heretical innovations that proved particularly disastrous, in his view, for the Twelver legal tradition. The first was the introduction into the Shi'ite tradition of Sunni *ḥadīth* methodology, particularly the classification of *ḥadīth*s under the categories of *ṣaḥīḥ* (strong, sound), *ḥasan* (good, reliable), and *ḍa'īf* (weak, unreliable). The second was the introduction of a strict division of the believers into two categories, *mujtahid*s (fully competent jurists) and *muqallid*s (laymen).[14] Neither of the statements can be taken to represent the history of Twelver scholarship accurately. Jamāl al-Dīn Aḥmad b. Mūsā Ibn Ṭāwūs (d. 673/1274–75) had already used Sunni *ḥadīth* methodology in the analysis of Shi'ite *ḥadīth*s a generation or two before al-'Allāmah al-Ḥillī,[15] and the leading jurists of Buwayhid Iraq, al-Sharīf al-Murtaḍā (d. 436/1044) and al-Shaykh al-Ṭūsī (d. 460/1067), had argued for the exclusive authority of the jurists, though they did not use the terms *mujtahid* and *ijtihād* in this context.[16] Nevertheless, al-Astarābādī's presentation gives the initial impression that *al-Fawā'id al-madanīyah* is in essence a polemic against the thought of al-'Allāmah al-Ḥillī in particular.

While al-Astarābādī focuses blame on al-Ḥillī as an innovator, he clearly has more recent Uṣūlī scholars in mind as targets for criticism. Chief among these later scholars, one gathers from the text, are al-Shahīd al-Awwal (d. 786/1384), 'Alī b. 'Abd al-'Ālī al-Karakī (d. 940/1534), and al-Shahīd al-Thānī (d. 965/1558). He consistently detracts from their stature by describing them as mere followers and imitators of al-'Allāmah, calling them his "pupils" (*talāmīdh*) and commentators on his works.[17] The most recent representative of this group, closest to the time of al-Astarābādī himself, was of course al-Shahīd al-Thānī. Al-Astarābādī is arguing, I would claim, more directly against the thought and works of al-Shahīd al-Thānī than against those of al-'Allāmah himself. He avoids saying so explicitly, preferring to lay blame on a much earlier scholar. This tactic presumably served to belittle the intellectual stature of his opponents but also to soften his criticisms of a more recent jurist whose descendants, both biological and intellectual, might find his deprecatory remarks offensive. Al-Astarābādī himself had studied with al-Shahīd al-Thānī's son Ḥasan, after all.

This strategy of oblique criticism was typical of academic discourse in the premodern period and would have been easily understood and interpreted by the contemporary audience. That al-Shahīd al-Thānī is the real target of al-Astarābādī's text seems likely not simply because he is the most recent scholar mentioned in this text as an unquestioning representative of al-ʿAllāmah al-Ḥillī's thought. More importantly, al-Shahīd al-Thānī was a major proponent of the two "innovations" that al-Astarābādī considers the Uṣūlīs' mortal sins: the use of Sunni methodology for the critical evaluation of Shiʿite *ḥadīth*s and the exclusive authority of the jurists. It is telling that the first opponent that al-Astarābādī cites at length in his work is al-Shahīd al-Thānī, whose discussion on the conditions for *ijtihād* from the chapter on judges in his legal commentary *al-Rawḍah al-bahīyah* is quoted verbatim.[18]

THE RELIABILITY OF SHIʿITE *ḤADĪTHS*

A crucial facet of the Akhbārī agenda was the strong acceptance of the authenticity of the four Shiʿite *ḥadīth* collections that had become canonical since the fifth/eleventh century: *al-Kāfī* by Muḥammad b. Yaʿqūb al-Kulaynī, *Man lā yaḥḍuruhu al-faqīh* by Muḥammad b. Bābawayh al-Qummī, and *Tahdhīb al-aḥkām* and *al-Istibṣār* by Muḥammad b. al-Ḥasan al-Ṭūsī. In stressing the reliability of these collections, the Akhbārīs were opposing what they saw as an attack on Shiʿite sacred texts that stemmed from the application of historical criticism to Shiʿite *ḥadīth*s. This type of criticism was to them both blatantly rationalist and patently Sunni in origin. While Ibn Ṭāwūs and al-ʿAllāmah al-Ḥillī had made some steps in this regard, the main proponents of the historical criticism of Shiʿite *ḥadīth*s (particularly from the perspective of Safavid scholars of the early seventeenth century) were al-Shahīd al-Thānī and his student and companion Ḥusayn b. ʿAbd al-Ṣamad al-ʿĀmilī. In the mid-sixteenth century, these two jurists had written major works of *ḥadīth* criticism, clearly inspired by and drawing on Sunni works in the field. Al-Shahīd al-Thānī completed the text and commentary of *al-Bidāyah fī ʿilm al-dirāyah* (Introduction to the Science of *Ḥadīth* Criticism) on 5 Dhū al-Ḥijjah 959/November 22, 1552, in Jabal ʿĀmil,[19] and Ḥusayn completed a similar text, *Wuṣul al-akhyār ilā uṣūl al-akhbār* (The Approach for Excellent Scholars to the Sources of Oral Reports), ca. 960/1552–53 in Mashhad.

These two works are on the whole quite similar in conception and organization, with the difference that Ḥusayn b. ʿAbd al-Ṣamad's work contains a long diatribe against the Companions Abū Bakr, ʿUmar, ʿUthmān, ʿĀ'ishah, and Muʿāwiyah, explaining why the Shiʿites do not accept the *ḥadīth*s that they transmit.[20] Al-Shahīd al-Thānī's work lacks such a polemical essay. The discrepancy between the two can undoubtedly be attributed to the contexts in which they were written: al-Shahīd al-Thānī was living under the rule of the Sunni Ottomans in what is now Lebanon, while Ḥusayn had just emigrated to Iran and was seeking employment from Shah Ṭahmāsb. Writing for the shah, secure in Safavid territory, Ḥusayn could impugn the character of Companions revered by the Sunnis without fear of retaliation and may even have expected to be rewarded all the more for doing so. A fundamental principle espoused in both works was that only *ḥadīth*s with an unbroken chain of reliable Imami Shi'ite transmitters whose probity (*'adālah*) is attested by authoritative sources may be accepted as sound (*ṣaḥīḥ*). This restrictive principle had the effect of calling into question the reliability of a large portion of the *ḥadīth* corpus included in the four canonical books of Twelver *ḥadīth*s, for many traditions had been transmitted by Sunnis, Shi'ites of questionable character, Shi'ite adherents of heretical sects, transmitters whose probity was not specifically attested, or transmitters who were essentially unknown. Many other scholars in the Twelver traditions had accepted the absence of negative reports as sufficient evidence to establish the probity of a transmitter, a position that al-Shahīd al-Thānī and Ḥusayn insisted was wrong. Both authors made explicit statements implying that the scholar could not rely uncritically on the standard *ḥadīth* compilations that Shi'ite jurists generally accepted on blind faith. They applied a strict, rationalist criticism to Shi'ite *ḥadīth*s.

Al-Shahīd al-Thānī's preoccupation with historical criticism may be seen in a dream he recorded. Near Sivas while on route from Istanbul to the Shi'ite shrines in southern Iraq, on the night of 2 Ramaḍān 952/November 7, 1545, he dreamt of meeting none other than al-Kulaynī, compiler of *al-Kāfī,* the earliest of the four canonical collections of Shi'ite *ḥadīth*s. In the course of the dream, al-Kulaynī complains to him bitterly about the horrible state of the available copies of his work—badly written, in poor condition, and riddled with copyists' errors. Al-Shahīd al-Thānī reassures the compiler and describes a rescue operation that he and his companions undertook in an effort to restore the text to its original excellent condition:

> A strange thing occurred to me that night. I dozed off for a short time and dreamed that I was in the presence of our magnificent Master, Muḥammad b. Ya'qūb al-Kulaynī—May God have mercy on him! He was a striking, older man with a handsome face, surrounded by the aura of great learning. About half of his sideburns were white. With me was a group of my advanced students, including my companion and friend, Shaykh Ḥusayn b. 'Abd al-Ṣamad, and we asked the Master, the above-mentioned Abū Ja'far al-Kulaynī, for the original copy of his book, *al-Kāfī,* so that we might copy it. He entered the house and brought out to us its first fascicle,

> copied on Syrian paper in quarto. When he opened it, we saw that it was written in an excellent hand with the vowels marked, the text corrected, and the symbols written in gold ink. We expressed our surprise at the fact that the original copy was like this, and we were extremely overjoyed thereat, because we had hitherto suffered a great deal from the poor quality of the copies. I requested the other fascicles from him, upon which he expressed his distress at people's lack of care in their treatment of the manuscripts and their poor copying of them. "I don't know where the rest of the fascicles are," he said, uttering these words as an expression of his grief at people's carelessness in copying the book and correcting the copies. He told us, "Busy yourselves with this fascicle while I find others for you," entering his house to retrieve the remaining fascicles. He returned to us with a fascicle in his hand that had been copied by someone else on Syrian paper in folio. It was unwieldy and the script was poor. He handed the fascicle to me and started complaining to us, venting his grief over the copying of his book in this manner. Among those present in the gathering was our pious brother, Shaykh Zayn al-Dīn al-Faqʿānī—May God benefit us with his blessings—who said, "I have another fascicle of the original copy of the type described above." He handed it to me, and I was overjoyed. Then he searched the house and brought out another fascicle until he had eventually unearthed four or more of the same type. We were extremely happy and went out to meet the magnificent Master, the author, who was still sitting in his former place. When we sat there before him, we again commiserated over the copying of the book and people's lack of care in doing so. Then I said, "O Master, in the city of Damascus, there is a Twelver Shiʿite named Zayn al-ʿĀbidīn al-Gharābīlī who has coped this book of yours in an excellent copy, on good paper. He has bound the book in two volumes, each one the size of *al-Sharāʾiʿ*.[21] This copy is a point of pride for us in the eyes of both friend and foe." The face of the Master—May God have mercy on him!—then lit up with joy. He expressed his happiness, opened his hands, and said a magnificent[22] blessing for [al-Gharābīlī], the text of which I do not remember. Then I awoke.[23]

This dream reveals al-Shahīd al-Thānī's deep concern with the issues of textual criticism and the textual integrity of the canonical *ḥadīth* collections. He realized that the scriptural texts on which Twelvers relied for derivation of the law were fallible and indeed in poor condition. He expressed hope that the situation could be remedied, but only through painstaking collection and edition of the extant manuscripts. It is inconceivable that with this perspective he would have argued, as did the Akhbārīs, for the authenticity of all the *ḥadīth*s in the four compilations.

Ḥadīth criticism had not been a prominent feature of Twelver tradition from the time of al-'Allāmah on but was rather revived in the sixteenth century by al-Shahīd al-Thānī, his student and companion Ḥusayn b. 'Abd al-Ṣamad, and the latter's students in Iran. Mīrzā Makhdūm al-Shīrāzī (d. 995/1587) claims in his anti-Shi'ite polemic written in 987/1579 that the science of *ḥadīth* criticism (*uṣūl al-ḥadīth*) did not exist among the Shi'ites until the work of al-Shahīd al-Thānī, who realized that this was a terrible shortcoming in Twelver scholarship. He rectified it by writing his own work on the topic, which Makhdūm claims he plagiarized from a Sunni work, the *Khulāṣah* of al-Sharīf al-Jurjānī (d. 816/1413), Makhdūm's ancestor.[24] Ḥusayn carried on the teachings of al-Shahīd al-Thānī after emigrating to Safavid Iran and is recognized as responsible for the revival of the study of the Shi'ite *ḥadīth* books there.[25] This project was carried on by 'Abd Allāh b. al-Ḥusayn al-Tustarī (d. 1021/1612), who wrote a number of works in the field of *ḥadīth*s. According to one account, when al-Tustarī arrived in Isfahan ca. 1007/1598, there were only fifty students of the religious sciences in the city; but when he died fourteen years later, there were over one thousand.[26] He was particularly well-versed in the biographies of *ḥadīth* transmitters (*rijāl*), and several of his students wrote *rijāl* works and commentaries on the *ḥadīth* books, including Muḥammad Qāsim al-Quhpā'ī (d. ?), Muṣṭafā al-Tafrīshī (d. ca. 1030/1621), Muḥammad Taqī al-Majlisī (d. 1070/1659–60), and Mīrzā Rafī' al-Dīn Muḥammad al-Nā'inī (d. 1082/1671–72). Al-Tustarī also wrote glosses on al-Ṭūsī's two famous *ḥadīth* collections, *al-Tahdhīb* and *al-Istibṣār*.[27]

While the study of *ḥadīth*s remained popular, writers of the subsequent generation attempted to soften the rationalist criticisms of al-Shahīd al-Thānī and Ḥusayn b. 'Abd al-Ṣamad in this field, claiming the authenticity of a relatively larger portion of the *ḥadīth* corpus and arguing that al-Shahīd al-Thānī's strict rule of *ḥadīth* criticism had been overstated. The most important works to do this were written by al-Shahīd al-Thānī's son Ḥasan al-'Āmilī and Ḥusayn b. 'Abd al-Ṣamad's son Bahā' al-Dīn al-'Āmilī. Ḥasan b. Zayn al-Dīn's work *Muntaqā al-jumān fī al-aḥādīth al-ṣiḥāḥ wa'l-ḥisān* (Select Pearls on Sound and Reliable Oral Reports), probably completed toward the end of the sixteenth century, presents the *ḥadīth*s of the categories *ṣaḥīḥ* and *ḥasan* on which Twelver legal rulings are commonly based. It selects from the relevant *ḥadīth* reports included in the four standard collections, restricting discussion to those reports whose chains of authority meet strict standards of authenticity.

Similar is Bahā' al-Dīn al-'Āmilī's *al-Ḥabl al-matīn fī iḥkām aḥkām al-dīn* (The Sturdy Cable, on the Sound Establishment of the Rulings of the Faith), which was completed on 18 Shawwāl 1007/May 14, 1599, in Mashhad. In this compendium of law, divided into four sections: *'ibādāt* (devotions), *'uqūd* (bilateral obligations), *īqāʿāt* (unilateral obligations), and *aḥkām* (rules), Bahā' al-Dīn sets out to present and comment on the *ḥadīth*s of the categories *ṣaḥīḥ* (sound) and *ḥasan* (reliable) on which Twelver legal rulings are based. It is thus like a work of *āyāt al-aḥkām,* a commentary on the verses of the Qur'ān with legal content but focusing on *ḥadīth* reports and (most importantly for present purposes) restricting itself only to those *ḥadīth*s whose chains of authority pass a test of authenticity rather than including all, or choosing freely from, the relevant *ḥadīth* reports from the four canonical collections.[28] Bahā' al-Dīn's work *Mashriq al-shamsayn wa-iksīr al-saʿādatayn* (The Rising of the Two Suns and the Elixir of the Two Joys), completed on 14 Dhū al-Qaʿdah 1015/March 13, 1607, in Qum, resembles *al-Ḥabl al-matīn* except that it includes the verses of the Qur'ān with legal content as well as *ḥadīth* reports. It, too, limits itself to *ḥadīth* reports of the *ṣaḥīḥ* and *ḥasan* categories.[29] Al-Astarābādī mentions this work prominently in *al-Fawā'id al-madanīyah.*[30] It includes an introductory discussion of *ḥadīth* methodology that argues against al-Shahīd al-Thānī's rule that the probity of a transmitter must be attested by two witnesses of recognized probity in order for him to be considered reliable, a view that would allow a larger percentage of Shiʿite *ḥadīth* reports to be considered authentic.[31]

These three works reflect a concern on the part of the authors to defend the role that Shiʿite *ḥadīth*s played in the elaboration of the law. The stringent critical criteria presented by al-Shahīd al-Thānī and Ḥusayn b. ʿAbd al-Ṣamad threatened to undermine many of the traditional Twelver legal rulings. Ḥasan b. Zayn al-Dīn and Bahā' al-Dīn were anxious to show, however, that even if one were limited to those *ḥadīth* reports of the *ṣaḥīḥ* and *ḥasan* categories one would have adequate scriptural proof-texts on which to construct the edifice of the law. They thus accepted al-Shahīd al-Thānī's general principles, admitting, for example, that the standard *ḥadīth* collections included "unreliable" (*ḍaʿīf*) *ḥadīth*s; but they reduced the stringency of certain restrictions and aimed to defend Twelver legal positions against a perception of general invalidity.

An exception to this trend to soften al-Shahīd al-Thānī's critical position can be found in the work of Sayyid Muḥammad al-ʿĀmilī (d. 1009/1600), known in the Shiʿite scholarly tradition as "the Author of *al-Madārik*" after his famous commentary *Madārik al-aḥkām,* on the legal text *Sharā'iʿ al-Islām* by al-Muḥaqqiq al-Ḥillī (d. 676/1277). As mentioned above, al-Astarābādī studied in Iraq under this scholar, as well as under Ḥasan b. Zayn al-Dīn al-ʿĀmilī. In *Madārik al-aḥkām,* Sayyid Muḥammad rejected many *ḥadīth* reports and transmitters as a consequence of his adherence to the critical method proposed by al-Shahīd al-Thānī.[32] This led one later Akhbārī author, Yūsuf b. Aḥmad al-Baḥrānī (d. 1186/1772), to write a corrective commentary on the work, entitled *Tadāruk al-Madārik.*[33]

With *al-Fawā'id al-madanīyah* came an outright refutation of al-Shahīd al-Thānī's work and the methodology of *ḥadīth* criticism as it had been applied to Shi'ite *ḥadīth*s. Al-Astarābādī, and later Akhbārīs as well, argued for the unquestionable reliability of all the *ḥadīth*s contained in the four canonical works. Anything less was perceived as an affront to the sacred texts of the Shi'ites and an attack on the bases of their religion. For the Akhbārīs, the compilers' knowledge and discernment, their chronological proximity to the transmitters, and their reliance on earlier written sources such as the "four hundred *uṣūl*" recorded by companions of the Imams all ensured the authenticity of the *ḥadīth*s in this corpus.[34] This aspect of the Akhbārī revival can be reliably viewed as a direct response to the *ḥadīth* methodology of al-Shahīd al-Thānī and the threat it posed to Twelver Shi'ite law.

RATIONALIST LEGAL METHODOLOGY

The second major criticism that al-Astarābādī and later Akhbārīs leveled against their opponents had to do with the science of jurisprudence. In their view, Twelver Shi'ite jurists had adopted Sunni legal methodology wholesale and in particular relied on rational proof and speculation to an unprecedented and unwarranted extent, going so far as to reject a *ḥadīth* report if it contradicted some rational consideration. If one examines the history of Twelver Shi'ite jurisprudence, one finds that Shi'ite legal methodology, from the tenth century on, grew gradually closer to that developed by the Sunni jurists. This trend reached a high point in the work of al-Shahīd al-Thānī, for whom Twelver Shi'ite legal methodology differed little indeed from that of the Sunnis. Al-Astarābādī's refutation of these legal methods should be seen as a reaction primarily to al-Shahīd al-Thānī's work in particular and not merely to the tradition of Shi'ite jurisprudence in general.

Al-Astarābādī argues against the division of the community of believers into *mujtahid*s (master jurists) and *muqallid*s (laymen), who are bound to practice the religion according to the dictates of a living master jurist. From the Akhbārīs' point of view, this theory created a class of religious specialists with claims to exclusive religious authority, but whose authority is completely invalid because it is based, ultimately, on human reason and not on divine command. The expertise of the master jurist is not grounded in scripture but in dialectic and speculation, which are fallible, human methods and cannot legitimately serve as the basis for rulings in the sacred law. Again, al-Astarābādī singles out al-'Allāmah al-Ḥillī as the innovator of this heresy, but al-Shahīd al-Thānī stands out as a strong and much more recent proponent of the theory. Together with 'Alī b. 'Abd al-'Ālī al-Karakī, al-Shahīd al-Thānī was one of the first jurists in the tradition to endorse the theory of *niyābah 'āmmah* (general deputyship), whereby the *mujtahid*, or the class of *mujtahids* as a whole, is said to be the "general representative" (*nā'ib 'āmm*) of the Twelfth Imam. This claim justifies the *mujtahids*' exclusive authority, holding that they stand in place of the Imam during the Greater Occultation. They are thus entitled to serve a number of functions normally reserved for the direct control of the Imam himself, such as the appointment of judges, the performance of *ḥudūd* punishments, and the collection and distribution of *khums* funds. Al-Shahīd al-Thānī made strong arguments for these positions in his legal works, and it is no surprise that (as mentioned above) al-Astarābādī begins his discussion of *ijtihād* in the opening of *al-Fawā'id al-madanīyah* with an extensive quotation from the work of al-Shahīd al-Thānī.[35]

A particularly striking example of al-Shahīd al-Thānī's rationalist approach in jurisprudence is his criticism of the Twelver theory of consensus. According to standard Twelver legal doctrine from the tenth century until the present, consensus—whether that of the Muslim community (*ijmā' al-ummah*) or that of the Shi'ite minority (*ijmā' al-ṭā'ifah*)—is an incontrovertible proof (*ḥujjah*). It represents the truth, in Shi'ite theory, because any real consensus must include the opinion of the hidden Imam, and whatever concurs with the opinion of the Imam is necessarily valid. Al-Shahīd al-Thānī voices harsh criticisms of this theory. In his treatise on Friday prayer, completed in 962/1555, he sternly criticizes earlier Shi'ite scholars for claiming the ability to determine where the opinion of the hidden Imam lies. He poses the rhetorical question: "Where do they get this knowledge concerning such questions, when they have not come upon any news of [the Imam's] person, let alone his opinion?!"[36] He continues: "How do they arrive at this decisive certainty that [the Imam's opinion] coincides with the opinions of the Shi'ite scholars, despite the complete break and total separation between them, and their utter ignorance of his opinions for a period exceeding six hundred years?!"[37]

After explaining the Shi'ite view concerning the authority of consensus of the Muslim community, Al-Shahīd al-Thānī turns to the common Twelver principle according to which opinions held by jurists of known genealogies do not affect consensus, since none of them could be the Imam, while the opinions of jurists whose genealogies are unknown must be taken into consideration, since one of them could possibly be the Imam. He protests:

> I have strong reservations about all of this, which I have set down precisely in an independent discussion.[38] The disputed questions contained in the law that are based on this—an incalculable number—are clear. Moreover, [Shi'ite consensus] is one of the most important legal principles on which subsidiary rulings are based, yet [the Shi'ite jurists'] discussions of it have

not been carefully examined, and their opinions concerning it vary quite widely, as anyone who has read them carefully may attest.[39]

In al-Shahīd al-Thānī's view, the rule Shi'ite jurists use to determine which opinions to take into consideration for consensus is seriously flawed, and Shi'ite discussions of the point to his day are inadequate. This glaring shortcoming in the Shi'ite legal system stands out as deserving rectification particularly because it is used so often in the Shi'ite tradition to justify positions on particular points of law.

Al-Shahīd al-Thānī's conclusion seems to be that the Shi'ites cannot rely so heavily on Shi'ite consensus during the Occultation, for it is simply impossible to determine where the Imam's opinion lies. They must pay more attention to other evidence.

> When the Infallible Imam is manifest, certitude is reached upon knowing his opinion or establishing that it is included among the opinions of his followers [*shī'ah*]. This was the case with his forefathers with regard to many questions on which the opinions of the Shi'ite scholars concurred with the reports transmitted from [the Imams], such as the opinion that it is obligatory to wipe the feet in performing ablutions, the prohibition against wiping the inner shoes (in performing ablutions), the prohibition of obligatory shares [*'awl*] and the agnatic distribution of excess [*ta'ṣīb*] in inheritance law, and other similar matters. In legal cases that first occurred during the time of the Occultation, and concerning which conflicting opinions have been voiced, one must refer to the dictates of the Qur'ān and the Sunnah and other legally permissible evidence, and not to completely unfounded claims such as these.[40]

It is not possible, al-Shahīd al-Thānī holds, to determine the opinion of the Imam during the Occultation. Therefore, one cannot look to the concept of Shi'ite consensus, which has been widely abused, to provide answers to all problems. In these statements, al-Shahīd al-Thānī seems to be voicing objections that one would expect from a Sunni opponent using rationalist methods.

Al-Shahīd al-Thānī's theory of consensus did not win many converts in later generations of Twelver jurists. Ḥasan b. Zayn al-Dīn discusses consensus in his manual of jurisprudence, *Ma'ālim al-dīn wa-malādh al-mujtahidīn,* and in doing so rejects most of his father's radical revisions.[41] The same is true for Bahā' al-Dīn al-'Āmilī's text on jurisprudence, *Zubdat al-uṣūl,* completed on 12 Muḥarram 1018/April 17, 1609.[42] The exception seems, again, to be Sayyid Muḥammad b. 'Alī al-Mūsawī, who adopted some of the major features of - al-Shahīd al-Thānī's theory of consensus in his work *Madārik al-aḥkām.* He questioned the assumption that a report of an earlier consensus in the sources can indicate the opinion of an earlier generation of Shiʿite jurists and can therefore identify the opinion of the Twelfth Imam himself.[43] For the Akhbārīs, this view would threaten the transmission and authority of many standard legal positions in the Twelver tradition that had been handed down from earlier generations of jurists but could not be linked directly with specific statements of the Imams.

Al-Astarābādī argued directly against these rationalist features of al-Shahīd al-Thānī's jurisprudence. He rejected outright the claim that the *mujtahid*s had any legitimate claims to exclusive religious authority during the Greater Occultation and along with it the theory that the jurists were endowed with the "general deputyship" of the Twelfth Imam. Al-Astarābādī also rejected the theory of consensus, holding that the Twelvers had adopted this concept from the Sunnis and that the chance coincidence of opinions provided no guarantee of the correctness of a ruling. A report of the agreement of Shiʿite scholars from the early Islamic centuries on a specific question would, however, be like a *ḥadīth* report in the standard compilations. Its authenticity would be guaranteed by the same factors that guaranteed the authenticity of the *ḥadīth,* such as the chronological proximity of these scholars to the Imam, their reliance on early written sources recorded by the Imam's companions, the assiduous attention they paid to the Imam's rulings, and so on.

ASSIMILATION TO SUNNISM IN THE TWELVER LEGAL TRADITION

Within the broad spectrum of the Twelver legal tradition as a whole, al-Shahīd al-Thānī and Ḥusayn b. ʿAbd al-Ṣamad stand at the far end toward assimilation with Sunni jurisprudence. By and large, it appears that they believed Sunni and Shiʿite jurisprudence operated in such a similar manner that the jurists of one group could draw on the legal works of the other group and apply many of the same rules and principles in their own legal system. Both al-Shahīd al-Thānī and Ḥusayn b. ʿAbd al-Ṣamad participated in a long and established tradition among Twelver Shiʿite scholars of participation in the Shāfiʿī legal *madhhab.* They spent many years studying Sunni *ḥadīth*s, law, and other religious sciences under Sunni teachers in Damascus and Cairo. In Cairo between 942/1535 and 943/1537, they studied under a number of Shāfiʿī law professors, including Abū al-Ḥasan al-Bakrī (d. 953/1546–47), Shihāb al-Dīn Aḥmad b. ʿAbd al-Ḥaqq al-Sinbāṭī (d. 950/1543), and Shihāb al-Dīn Aḥmad al-Ramlī al-Anṣārī (d. 957/1550), the leading Shāfiʿī jurist of the time. They studied standard works in the Shāfiʿī legal curriculum, including, on law, *Minhāj al-ṭālibīn* of al-Nawawī (d. 676/1278); and, on jurisprudence, *al-Waraqāt* by al-Juwaynī (d.

478/1085), the *Mukhtaṣar* of Ibn al-Ḥājib (d. 646/1249) with the commentary *al-Sharḥ al-ʿAḍudī* by ʿAḍud al-Dīn al-Ījī (d. 756/1355), and *Jamʿ al-jawāmiʿ* by Tāj al-Dīn al-Subkī (d. 771/1370) with the commentary of Jalāl al-Dīn al-Maḥallī (d. 864/1459). They must have completed these studies in Sunni *madrasahs*, perhaps even at al-Azhar itself, and it is likely that they received stipends designated for Shāfiʿī law students.

Subsequently, they were able to obtain posts as professors of Shāfiʿī law in Sunni *madrasahs*. In order to do so, they presented themselves as Shāfiʿī jurists to officials connected with the court of the Ottoman Sultan Suleiman (926–74/1520–66) and wrote works that confirmed their identity as Sunni jurists educated in the Shāfiʿī *madhhab*. Though the work al-Shahīd al-Thānī presented to Ottoman officials is not extant, Ḥusayn's work *Nūr al-ḥaqīqah wa-nawr al-ḥadīqah* (The Light of Truth and the Blossoms of the Garden), on ethics, shows that he claimed to be a Shāfiʿī jurist. It includes a flowery dedication to Sultan Suleiman and is signed "Ḥusayn b. ʿAbd al-Ṣamad *al-Shāfiʿī* al-Ḥārithī al-Hamdānī." Ḥusayn made such a petition twice, in 945/1539 and 952/1545, while al-Shahīd al-Thānī did so once, in 952/1545. The results of Ḥusayn's first petition are not revealed in the extant sources; but on the second occasion he was offered a position as professor of law at a Sunni *madrasah* in Baghdad. He apparently declined the post after finding that the endowment lacked adequate funds. Al-Shahīd al-Thānī was awarded a position as professor of Shāfiʿī law at the Nūrīyah *madrasah* in Baʿlabakk and taught there for nearly two years. Al-Shahīd al-Thānī and Ḥusayn b. ʿAbd al-Ṣamad both clearly went to great lengths to participate, as Sunni jurists, in the Sunni legal tradition.[44]

Both scholars tended to advocate peaceful coexistence with Sunnis and encouraged debate and intellectual exchange between the two groups. Al-Shahīd al-Thānī in particular followed Sunni methods, adopted Sunni innovations, and incorporated Sunni theories into his own works on the religious sciences. One very clear example of the type of borrowing he undertook was his introduction of the *sharḥ mazj* (interwoven commentary) into Shiʿite legal studies. By the fifteenth century, this technical innovation in the writing of commentaries had become popular in the Sunni legal curriculum and in other texts. Instead of presenting the original text at the top of the page, with the commentary underneath, or in the center of the page, with the commentary in the margins, this new type of commentary involved writing the clauses of the original text (overlined so that it might be distinguished) into the explanatory sentences of the commentary itself. This type of commentary has the advantage of saving a tremendous amount of time for the reader, who would otherwise have to jump back and forth continually between the original text and the commentary. (The danger, though, is that it threatens to blur the distinction between the original text and the commentary.) Perhaps the best-known work to use this method is the famous Qur'ānic exegesis *Tafsīr al-Jalālayn* by Jalāl al-Dīn al-Maḥallī (d. 864/1459) and Jalāl al-Dīn al-Suyūṭī (d. 911/1505). Al-Shahīd al-Thānī's student Bahā' al-Dīn Muḥammad Ibn al-'Awdī reports that zealous pride led the master to write interwoven commentaries when he saw that the Sunnis had them while the Twelvers did not. One work written in this manner that al-Shahīd al-Thānī certainly studied was Jalāl al-Dīn al-Maḥallī's commentary on Tāj al-Dīn al-Subkī's *Jam' al-jawāmi'*. Al-Shahīd al-Thānī wrote his legal works *al-Rawḍah al-bahīyah,* a commentary on *al-Lum'ah al-dimashqīyah* by al-Shahīd al-Awwal, and *Rawḍ al-jinān,* a commentary on al-'Allāmah's *Irshād al-adhhān,* in this fashion.[45]

Many other works by al-Shahīd al-Thānī draw extensively on Sunni works. His *Munyat al-murīd fī ādāb al-mufīd wa'l-mustafīd,* on education; *Musakkin al-fu'ād 'inda faqd al-aḥibbah wa'l-awlād,* on the loss of children and loved ones; *Tamhīs al-qawā'id,* on legal and grammatical maxims; and *Masālik al-afhām ilā tanqīḥ Sharā'i' al-Islām* all contain material that indicates a heavy debt to Sunni sources.[46] One indication of al-Shahīd al-Thānī's belief in the essential compatibility of Sunni and Shi'ite jurisprudence is his statement that the student of law need not expend great efforts mastering the methods of logical proof, since most of the relevant information is provided in standard works on jurisprudence such as *Tahdhīb al-wuṣūl* by al-'Allāmah al-Ḥillī and the *Mukhtaṣar* of Ibn al-Ḥājib.[47] The fact that he cites Ibn al-Ḥājib's famous text of Sunni jurisprudence in one breath with a Shi'ite text as a reliable reference for the Twelver student of law suggests that he saw Sunni and Shi'ite legal methodology as largely if not completely compatible.

An assimilationist posture was anathema to the Akhbārīs.[48] Al-Astarābādī and later Akhbārīs advocated the complete avoidance of Sunni scholarship, especially that concerned with the religious sciences, and disapproved of any scholarly interchange between the two groups that would lead Shi'ites to think highly of the Sunnis' works or doctrines. They advocated the strictest adherence to the traditions of the Imams, even holding that Shi'ites should only understand Qur'ānic commentary through the *ḥadīth*s of the Imams. For this reason, the Akhbārīs looked on scholars such as al-Shahīd al-Thānī with the utmost circumspection. Indeed, while a number of the greatest Shi'ite jurists of the past (particularly al-'Allāmah al-Ḥillī and al-Shahīd al-Awwal) were known for similarly mixing with Sunnis and using Sunni scholarship in their own legal and other works, al-Shahīd al-Thānī seems, in some respects, to have moved further along the road to assimilation than they did, at least in the view of the Akhbārīs. The following statement concerning the study of Sunni works by Muḥammad b. al-Ḥasan al-Ḥurr al-'Āmilī, an Akhbārī who wrote in Mashhad in the late seventeenth century, is typical: "... the evils of studying their works are many and obvious; the least of them is approval of them concerning points that are not known to be in agreement with the Imams or are in contradiction to them."[49] Concerning al-'Allāmah, al-Shahīd al-Awwal, and al-Shahīd al-Thānī in particular, the same author comments: "There is no doubt that their intentions were sound. Nevertheless, the results of [their studies with Sunnis] are apparent to anyone who has examined and perused assiduously the books of legal methodology, legal derivation, and *ḥadīth*s." [50]

Al-Ḥurr al-ʿĀmilī means to imply here that Twelver Shiʿite works not only on *ḥadīth*s but also on jurisprudence and the points of law have become contaminated and corrupted with Sunni material, concepts, and methods. In his view, al-Shahīd al-Thānī, despite his good intentions, is one of the main culprits in this unfortunate development; and indeed (as we have seen) al-Shahīd al-Thānī was the most recent of the prominent scholars that al-Astarābādī singled out as having promulgated heretical innovations. The threat of assimilation was of great concern to al-Astarābādī, and al-Shahīd al-Thānī embodied that threat, given his career and scholarly production, more than any other jurist in Twelver history.

CONCLUSION

Modarressi's sketch of the genesis of the Akhbārī revival is in fact the most detailed available to date, but it remains a mere outline. He identifies two areas in which the ground was already prepared for the Akhbārī revival in the sixteenth century: an increased interest in *ḥadīth*s and a trend toward revising or questioning the bases of earlier Uṣūlī legal scholarship. While these observations are true, Modarressi's presentation implies that such figures as al-Shahīd al-Thānī and Ḥusayn b. 'Abd al-Ṣamad were on the same side of the intellectual fence as the Akhbārīs, when in fact they represent the opposite end of the spectrum of Twelver scholarship on law, jurisprudence, and the interpretation of sacred texts. This being the case, it is necessary to reconsider the purport of some material attributed to these two scholars that Modarressi cites as leading up to the Akhbārī revival.

Modarressi writes that al-Shahīd al-Thānī wrote a work arguing against following the legal judgments of earlier jurists without examining their bases.[51] In authoring this treatise, *Risālah fī taqlīd al-mayyit,* al-Shahīd al-Thānī was adopting a strongly Uṣūlī, rather than Akhbārī, position, arguing that one was obliged to follow the decisions of a living *mujtahid* instead of continuing to follow the opinions of earlier scholars. He completed the work on 5 Shawwāl 949/ January 12, 1543, for his father-in-law, meaning thereby to announce to the Shiʿite public that he was a fully qualified *mujtahid* able to serve as a guide for lay believers. This need would have been particularly pressing after the passing of ʿAlī b. ʿAbd al-ʿĀlī al-Karakī, the leading jurist of the previous generation, who had died in 940/1534. Al-Shahīd al-Thānī was certainly not arguing against adopting opinions arrived at through *ijtihād;* nor was he presenting a general critique of earlier Uṣūlī jurisprudence and legal methodology. Modarressi also cites this same treatise, observing that "[t]he value of logic and philosophy in Islamic scholarship had already come under question." Here the context must be taken into consideration. The passage of interest reads as follows:

> An even more heinous problem, a greater disaster, and a more damning sin for those who commit it is what is commonly practiced by many of those who call themselves men of learning among the people of Iran and adjacent regions, in that they consume their lives and spend all their time acquiring the sciences of logic, philosophy, and other things that are to be considered forbidden either in and of themselves or because they take one away from what is obligatory. If they but expended a fraction thereof on the acquisition of the religious sciences about which God—glory be to Him!—will ask them insistently on the Day of Resurrection and for the neglect of which He will address them very sternly, they would acquire the religious knowledge that is incumbent upon them.[52]

In this passage, al-Shahīd al-Thānī is complaining of the neglect of the study of *ḥadīths* and law during his own era in the Islamic tradition. He blames Iranian scholars in particular for paying too much attention to logic and philosophy while ignoring other sciences that are more important because of the religious duties they fulfill and the rewards they entail. He is not arguing, as the Akhbārīs did, that the application of rational principles in the interpretation of the law is inappropriate and a heretical innovation. The sin, rather, is neglect of legal studies altogether. Al-Shahīd al-Thānī took a moderately conservative approach to logic and philosophical theology similar to that adopted by Sunni jurists such as Ibn Taymīyah (d. 728/1328) and Jalāl al-Dīn al-Suyūṭī (d. 911/1505) but did not advocate the abandonment of rationalist jurisprudence.[53] That this work of his was not proto-Akhbārī but actually anti-Akhbārī in nature may be seen from the late seventeenth century treatise by Niʿmat Allāh al-Jazāʾirī (d. 1112/1701), *Kitāb manbaʿ al-ḥayāt wa-ḥujjīyat qawl al-mujtahid min al-amwāt* (essentially a refutation of the *Risālah fī taqlīd al-mayyit*), which argues that one may indeed adopt the opinion of a deceased authority, without reference to a living *mujtahid*.[54]

Modarressi reports that Ḥusayn b. ʿAbd al-Ṣamad criticized the legal methods of earlier Shiʿite jurists and blamed them for imitating the ancients in many of his works. Critical statements of this sort are often found in legal works that attempt to revise a view commonly accepted in contemporary scholarship. They do not in and of themselves suggest the kind of radical revision of the Shiʿite legal system the Akhbārīs advocated. Modarressi notes that Ḥusayn wrote a treatise in which he argued that "*ijtihād,* i.e. the normal method of legal reasoning which is based on rational argument, is not the only way to the discovery of legal norms." This statement seems to be based on the title of a treatise listed by Āghā Buzurg al-Ṭihrānī as *Maqālah fī wujūb al-iftā' wa-bayān al-ḥaqq ʿalā kull man ʿalima bihi mujtahidan kāna am lā* (Treatise on the Obligation of Issuing a Legal Opinion and Revealing the Truth on the Part of Anyone Who Knows It, Whether a *Mujtahid* or Not).

Here one should recognize that the author did not mean by *mujtahid* anyone who was capable of rational legal derivation. He probably intended a legal scholar of particularly high stature and innovation. Only this can explain how he could report in 970/1563 (after having served as Shaykh al-Islām or chief *muftī* at the Safavid capital, then Qazvin) that at the time he was writing there was no known living *mujtahid,* despite the fact that he himself was clearly a qualified legal authority.[55] Similar is the report cited by Modarressi that a *ṣadr* at Safavid court in the early seventeenth century claimed that that was no living *mujtahid* in Iran or the Arab regions at the time.[56] In fact, we might see such statements as expressions of modesty or invitations to followers or patrons to declare their authors in fact *mujtahid*s. The title of Ḥusayn's treatise cannot be taken as evidence that he rejected the legitimacy of *ijtihād* as a method of discovering the law or meant to propose alternatives. It most likely indicates an opinion that, though contemporary jurists were not extremely accomplished and could not compare with the giants of the past such as al-Shahīd al-Awwal and al-ʿAllāmah al-Ḥillī, they nevertheless were obliged to serve as legal consultants for laymen. The implication is that competent jurists should give opinions when questions arise and not hold back out of deference to senior jurists, modesty, or pious reluctance—and not that answers to legal questions can or should be discovered by methods other than *ijtihād.*

Modarressi has suggested that the work of al-Shahīd al-Thānī, Ḥusayn b. ʿAbd al-Ṣamad al-ʿĀmilī, and other sixteenth-century figures set the stage for the revival of Akhbarism in the next century by calling for more freedom in the interpretation of Shiʿite law and adopting a critical approach to earlier Shiʿite legal scholarship. While al-Shahīd al-Thānī's work played an important role in provoking the Akhbārī revival, it was not as a forerunner or part of the vanguard of the Akhbārī school. In attacking the theories of Uṣūlī jurists, al-Astarābādī was most likely reacting to the thought of al-Shahīd al-Thānī in particular, though he deemed it preferable to lay blame on the earlier jurist al-ʿAllāmah al-Ḥillī. Al-Shahīd al-Thānī had not only called into question the authenticity of many traditions contained in the four canonical Shiʿite *ḥadīth* collections but also espoused positions on legal theory that brought Shiʿite jurisprudence dangerously close to that of the Sunnis, as his remarks on consensus show. Al-Shahīd al-Thānī and the Akhbārīs certainly shared an interest in earlier works of *ḥadīth*s, but their intentions were poles apart: the Akhbārīs aimed to bolster the authority of the standard *ḥadīth* compilations and to gather as much pseudepigraphal material as possible, while al-Shahīd al-Thānī and Ḥusayn b. ʿAbd al-Ṣamad, drawing on the methods of historical criticism, sought to limit the material accepted as probative to that which could be proved authentic according to rationalist standards. Similarly, their criticisms of earlier Shiʿite legal scholarship were diametrically opposed. While Akhbārīs criticized Shiʿite jurists for following what they saw as Sunni methods, al-Shahīd al-Thānī criticized them for not applying these same methods consistently or correctly.

Through increased patronage, political and military stability, and ideological backing, the Safavid Empire brought about a renaissance in Shiʿite religious scholarship that proved formative for subsequent Iranian intellectual history and reached beyond the borders of Iran. Since the fall of the Buwayhids in Iraq and Iran and the Fatimids in Egypt and Syria, Shiʿite religious scholarship had been carried out on a relatively small scale in enclaves in Lebanon, Iraq, and Bahrain. With the advent of the Safavids, endowment funds, posts as religious functionaries, and the largesse of the shahs, members of the royal family, and high officials connected with the Safavid court caused a dramatic increase in Shiʿite scholarly production on law, *ḥadīth*s, Qurʾānic commentary, and other related fields. Among the results of this intellectual flowering over the course of the sixteenth and seventeenth centuries, one may distinguish three main accomplishments. First, the Safavid period witnessed the popularization of Shiʿite religious scholarship for a wide audience, not only in Iran but also in the Indian subcontinent, through translations of Arabic works into Persian, Persian commentaries, and the authorship of original works in Persian. Second, creative interaction took place between traditional Twelver scholarship in the religious sciences and Iranian scholarly traditions of mysticism, philosophy, and the natural sciences, creating a mix, at times uneasy, that has characterized much of Iran's subsequent intellectual production since that period. Third, this period produced a large body of scholarship directly connected with the Akhbārī revival.

Akhbārī methodology provoked a massive project to re-collect Shiʿite scriptural and related material from the early Islamic centuries. This project resulted in several of the most important Safavid works on the religious sciences, chief among which are *al-Wāfī* by Muḥsin al-Fayḍ al-Kāshānī (d. 1091/1680), *Wasāʾil al-shīʿah* by Muḥammad b. al-Ḥasan al-Ḥurr al-ʿĀmilī (d. 1099/1688), and *Biḥār al-anwār* by Muḥammad Bāqir al-Majlisī (d. 1111/1699), in addition to numerous commentaries on the standard *ḥadīth* compilations, most of which remain in manuscript. The Akhbārīs' more inclusive approach to scripture led to the preservation and dissemination of many texts and collections from earlier periods in Shi'ite history, including a great deal of material of questionable authenticity or doubtful orthodoxy. The efforts of the Akhbārīs to recuperate scriptural material and establish authoritative links between contemporary scholars and their forebears also brought about a heightened interest in the science of biography (*'ilm al-rijāl*), and it is to this trend that we owe the most important sources for the lives and works of scholars of the Safavid period, such as *Amal al-āmil* by al-Ḥurr al-'Āmilī and *Lu'lu'at al-baḥrayn* by Yūsuf al-Baḥrānī (d. 1186/1772).

In addition, the Akhbārī challenge led their opponents, the Uṣūlīs, to present strong and systematic arguments justifying the use of rationalist methods and the exclusive authority of the jurists. These arguments, which eventually won the day, served to bolster the authority of the jurists more solidly than had been the case in earlier centuries.[57] It is probable that the general use of the term *mujtahid* in the modern Twelver tradition to refer to any fully competent jurist—in keeping with the theoretical presentations of most Twelver and Sunni works on jurisprudence—and the regular granting of the license recognizing that competence (*ijāzat al-ijtihād*) both resulted from the Uṣūlī jurists' defense against the Akhbārī challenge.

The sixteenth century witnessed a high point of the assimilationist trend in Twelver scholarship on the religious sciences, and it was this development that brought about the Akhbārī revival. The Akhbārī reaction to this excess was ultimately defeated, but it had long-lasting effects on the subsequent intellectual history of Iran and Twelver legal scholarship. It ultimately failed to undermine the authority of the jurists, who came out of the conflict in an even stronger position. Nevertheless, the establishment of a Shi'ite majority state, the conversion of the Iranian masses to Shi'ism, and the consequent shift of focus of the Shi'ite scholarly community to Iran worked against an assimilationist stance on the part of Shi'ite jurists, curbing the ongoing importation of Sunni material and methods into Twelver *ḥadīth* and legal scholarship that such scholars as al-'Allāmah al-Ḥillī, al-Shahīd al-Awwal, and al-Shahīd al-Thānī had advocated.

NOTES

1. One among many indications of al-Shahīd al-Thānī's lasting legacy is the fact that his work *al-Rawḍah al-bahīyah,* a commentary on al-Shahīd al-Awwal's legal compendium *al-Lum'ah al-dimashqīyah,* remains a standard text in the Twelver legal curriculum today.

2. On the Akhbārīs in general, see the following sources: Said Amir Arjomand, *The Shadow of God and the Hidden Imam: Religion, Political Order, and Societal Change in Shi'ite Iran from the Beginning to 1890* (Chicago: University of Chicago Press, 1984), pp. 13–14,

145–47, 152–53; E. G. Browne, *A Literary History of Persia*, 4 vols. (Cambridge: Cambridge University Press, 1929), 4:374; Juan Cole, "Shī'ī Clerics in Iraq and Iran, 1722–1780: The Akhbari-Usuli Controversy Reconsidered," *Iranian Studies* 18 (1985): 3–34; idem, *Roots of North Indian Shī'ism in Iran and Iraq: Religion and State in Awadh, 1722–1859* (Berkeley: University of California Press, 1988), pp. 17–22, 31–39; Abdojavad Falaturi, "Die Zwölfer-Schia aus der Sicht eines Schiiten: Probleme ihrer Untersuchung," *Festschrift Werner Caskel* (Leiden: E. J. Brill, 1968), pp. 62–95; Etan Kohlberg, "Ak̲bārāya," in *Encyclopaedia Iranica*, 1:716–18; idem, "Aspects of Akhbari Thought in the Seventeenth and Eighteenth Centuries," in *Eighteenth-Century Renewal and Reform in Islam*, ed. Nehemial Levtzion and John O. Voll (Syracuse: Syracuse University Press, 1987), pp. 133–60; Wilferd Madelung, "al-Ak̲h̲bāriyya," in *Encyclopaedia of Islam*, 2nd ed., Supplement, pp. 56–57; Hossein Modarressi Tabataba'i, "Rationalism and Traditionalism in Shī'ī Jurisprudence: A Preliminary Survey," *Studia Islamica* 59 (1984): 148–58; idem, *An Introduction to Shī'ī Law: A Bibliographical Study* (London: Ithaca Press, 1984), pp. 52–57; Moojan Momen, *An Introduction to Shī'ī Islam: The History and Doctrines of Twelver Shiism* (New Haven: Yale University Press, 1985), pp. 117–18, 222–25; Andrew Newman, "The Development and Political Significance of the Rationalist (Uṣūlī) and Traditionalist (Akhbārī) Schools in Imāmī Shī'ī History from the Third/Ninth to the Tenth/Sixteenth Century" (Ph.D. dissertation, UCLA, 1986); idem, "The Nature of the Akhbari/Usuli Dispute in Late Ṣafawid Iran, Part I: 'Abdallāh al-Samāhijī's *Munyat al-mumārisīn*, Part 2: The Conflict Reassessed," *Bulletin of the School of Oriental and African Studies* (*BSOAS*) 15 (1992): 22–51, 250–61; Gianroberto Scarcia, "Intorno alle controversie tra Aḫbārī e Uṣūlī presso gli Imamiti di Persia," *Rivista degli Studi Orientali* 33 (1958): 211–50; Devin J. Stewart, *Islamic Legal Orthodoxy: Twelver Shiite Responses to the Sunni Legal System* (Salt Lake City: University of Utah Press, 1998), pp. 175–208; Aron Zysow, "The Economy of Certainty: An Introduction to the Typology of Islamic Legal Theory" (Ph.D. dissertation, Harvard University, 1984), pp. 501–8.

3. Stewart, *Islamic Legal Orthodoxy*, pp. 169–201.

4. Muḥammad Amīn al-Astarābādī, *al-Fawā'id al-madanīyah* (Tehran, 1904), pp. 17, 133.

5. Ibid., p. 295.

6. Ibid., pp. 133, 278. He reports in the first passage that he studied 'Aḍud al-Dīn al-Ījī's commentary on the *Mukhtaṣar* of Ibn al-Ḥājib in his youth (*fī awā'il sinnī*). In the second, he states that he had been in Shiraz twenty years prior to writing the *Fawā'id*. Since the work was completed in 1031/1622, this would place him in Shiraz ca. 1011/1602, after his studies in Karbala.

7. Ibid., pp. 17–18.

8. Ibid., p. 2; Āghā Buzurg al-Ṭihrānī, *al-Dharī'ah ilā taṣānīf al-shī'ah*, 4:433.

9. On al-Astarābādī's death date, see Stewart, *Islamic Legal Orthodoxy*, p. 181, n. 22.

10. Newman, "The Development and Political Significance of the Rationalist (Uṣūlī) and Traditionalist (Akhbārī) Schools."

11. Hossein Modarressi, *An Introduction to Shī'ī Law: A Bibliographical Study* (London: Ithaca Press, 1984), pp. 52–53.

12. Ibid., p. 52, n. 2.

13. Rula Jurdi Abisaab, "The Ulama of Jabal 'Āmil in Safavid Iran, 1501–1736: Marginality, Migration and Social Change," *Iranian Studies* 27 (1994): 103–22; here p. 106.

14. al-Astarābādī, *al-Fawā'id al-madanīyah*, p. 18.

15. Asma Afsaruddin, "An Insight into the Ḥadīth Methodology of Jamāl al-Dīn Aḥmad b. Ṭāwūs," *Der Islam* 72 (1995): 25–46.
16. Stewart, *Islamic Legal Orthodoxy*, pp. 210–17.
17. al-Astarābādī, *al-Fawā'id al-madanīyah*, p. 4 and passim.
18. Ibid., pp. 4–6.
19. *Sharḥ al-bidāyah fī 'ilm al-dirāyah* (Tehran, 1891–92), p. 175.
20. *Wuṣūl al-akhyār ilā uṣūl al-akhbār*, ed. 'Abd al-Laṭīf al-Kūhkamarī (Qum: Maṭba'at al-Khayyām, 1981), pp. 63–85.
21. This is the well-known legal text *Sharā'i' al-Islām* by al-Muḥaqqiq al-Ḥillī (d. 676/1277).
22. Reading *jalī* for *khafī* in the text.
23. 'Alī al-'Āmilī, *al-Durr al-manthūr min al-ma'thūr wa-ghayr al-ma'thūr*, 2 vols. (Qum: Maṭba'at mihr, 1978), 2:178–79.
24. Mīrzā Makhdūm al-Shīrāzī, *al-Nawāqiḍ fī al-radd 'alā al-rawāfiḍ*, MS Garrett Collection, 2629, Princeton University Library, fol. 99b.
25. Mīrzā 'Abd Allāh Afandī al-Iṣfahānī, *Riyāḍ al-'ulamā' wa-ḥiyāḍ al-fuḍalā'*, ed. Aḥmad al-Ḥusaynī, 6 vols. (Qum: Maṭba'at al-Khayyām, 1980), 2:118.
26. Muḥammad Bāqir al-Khwānṣārī, *Rawḍāt al-jannāt fī aḥwāl al-'ulamā' wa'l-sādāt*, 8 vols. (Beirut: al-Dār al-islāmīyah, 1991), 4:234–35.
27. Muḥsin al-Amīn, *A'yān al-Shī'ah*, 10 vols. (Beirut: Dār al-ta'āruf li'l-maṭbū'āt, 1984), 8:48; al-Khwānṣārī, *Rawḍāt al-jannāt*, 4:228–37.
28. Bahā' al-Dīn al-'Āmilī, *al-Ḥabl al-matīn*, MS Taymūr Ḥadīth 2190, Dār al-Kutub, Cairo.
29. Bahā' al-Dīn al-'Āmilī, *Mashriq al-shamsayn wa-iksīr al-sa'ādatayn*, ed. Sayyid Mahdī al-Rajā'ī (Mashhad: Islamic Research Foundation, 1993).
30. al-Astarābādī, *al-Fawā'id al-madanīyah*, pp. 68–69.
31. Bahā' al-Dīn al-'Āmilī, *Mashriq al-shamsayn*, pp. 19–104.
32. Muḥammad b. Abī al-Ḥasan al-'Āmilī, *Madārik al-aḥkām fī sharḥ Sharā'i' al-aḥkām*, 8 vols. (Beirut: Mu'assasat Āl al-Bayt, 1990).
33. Yūsuf b. Aḥmad al-Baḥrānī, *Lu'lu'at al-baḥrayn*, ed. Muḥammad Ṣādiq Baḥr al-'Ulūm (Najaf: Maṭba'at al-Nu'mān, 1966), pp. 447–48.
34. Etan Kohlberg, "al-Uṣūl al-arba'u mi'a," *Jerusalem Studies in Arabic and Islam* 10 (1987): 128–65.
35. See Norman Calder, "The Structure of Authority in Imāmī Shī'ī Jurisprudence" (Ph.D. dissertation, School of Oriental and African Studies, University of London, 1980), pp. 66–170; idem, "Judicial Authority in Imāmī Shī'ī Jurisprudence," *British Society for Middle Eastern Studies* 6 (1979): 104–8; idem, "Khums in Imāmī Shī'ī Jurisprudence from the Tenth to the Sixteenth Century, A.D.," *BSOAS* 45 (1981): 39–47; idem, "Zakāt in Imāmī Shī'ī Jurisprudence from the Tenth to the Sixteenth Century, A.D." *BSOAS* 46 (1982): 468–80; Aḥmad Kazemi Moussavi, *Religious Authority in Shi'ite Islam: From the Office of Mufti to the Institution of Marja'* (Kuala Lumpur: International Institute of Islamic Thought and Civilization, 1996), pp. 31–32, 103, 151, 223.
36. al-Shahīd al-Thānī, *Risālah fī ṣalāt al-jum'ah*, pp. 50–101, in *Rasā'il al-Shahīd Zayn al-Dīn b. 'Alī al-Juba'ī al-'Āmilī* (Qum: Maktabah-yi Baṣīratī, 1895–96), p. 88.
37. Ibid., pp. 88–89.
38. al-Shahīd al-Thānī is referring here to a treatise devoted exclusively to the issue of

consensus, entitled *Risālah fī taḥqīq al-ijmāʿ*, which is apparently not extant but was in the possession of his great-grandson ʿAlī b. Muḥammad al-ʿĀmilī in the seventeenth century. See *al-Durr al-manthūr,* 2:188.

39. al-Shahīd al-Thānī, *Tamhīd al-qawāʿid al-uṣūlīyah waʾl-ʿarabīyah li-tafrīʿ fawāʾid al-aḥkām al-sharʿīyah* (Tehran, 1855), p. 34.

40. al-Shahīd al-Thānī, *Risālah fī ṣalāt al-jumʿah,* p. 89.

41. Ḥasan b. Zayn al-Dīn al-ʿĀmilī, *Maʿālim al-dīn wa-malādh al-mujtahidīn* (Tehran, n.d.), pp. 191–201.

42. Bahāʾ al-Dīn al-ʿĀmilī, *Zubdat al-uṣūl* (Isfahan: Dār al-ṭibāʿah, 1899), pp. 75–86.

43. Muḥammad b. Abī al-Ḥasan al-ʿĀmilī, *Madārik al-aḥkām,* 1:43; Muḥammad Bāqir al-Bihbihānī, *al-Fawāʾid al-ḥāʾirīyah* (Qum: Bāqirī, 1995), pp. 387–89.

44. Stewart, *Islamic Legal Orthodoxy,* pp. 61–109, esp. pp. 86–94; idem, "Ḥusayn b. ʿAbd al-Ṣamad al-ʿĀmilī's Treatise for Sultan Suleiman and the Shīʿī Shāfiʿī Legal Tradition," *Islamic Law and Society* 4 (1997): 156–99.

45. Stewart, *Islamic Legal Orthodoxy,* pp. 18–19.

46. Zayn al-Dīn al-ʿĀmilī, *Munyat al-murīd fī ādāb al-mufīd waʾl-mustafīd* (Najaf: Maṭbaʿat al-Gharī, 1950–51); idem, *Tamhīṣ al-qawāʿid al-uṣūlīyah waʾl-ʿarabīyah li-tafrīʿ fawāʾid al-aḥkām al-sharʿīyah* (Tehran, 1855); idem, *Masālik al-afhām ilā tanqīḥ Sharāʾiʿ al-Islām,* 6 vols. (Qum: Muʾassasat al-maʿārif al-Islāmīyah, 1992).

47. Zayn al-Dīn al-ʿĀmilī, *al-Rawḍah al-bahīyah fī sharḥ al-Lumʿah al-dimashqīyah,* 10 vols. (Najaf: Maṭbaʿat al-ādāb, 1967), 3:65.

48. For this reason, Momen's view that the Akhbārī tendency is actually closer to Sunni Islam than the Uṣūlī tendency is not accurate; Momen, *An Introduction to Shīʿī Islam,* p. 222.

49. Muḥammad b. al-Ḥasan al-Ḥurr al-ʿĀmilī, *al-Fawāʾid al-ṭūsīyah,* ed. Mahdī al-Lājiwardī al-Ḥusaynī and Muḥammad Durūdī (Qum: al-Maṭbaʿah al-ʿilmīyah, 1983), p. 341.

50. al-Ḥurr al-ʿĀmilī, *Amal al-āmil fī ʿulamāʾ Jabal ʿĀmil,* 2 vols. (Baghdad: Maktabat al-Andalus, 1965–66), 1:89.

51. Modarressi, *An Introduction,* p. 52, cites Āghā Buzurg al-Ṭihrānī, *al-Dharīʿah ilā taṣānīf al-shīʿah,* 10:42, as well as MS M169/3, UCLA, Los Angeles. Āghā Buzurg gives the title *Dhamm al-taqlīd waʾttibāʿ al-ābāʾ wa-tark al-istidlāl* (Censure of the Blind Adoption of Opinions, Following One's Ancestors' Way, and Abandoning Proof of Legal Rulings). Modarressi's characterization of this particular work seems based primarily on this title. The incipit cited, however, is the same as that found in the UCLA MS, which has the title *Risālah fī taqlīd al-mayyit. Dhamm al-taqlīd* is thus in all probability the same work Āghā Buzurg cites under the title *Risālah fī taqlīd al-mayyit* (*al-Dharīʿah,* 4:392). The manuscript Āghā Buzurg mentions under the title *Dhamm al-taqlīd,* however, may be abridged or incomplete, because he reports that it is about 230 lines long, while the UCLA MS is about twice that length.

52. *Risālah fī taqlīd al-mayyit,* MS M169/3 UCLA, Los Angeles, fol. 31b.

53. See Zayn al-Dīn al-ʿĀmilī, *al-Iqtiṣād waʾl-irshād ilā ṭarīqat al-ijtihād fī maʿrifat al-hidāyah waʾl-maʿād wa-aḥkām afʿāl al-ʿibād,* pp. 162–205, in idem, *Ḥaqāʾiq al-īmān,* ed. Sayyid Mahdī al-Rajāʾī (Qum: Maṭbaʿat Sayyid al-Shuhādāʾ, 1989), esp. pp. 176–82; Ibn Taymīyah, *al-Radd ʿalā al-manṭiqīyīn,* ed. ʿAbd al-Ṣamad Sharaf al-Dīn al-Kutubī (Bombay: Maṭbaʿat al-qayyimah, 1949); Wael Hallaq, *Ibn Taymiyah against the Greek Logicians* (Oxford: Clarendon Press, 1993). Al-Suyūṭī wrote a work entitled *Ṣawn al-manṭiq waʾl-kalām ʿan fann al-manṭiq waʾl-kalām* (Defending Reason and Speech against the Disciplines of

Logic and Dogmatic Theology); Elisabeth Sartain, *Jalāl al-Dīn al-Suyūṭī,* 2 vols. (Cambridge: Cambridge University Press, 1975), vol. 2: Jalāl al-Dīn al-Suyūṭī, *Kitāb al-taḥadduth bi-ni'mat Allāh,* p. 106.

54. al-Jazā'irī, *Kitāb manba' al-ḥayāt wa-ḥujjīyat qawl al-mujtahid min al-amwāt* (Beirut: Mu'assasat al-a'lamī li'l-maṭbū'āt, 1981).

55. Ḥusayn b. 'Abd al-Ṣamad al-'Āmilī, *al-'Iqd al-ḥusaynī,* ed. al-Sayyid Jawād al-Mudarrisī al-Yazdī (Yazd: Chāp-i gulbahār, n.d.), p. 31; Devin J. Stewart, "The First *Shaykh al-Islām* of the Safavid Capital Qazvin," *Journal of the American Oriental Society* 116 (1996): 387–405.

56. Modarressi, *An Introduction,* p. 53.

57. It is wrong, though, to assert that Shi'ite arguments for the exclusive authority of the jurists are a recent phenomenon. One may find such arguments in the works of the eleventh-century jurists al-Sharīf al-Murtaḍā and al-Shaykh al-Ṭūsī. See Stewart, *Islamic Legal Orthodoxy,* pp. 210–14.

Contributors

Hamid Algar
Department of Near Eastern Studies, University of California, Berkeley

Juan R. I. Cole
Department of History, University of Michigan

Stephen Frederic Dale
Department of History, Ohio State University.

Shireen Mahdavi
Department of History, University of Utah

Rudi Matthee
Department of History, University of Delaware

Michel Mazzaoui
Department of History, University of Utah

R. D. McChesney
Department of History, New York University

Vera B. Moreen
Department of Religion, Swarthmore College

Devin Stewart
Department of Middle East and South Asian Studies, Emory University

Index

'Abbās, Hazrat-i, 150

'Abbas I, Shah. *See* 'Abbās I, Shah

'Abbās I, Shah, 67, 89, 99*n*, 155*n*; and hajj routes, 145, 146, 147, 149; historians in reign of, 2, 4; and Isfahan, 44*n*, 170; and Jahangir, 49–50, 57–60, *58*, 136; and poetry, 66; and religious sects, 26, 48*n*, 166; and Russia, 103, 110–21, 125*n*, 126*n*, 127*n*, 128*n*; territory of, vii, viii, 18

'Abbās II, Shah, 150, 156*n*

'Abd Allāh. *See* Khān, 'Abd Allāh

'Abd Allāh Khān Madrasah, 141

'Abd al-'Azīz. *See* Khān, 'Abd al-'Azīz

'Abd al-Vahhāb Hamadānī, Mīr Sirāj al-Dīn. *See* Hamadānī, Mīr Sirāj al-Dīn 'Abd al-Vahhāb

Abdî, 24

Abdülkerim Efendi, 20

Abī 'l-Khayr, Abū Sa'īd b., 16, 44*n*

Abisaab, Rula Jurdi, 172

Abī Ṭālib, 'Alī b., 45*n*

Abraham, 39*n*

Abu 'l-Hasan, 58, 59

Abū 'l-Khayr, Bū Sa'īd-i. *See* Abī 'l-Khayr, Abū Sa'īd b.

Âcizî, 20

Afghanistan, 47*n*, 67, 76, 135, 139, 140

Aflākī, Aḥmad, 24

Agra, 56, 67, 68, 74, 76; and hajj routes, 135, 136, 140, 141, 148

Ahaz, King, 164

Ahmad, Aziz, 66

Aḥmad, Maulānā Ghiyāṣ al-Dīn, 23

Ahmed (son of Şeyh Aziz), 19–20

Ahmed I, Sultan, 143

Ahmednagar, 56

Ahmed Paşa, Dukakinzade, 11

Aḥrār, Khwājah 'Ubayd Allāh. *See* Aḥrār, Khwāja 'Ubaydullāh

Aḥrār, Khwāja 'Ubaydullāh, grandson of, 140; and Jāmī, 25, 37*n*; and Naqshbandīs, 7, 21–22, 23, 28, 35*n*, 44*n*; pupils of, 8, 9, 13, 32, 34*n*

'Ā'ishah, 174

'Ājizī, Sayyid Abvābī, 18

Akbar, and the arts, 50, 51, 68; and hajj routes, 136, 137, 140, 141, 143; and Jahangir, 52, 54, 57, 67; rebellion of, 75

Akhtarīn, 15

Akşehir, 9, 13

'Alam, Khan, 56

Alam, Muzaffar, 68, 78*n*

'Alam, Shah, 65

Albo, 159

Aleppo, 15, 16

Alexander, King, 112, 113, 116, 127*n*, 128*n*